KARMA QUEENS,
GEEK GODS
& INNERPRENEURS

KARMA QUEENS,
GEEK GODS
&INNERPRENEURS

Meet the 9 Consumer Types
Shaping Today's Marketplace

RON RENTEL
WITH JOE ZELLNIK

McGraw-Hill
New York ▪ Chicago ▪ San Francisco ▪ Lisbon
London ▪ Madrid ▪ Mexico City ▪ Milan ▪ New Delhi
San Juan ▪ Seoul ▪ Singapore ▪ Sydney ▪ Toronto

1 2 3 4 5 6 7 8 9 0   DOC/DOC   0 9 8 7

ISBN-13: 978-0-07-147791-8

ISBN-10:0-07-147791-8

This publication is designed to provide accurate and authoritative information in regard to the subject matter covered. It is sold with the understanding that the publisher is not engaged in rendering legal, accounting, or other professional service. If legal advice or other expert assistance is required, the services of a competent professional person should be sought.

–From a declaration of principles jointly adopted by a committee of the American Bar Association and a committee of publishers.

■　■　■　■

McGraw-Hill books are available at special quantity discounts to use as premiums and sales promotions, or for use in corporate training programs. For more information, please write to the Director of Special Sales, Professional Publishing, McGraw-Hill, Two Penn Plaza, New York, NY 10121-2298. Or contact your local bookstore.

For Barb, Brandt, Jack, Willa, and Maccray

Contents

ACKNOWLEDGMENTS

As with everything we've ever done at Consumer Eyes, collaboration is the order of the day. This book reflects the work and energy of many different people.

From the beginning, my wife, Barb, and my kids, Brandt, Jack, Willa, and Maccray, have supported my vision for this project and have given me the time and space to work on it. Without the solid support and love of my family I could never have done this.

Thanks to Adam Rothberg, who sparked the whole chain of events that led to getting things off the ground. A special thanks goes to my agent, Jim Levine, for working to get the deal done, and to Mary Glenn, my editor at McGraw-Hill, for advocating on my behalf throughout the process and helping make it all seem fairly painless.

Making ideas come alive with words is not easy, but my collaborator and coauthor, Joe Zellnik, made it seem so. He worked hard, took criticism well, and stuck with it, even when things got bumpy. And beyond his writing contribution, Joe's hand has been present throughout so many of the details of this project, far too numerous to mention.

I owe a big debt of gratitude to Consumer Eyes team members past and present, including Krista Pinter, Steve Zimet, Susan Sokirko, Cecile Mirman, Marc Weissman, Sharon Park, Teri Patane, Candie Broxson, David Cory, Linda Castrilli, Karen Newman, Francisco Staton, Keisha Pottinger, David Zellnik, Angelina Ho, Emily Kozlow and, last but not least, Emilie Dishongh, who designed the cover of the book, and Amber Davis, who researched tirelessly, poring over stats, facts, and sites, and finding quotes and support that tied everything together. Special thanks to my friend Mark Thomas for the back jacket photo.

Thanks also to my partners at BuzzBack Market Research, Carol Fitzgerald and Sylvia Stein, who have helped shape an exciting business that continues to grow and evolve.

To two of my lifelong friends who have supported me throughout my career and helped me to see promise and opportunity, and who have always been there with wise counsel and advice, Rob Grubman and Lee Ackerley . . . thanks for everything you do.

And most importantly, thanks to the clients of Consumer Eyes. You know who you are! For over 16 years, we have had the honor of working with you to develop brand strategies and new product innovations. Without you, we do not exist. Thanks for allowing us to take chances as we develop new tools and constructs for capturing and reflecting consumer insights. You are the reason we have fun at work each and every day.

kay, you picked this book up. Presumably that means you have some interest in consumers and what we have to say about them. Maybe you're a marketer, maybe you're an innovator or entrepreneur, or maybe you're just fascinated by what makes consumers tick. Perhaps you're still standing in a bookstore, reading this introduction trying to decide whether or not to buy the book. (Go ahead, you won't regret it.) Whoever you are, you probably want to know what exactly we mean by consumer types (C-Types). That isn't what this introduction is about. (Skip ahead to Part 1.) This introduction is about us, and how and why we came to write this book.

"We" refers to Consumer Eyes, Inc. We're a New York-based marketing and innovation consultancy. Since 1991, we've been helping companies grow their brands and fill their new product pipelines with breakthrough, business-building ideas and concepts. Every single year, Consumer Eyes probes, explores, and processes the attitudes and behaviors of literally thousands of consumers, of every stripe and variety, in everything from in-depth, at-home ethnographic interviews to 60-second curbside surveys. After tens of thousands of interactions, we think that nobody knows consumers like we do.

Our clients have included some of the top companies in the world, and over the years we've had a hand in creating a number of successful and influential new products, across myriad categories.

Over a decade ago we began tracking trends—looking at how and why they emerge, and where they're headed next—so we always stay one step in front of the consumer. Then we pioneered a process called Consumer Immersion, which involves tours of category-related hot spots, expert interviews, hands-on experiential visits, and a multitude of real-world consumer interactions. During our Immersions we break bread with consumers in cutting-edge restaurants, sip cocktails with them in their favorite bars, and query them on the street, at the gym, and in the supermarket. Together with our clients, we see how life looks from the consumer's perspective and let that learning inform all of the brainstorming and insight building that follows.

C-Types grew out of our Consumer Immersion work. We noticed similarities among many of the consumers with whom we interacted, seeing the same types of consumers showing up again and again, across different product categories. Eventually we developed a new way of categorizing consumers according to the similarities we noticed. This book is the result. It's an in-depth exploration of the nine most interesting consumer types we've uncovered. These are the types we think are and will be influential going forward: the consumers who will set the trends in art, music, technology, consumer products and services, and more. Hopefully you'll find it useful and, more importantly, interesting and insight-inspiring.

KARMA QUEENS,
GEEK GODS
& INNERPRENEURS

WHAT'S A C-TYPE AND WHY SHOULD I CARE?

1.1 C-TYPES DEFINED

Do you know a couple who shops only at Whole Foods, who proudly drives a Prius, and who took three vacations last year, all to exotically remote locales? You may just know some E-litists.

Who's the person you turn to when you need to make a decision about buying a new computer, flat screen plasma TV, or pda? Most likely, your friendly local Geek God.

Are you a guy who's changed a week's worth of diapers? Taken the 3 a.m. feeding? Been the one who your preadolescent daughter turns to when she needs social advice or emotional support? Congratulations, you may just be a Denim Dad.

In today's world, it's a truism that there's simply no mass audience out there that shares common goals, values, and interests. So it's more important than ever to find ways of understanding the whole through its component parts. C-Types are a valuable tool in this effort.

So what exactly is a C-Type? It's a rich, three-dimensional portrait of a type of consumer derived from their key attitudes and behaviors, their social status, and other demographic factors. It's a portrait combining quantifiable data backed up by real-world expressions of personality. C-Types are not flat, factual constructs; each type has a multifaceted persona—a face, if you will—that makes him or her easier for marketers to interact with, to understand on a deeper level, and to figure out how to reach effectively.

C-Types are not essentially demographic constructs, though demographics do play a part. Some C-Types, it's true, are defined in great part by age and/or gender, or are found more frequently in certain regions of the country or in a certain economic bracket. But C-Types are not to be confused with the rough groupings of consumers categorized by "life stages" or "lifestyles." (A generational swath as massive as the Boomers, for instance, is made up of lots of different and overlapping C-Types, while Gay Americans or Evangelical Christians, to choose two wildly divergent lifestyle groups, contain multiple C-Types within their somewhat self-defined ranks.)

Psychographics are closer to the C-Type model, but C-Types are not merely psychographic profiles by another name. In general, psychographic profiling is a distillation process that looks at all the features of a particular market segment and, finding the points of commonality, casts off oddities and irregularities that don't fit, ending up with a portrait of a generic everyman that in truth resembles no real man (or woman).

C-Types, on the other hand, are all about the idiosyncratic characteristics that make consumers distinct. C-Types take contradictions into account. They are also defined with the help of immediately recognizable, everyday references (e.g., what stores these consumers shop in, what brands or designers they associate themselves with, which foods and beverages they consume) or through illuminating examples of the type drawn from popular culture.

C-Types emerged when we looked at where demographics and psychographics intersected, informed by a whole lot of real-world experience on our part. They are a conceptual space where "who consumers are," "what consumers think," "what consumers do" and "how consumers express themselves in today's marketplace" all come together.

There are obviously precedents for this construct. "Soccer Moms" were a type that came to prominence during the political campaigns of the 90s, but it personified something so immediately recognizable that it remains with us 15 years later. "Metrosexuals," another recent type that made a splash (debased by use as a pop culture punch line, and perhaps a more dubious construct to begin with) have not proved as durable. But the notion of definable types goes back even further than that. If someone says "Beatnik" to you, you probably still immediately picture black turtlenecks, goatees, bongos, and Maynard G. Krebs. "Flapper" still carries associations as disparate as bobbed hair, the Charleston, women in the workplace, and the first era of sexual liberation. The list could go on. How about "Hippie" or "Astronaut's Wife" or even "The Man in the Gray Flannel Suit"? In all these cases, the image evoked is of a three-dimensional being. This distinguishes consumer types from mere advertising characters ("the Arrow shirt collar man") or comic stereotypes ("valley girl") whose very essence is flat, and whose power comes from their simplicity and lack of nuance. True consumer types are rich with resonances, which is what makes consumer typing such a powerful tool. When you describe a consumer with a term like "Hippie," you can picture his hair and clothing, understand his political views, his attitudes toward social issues, almost hear his favorite tunes on the radio. Maybe even smell some fragrant smoke in the air.

1.2 WHY C-TYPES MATTER

For some time now, there has been a proliferation of marketing consultants and pundits touting trends as a way to stay ahead of the consumer. Trends are valuable in making certain that you're up to speed on the present, but they are not very helpful in guessing where consumers might turn next. Trends inform you about consumer behavior without necessarily helping you understand the reasons behind it. C-Types go further because they identify the consumers who set the trends. Types illuminate the consumer psyche, while trends merely articulate consumer behavior.

As an example, let's take a look at one behavioral category: safety and security. We can all agree that today's consumers feel the need for a safe haven in a world that has become increasingly uncertain. First, some trends: worried parents are now giving all their kids cell phones. Useful? Yes, definitely. It's a behavior that will surely increase, and one that has many new product and service implications (cell phones designed for very young children, new phone service family plans, two-way-only phone service between parent and child phones, etc.) Another trend: many parents always call the doctor at the first sign that one of their children is sick. Again, this could be useful knowledge (a productive trend if you were trying to create a 24-hour help line for nervous parents, or market publications offering medical advice, etc.) but not, perhaps, particularly wide-ranging.

Now let's look at the C-Type informed by safety and security—Parentocrats (see Chapter 2.2). Talk to Parentocrats about their ideas on child rearing and keeping kids protected, and the conversation will likely go much further than the trends above. You may find that they actually have tracking devices on their children and pets. They probably have back-up prescription antibiotics on hand "just in case." They may use a toothbrush sanitizer to ensure that toothbrushes stay germ free. Extreme? Yes. But insightful and likely to stir up some creative juices if you are trying to develop a new product targeted to families. And even if your primary area of interest is safety and security, you will glean practically as much insight from other facets of the Parentocrat C-Type. The conversation may reveal that the Parentocrat's son plays on three soccer teams and is learning conversational Japanese, while her daughter plays two sports, is involved in school theater, and goes to Kumon. You may come to understand that the Parentocrat impulse to protect kids physically is twinned with the impulse to push them intellectually. This kind of insight informs more than just the creation of truly breakthrough new goods and services. It can also help you as you think about the messaging and imagery that should surround the marketing of your new product.

Here's a practical example: say you're an auto manufacturer challenged to create a compelling new vehicle feature. The safety and security trend might lead you to create OnStar (a good idea). Approaching the same goal through the lens of the Parentocrat might have ended in a souped-up OnStar whose global satellite connections would be combined with a high-tech on-board electrical system to allow remote Web access for kids who are doing their homework on laptops in the car.

C-Types force you to challenge assumptions about trends and where they originate. They open you up to understanding your consumer holistically, so you can more readily develop ideas on a functional level. Moreover, consumer typing is awesome for helping you ladder up to the emotional end benefits and higher order needs that are more likely to create a strong consumer connection and long-term affinity.

C-Types allow you an easy way to take the totality of your consumer into account when innovating. Imagine developing a new lunch offering targeted to Metrosexuals (think: urban, fashion-conscious, hip, sexy). Using the multidimensional facets of C-Types, it's easy. Intrinsics come first, no problems there: Low calorie? Yes; chicken or salmon, not beef; whole-grain pita; balsamic vinaigrette dressing, and a bit of mesclun salad (not iceberg lettuce!) on top. And thanks to consumer typing, the extrinsics come easy, too. The message of the introductory ad: "Don't Live to Eat . . . Eat to Love." The media buy? GQ. You'll find that the better you know the C-Types that make up your target, the more effectively you'll be able to create breakthrough marketing strategies and tactics. Even better, you will understand how they think and feel even beyond the bounds of your category.

Understanding the aspirations and preoccupations of all the various C-Types who interact with your brand—whether they embrace it or reject it—is vital to understanding the future and your company's or brand's place in it. Taken together, the C-Types profiled in this book represent the changing face of the American consumer. Though some of their choices and characteristics might seem extreme, these consumers are the ones driving societal changes, and they best exemplify the attitudes and behaviors which, though perhaps still in their infancy, will define tomorrow. If you can reach these key C-Types, you can not only win them over but their entire social network as well.

Malcolm Gladwell's *The Tipping Point* has made the notion of market influencers commonplace. It is now widely accepted that there are some consumers who are always the first to try and adopt new behaviors or products, and these consumers are instrumental in influencing friends, family, and even distant acquaintances to try and adopt these things, too. More recently, Boston marketing firm BzzAgent has managed to create substantial word-of-mouth marketing campaigns simply by providing their "agents" (who are all untrained consumer volunteers) with key talking points to bring up in their everyday conversations. The success of their campaigns proves that spreading marketing messages through person-to-person contact is as effective as traditional advertising, if not more so.

The nine C-Types covered in detail in the following chapters each represent a large and growing behavioral and attitudinal segment of the U.S. population. They will prove invaluable for marketers, advertisers, re-tailers, editors, innovators, and anyone else who has an eye focused on the future. Even if at first glance it seems that one or more of the types has no relevance to your line of work, keep an open mind. All of the Con-sumer Eyes' C-Types have proved useful in our work across a range of categories and industries, and will surely continue to do so. Conversely, whatever your category or industry, there are always more than a few different and overlapping C-Types within your core consumer target.

1.3 GENESIS OF THE TYPES

The goal isn't new. From segmentation studies to target definitions, mar-keters have continuously tried to sort consumers into buckets to make it easier to develop advertising or understand brand equity. C-Types are a way of bringing a dose of reality to the process, allowing you deeper ac-cess to consumers' psyches so that you really feel like you've gotten to know your target and gotten a handle on where they are going. Reality— that's the key. In all our years of providing our clients with insights, strate-gies, platforms, and concepts, we have stayed true to a credo which puts real-world experience ahead of traditional qualitative research.

The first attempt to inject the real world into marketing was the fo-cus group. Now, we've conducted our fair share of focus groups over the last 16 years, and we still enjoy interacting with consumers in markets all across the country. But, at the same time, we have come to believe that today the focus group is overly relied upon and often takes mar-keters down a path of sameness which does not help foster creativity or insight. Are we suggesting that focus groups be abandoned altogether? Certainly not. Don't misunderstand: focus groups can still be a valuable tool if what you are seeking is a reaction to an already defined idea (to determine its strengths and weaknesses or to build and refine it), but they have unfortunately become less effective in achieving their originally stated goal—that of pointing up need gaps and unmet desires.

Here's why. First off, consumers have become armchair-marketers, often evaluating a problem or idea with too much judgment and distance. When it was developed, the focus group was a fine way to get inside consumers' thoughts and lives, but unfortunately you now often hear consumers say things like, "If you want to position this to me," or, "I think the target for that is. . . ." The general consumer has become too sophisticated to be trusted for an unfiltered opinion. Even the most well-intended respondents misremember or paint a reinvented picture of their life. "Focus group speak" has reached epidemic proportions. A good moderator might try to make the conversation as honest and real as possible, but it can be a losing battle. Perhaps the focus room itself, complete with mirrors and a sterile, conference-room ambience, engenders this retreat into theorizing or show-off cleverness. Whatever the reason, data gleaned from a group like this can be misleading at worst, unproductive at best.

Finally, today's mainstream, middle-class U.S. population lives high on Maslow's hierarchy of needs. Most of their broad needs are being nicely met, and most of their niche needs as well. In a society dominated by consumerism, where abundant choices are available in virtually every category, talking to mainstream consumers about their needs in order to identify gaps seems almost pointless. Which means that these focus groups invariably yield very little that could not have been identified through secondary data or a good look at the history of the category.

This dissatisfaction with focus groups led us to develop our real-world brand and innovation process, termed Consumer Immersion, in the mid-1990s. Since we began working in this fashion, our competitors and clients alike have adopted the Immersion handle too, each defining it their own way. Our view of Consumer Immersion is that the best place to investigate consumers' lives is to speak to consumers where they live, to follow them as they go through daily chores and errands, and to interact with them in a variety of real-world settings. Informally stopping a consumer in the supermarket as she ponders your category is amazingly enlightening. Hanging out with 21-year-olds in their favorite club will enable you to examine both their emotional lives and drinking habits at once. Drinking rituals are highly communal, and watching patrons order drinks in a bar can shed a lot of light on how drink choices change over the course of the evening. In these situations, there is also no lapse between what consumers say they do and what really goes on. No matter what a consumer might say about her condiment usage, there's no substitute for opening up her fridge and seeing a crusty bottle of hot sauce on the back of the shelf and a well-used bottle of mayonnaise up front.

So that's what we do—together with our clients we interview, observe, and join consumers in their activities everywhere from a kitchen table in Boston to behind the counter of a juice bar in Malibu. If we want fodder for new automotive ideas, we travel with consumers as they commute to work. When we helped V8 develop V8 Splash, the key insights surfaced at a juice bar in Walnut Creek, California. When we helped Goodyear create its new Assurance tire, we called the Automotive Hall of Fame in Detroit our home base. From a cafe to a doctor's office, from a spa to a sex shop, all our insights are filtered through the world we live in, and we think they're that much richer because of it. Because of the Immersion process there's a context for every action, a touchstone to help put consumer behavior in perspective.

In the course of our Immersion work, in order to make the consumer interactions more meaningful, we began to type consumers informally. Using these rough types, we were better able to narrow our focus to suit particular clients and categories. For a global exploratory for a communications company, this meant seeking out Shopaholics and Gadgetheads. For an innovation pipeline project for a beverage brand, it meant Organic Shoppers and Hyperphobics. Segmenting in this new way was inspiring. Then one day, with the idea of Soccer Moms in mind, we challenged ourselves to put this informal, behavior-oriented consumer typing into a bigger context. Could we identify big, interesting buckets of people that our clients should know as they generated brand strategies and innovations? Could we bring real depth and a third dimension to traditional consumer segmentation? Would it be worth anything if we did?

Yes, Yes, and Yes! At this point we found we were not alone in this quest. We saw an article labeling young, urban, fashion-conscious men "Metrosexuals," and before we knew it the word was everywhere. In our work, we had been speaking about a type of male we called "Venus Enviests," which was essentially the same thing. At that eureka moment it became clear to us that indeed, if properly identified, consumer types could be of interest to a wide audience. And this theory has proved to be correct. The first of these new types we came up with, Karma Queens (see Chapter 2.1), has already proved its worth and its applicability, time and time again. And not in just the obvious categories like food, drink, and personal care, but in research into banking services, pharmaceuticals, and cell phones, too.

A few caveats as to the C-Types detailed in this book. First, our decision to include full chapters on only nine C-Types should make it clear that this book is not meant to be a comprehensive study of all the types of consumers in existence. Not even close. There are numerous C-Types out there, and the ground is constantly shifting beneath them. The demographic numbers for some types are growing, for some types are waning. Outmoded types are always making way for new ones. So the types in this book are ones that we think are most important now, and ones that will remain so for a good while. Put simply, this book represents our spin on nine consumer groupings we think you'll want to know about. That said, among the types we didn't include are some of the potentially largest. Empty Nester Boomers, to name one glaring omission, is an example of what we're talking about. Let's face it; there's no denying the impact this group of aging Boomers has had and will continue to have. But there has already been so much written about them. Truthfully there seemed to be very little new we could offer on the subject. (If you're interested in doing a little digging on your own, we recommend "The Second 50 Years," a great online clearinghouse for all things "aging boomer" at www.second50years.com.) This is not to imply that we've disregarded any type that has been written about; some of our types have been fomenting in popular literature and culture for a while. In fact, most have some sort of roots in articles or thinking that has come before.

What all the chosen types share, however, is that they are all consumers we have come across ourselves in the course of our work. None of what follows is based purely on secondhand sources. And each C-Type in this book reflects our collected wisdom around which, of all the consumer behaviors currently evolving in the mainstream or on the leading edge, are the ones to watch. These types have emerged through thousands of interviews with consumers and experts, and (after poring over many, many Web sites and blogs and virtually every magazine on the planet) we think they are the types you will need to know about if you want to be forward-thinking.

So, are C-Types a black box to success? No.

C-Types should be used to challenge your own thinking, not to replace it. It is our hope that you will use them to spark creativity that leads to more powerful and insightful marketing. Use them as a filter (one of many) for your brand or target. Try picking a type that seems an unlikely consumer for your brand or category and then challenge yourself to make a connection. What you come up with may just lead to an incremental idea that leads to a truly breakthrough one. Use the types to inform your marketing judgment so that you begin to think and react like your consumer. Think about what C-Types indicate about how the consumer landscape is shifting and how you can evolve your product to keep pace.

Beyond that, we hope that you will become inspired to identify a consumer type for your own brand. Doing so will help you in every aspect of your marketing, from choosing actors for your ads through identifying innovations that are consistent with your brand and target.

Let's suppose you market an upscale cosmetics line. Traditional segmentation might identify your core target as a working female, 25 to 40, with an income of $45,000+. Brand development indices might further indicate that she is most likely an urban dweller. But what do you really know about her? Is she sports focused? Which sports? Confident about her looks? Likely to visit a spa more frequently than the typical woman in her age demo? Could you pick her out at a cocktail party?

That's what consumer typing is all about. If you take our premise as a starting point and use it to develop a C-Type of your key consumer, you'll not only gain insight into your brand and business, but you'll also become empathetic with your user in ways that can help make your decision-making process easier and more automatic. It is our hope that as you read through the C-Types we have highlighted, you'll begin to internalize this kind of thinking and take the steps that will help you uncover your own brand type.

NINE C-TYPES YOU SHOULD KNOW

KARMA QUEENS

"

We're not talking Berkeley. We're not talking New Age. We're talking Pike County and Letcher County and Perry County and places like that . . . in Central Kentucky.

Dr. Maureen Flannery, a board-certified acupuncturist on the subject of widespread acceptance of alternative medicine

If you take a vitamin supplement, that's considered to be alternative medicine; if you take a yoga class, you're doing alternative medicine. If you listen to a relaxation audio tape, that's considered alternative medicine. It's the great American principle of freedom of choice.

Dr. Kenneth R. Pelletier, author of *The Best Alternative Medicine*

More consumers are looking at organic food as a health issue. It's not a hippie culture. Organic is now mainstream.

Terra Brockman, founder of The Land Connection

Have you ever noticed a woman of a certain age walking through a mall dressed in Birkenstocks and Eileen Fisher? Or a woman putting her groceries — a mix of organic produce, gourmet teas, and high-end bath products — into the trunk of her VW Beetle? How about the older woman leaving the gym with a rolled-up yoga mat in her hand and a satisfied smile on her face?

It's very likely you've just seen a Karma Queen.

There are a number of vaguely derogatory terms out there for these women, such as crunchy, granola or aging hippie, but these veiled insults don't mean much to the Karma Queen. Karma Queens are individuals with a strong sense of self, trying their best to achieve harmony with the universe. And no matter what others think, they continue to march to their own drum.

Typically in their forties or fifties, these are women who have lived long enough to know who they are, what they want, and what they believe in. Although age is a less important consideration than outlook and attitude; Karma Queens can be found as young as 20 or as old as 70. They need not be wealthy, but most are at least comfortably well-off. Their purchase decisions are, generally speaking, not constrained by financial considerations. Rather, this type puts her money where her ideals are, choosing to patronize companies that are as ecologically minded and socially conscious as she is. And her discretionary income is likely to be spent on intangible services like spa treatments or visits to retreats, rather than on status markers like a big house or expensive jewelry.

While the heart of every Karma Queen lies in unspoiled countryside, you are more likely to find Karma Queens concentrated in urban centers or in the densely populated regions surrounding cities. Is it because they can find a wider range of organic and/or alternative products and services there? Or is it because the underlying impulse to embrace a Karma Queen outlook comes from some sort of "civilization backlash" unlikely to be encountered in a more remote area? It could simply be that Karma Queens are social creatures who believe in the value of human interaction.

Wherever they reside, you're likely to find the Karma Queen at the center of an extended network of family and friends. She is often the glue that binds together a community, or she stays in touch with far-flung relatives. As such, her sphere of influence is large, and (make no mistake about it) she can be very influential. Karma Queens enjoy spending their money, and they like to spend it on pampering themselves and those closest to them. Their daily purchases set the pattern for their households, and their gifts to others (which lean toward the cutting edge and often come from the health and wellness or natural foods categories) can expose these consumers to goods and services with which they were previously unfamiliar.

The origins of the Karma Queen type lead inexorably back to the sixties. Even Karma Queens too young to have taken part in the Summer of Love are at least spiritual descendents of those tumultuous times. For aging female Boomers, the Karma Queen outlook marks a return to the idealism and spiritualism of their vanished youth. After the excesses of the greed-is-good eighties and the dot-com nineties, Karma Queens happily embrace the ethos of the early women's movement with its "rap sessions," Women's Lib, and bestsellers like *Our Bodies, Ourselves*. Karma Queens, like the hippies of the sixties, are interested in the exploration and exaltation of the individual, but remain cognizant of every individual's effect and impact on society, community, and the planet as a whole.

> If you look carefully at what you are doing, you can ask, "Am I making the world better or worse?" We pretty much have that choice about everything in life.
>
> **Hana Newcomb, *The Washington Times*, 7/6/03**

KARMA QUEENS: HEALTH AND WELLNESS

Health and wellness is perhaps the primary arena in which the Karma Queen mentality has altered the larger consumer landscape. Karma

Queens see health and wellness not as an occasional, situational concern but as a lifelong goal. The current worldwide wellness movement, if it cannot be directly attributed to the relatively small number of core Karma Queens, was certainly due in part to their influence. It is important to remember that Karma Queens are usually wives and mothers in addition to being individuals and therefore are the key decision makers and influencers when it comes to matters of well-being for their families.

To a Karma Queen, good health is as much a continual mindset as a person's state of being at any given moment. Health care, or more properly, taking care of one's health, is a holistic matter and goes far beyond the treatment of isolated illnesses. Treatment *and* prevention are critical to the Karma Queen, and in both instances she will seek out alternative therapies rather than conventional or mainstream ones. Increasingly, though, what was once alternative has now become mainstream, thanks again to the Karma Queen. A recent study from Taylor Nelson Sofres Intersearch found that 70 percent of Americans have tried or are currently using some kind of alternative medicine.[1]

> I don't trust the pharmaceutical companies; I don't trust the FDA. I just always felt natural is better. It's something God intended for this use. Why not use it?
>
> **Janice, age 48**

> I go to MDs mostly, but I understand their limits. I take baths for aching muscles—water relaxes. And I have done some work with the Alexander Technique, which has helped chronic back and shoulder aches.
>
> **Kappy, on womenshealth.com**

Aromatherapy in particular has made an enormous leap into the consciousness of mainstream consumers, and is showing up across a wide range of products and categories. It is now a $300 million a year business, and it's estimated that it could even quadruple over the next five years.[2] While it may not yet have been taken up by the majority of the country in any substantive way, aromatherapy (as well as acupuncture, meditation, etc.) can no longer be referred to as obscure or offbeat.

> I tell you, it's all about that smell . . . [Lavender is] just so darned nice.
>
> **Jennifer, homemaker, quoted in the *Chicago Tribune*, 4/29/05**

> If you have a cleaner in the kitchen that smells of cucumber and sage, probably just the novelty alone can make some of the job you have to do seem less like drudgery
>
> **Pamela Dalton, research psychologist, quoted in the *Chicago Tribune*, 4/29/05**

When it comes to overall health maintenance, Karma Queens use exercise and nutrition as their preferred preventive and everyday "feel-good" method. To this C-Type, the emotional benefit of "feeling good" cannot be separated from the restorative or healing benefit of a specific regimen. Products and services targeted to them must play to this multilayered, mind-body-spirit approach to wellness. In keeping with this attitude, ancient, Eastern, and/or more natural and gentle exercise options are their favorite practices. Most notably, Karma Queens have helped popularize yoga and Pilates. More than 20 million people in North America now practice yoga as exercise for the mind and body, and as many as 80 percent of health clubs and fitness centers now offer yoga classes.[3]

> After my cancer surgery, I thought I might never lift my arm again . . . but yoga helps compensate for the loss. It impels you to do things you never thought you were capable of doing.
>
> **Sue, breast cancer survivor and yoga student**

> It's important for me to meditate every morning, if only for 10 minutes, to touch base with myself. Sometimes during the day,

when I'm silent or alone, I find myself automatically feeling the tranquility I experience during meditation.

Jane, 38, advertising executive

While, previously as noted, there are some younger Karma Queens, the core group for this type is well past youth and the aura of invulnerability that comes with it. Therefore their major preoccupations are maintaining health while staying vital and young-at-heart. As middle-aged women, menopause is one of the primary concerns of this C-Type. And as Karma Queens face "the change," they have helped alter our society's collective attitude toward it, shifting it toward a view that the mental and physical baggage associated with menopause is perfectly natural. In 2000, the retail sales of natural products for menopause in the United States were approximately $600 million[4] (out of a $2.4 billion a year category).[5] According to the North American Menopause Society, 30 percent of women now use acupuncture as a menopause treatment. Barring serious problems, most Karma Queens do not believe hormone replacement therapy is necessary. And this attitude extends well beyond menopause. It's worth remembering that, no matter the ailment or health issue, Karma Queens will gravitate toward the natural solution over the chemical one.

MARKETPLACE EVIDENCE

Clairol Natural Instincts
This brand, from marketing behemoth Procter & Gamble, aimed to capture Karma Queen hearts (and hair) by stressing whole body wellness and the benefits of yoga by sponsoring "Find Your Balance" festivals across the country. A spring 2006 festival in New York's Central Park attracted 3,000 women interested in yoga for all levels (including actress Mariel Hemingway, who also led a class). After the workout, healthy snacks and beauty goodies from Olay were passed around.

Karma Queens: Beauty, Fashion, and Home

Nothing could seem further removed from the world of the Karma Queen than a glossy fashion magazine. But surprisingly there is reason to think the latter is moving closer to the former, rather than farther apart. While there will always be a segment of the fashion and beauty world that celebrates artifice and an unnatural exaggeration of face and form, experts are seeing a shift toward natural beauty, with an emphasis on the "natural." Emily Dougherty, the beauty editor of *Elle* magazine, notes, "Natural ingredients are the key 'new harvest.'" In fact, sales of body-care products made exclusively or nearly exclusively from natural ingredients rose by 10 percent in 2005, to $4.5 billion.[6] For many Karma Queens, the entirety of their beauty regimen consists of protecting their skin and body, rather than trying to enhance it. Sunscreen is a Karma Queen must, and Karma Queens are among the vanguard of consumers embracing ellagic acid. This is a totally natural derivative of pomegranate that boosts the sun-blocking power of chemical SPFs (sun-protecting factors,) thus lowering the amount of human-made compounds needed. Mother Nature always trumps human-made for a Karma Queen.

Supermodel Christy Turlington is one personality from high fashion who is making overtures in the direction of Karma Queens. Turlington has cofounded a luxury skin care line called Sundāri, created according to the ancient Indian medicinal practice called Ayurveda. All Sundāri products are made with essential oils ("the most concentrated and refined form of a plant") and, for a price, will ensure Karma Queens the beautiful, clear, and natural-looking skin they desire.

If your product is made with natural ingredients, be sure to highlight that in your advertising and marketing. Tell the story of the raw materials that make up your goods because Karma Queens care. Even something as subtle as the paper upon which your ads or press materials are printed can have an effect on the Karma Queen response. Is the paper glossy and slick or natural and organically textured? Guess which paper this C-Type prefers?

One of the Karma Queen's favorite beauty rituals and indulgences is going to the spa. With yoga-packed schedules and other therapies such as biofeedback, acupuncture, and cupping (an ancient healing method in which heated cups are attached by suction to pressure points on the skin), the spa is a haven for Karma Queens. Spa revenues more than doubled from 1999 to 2003, to over $11 billion, and there has also been an increase in the number of spas in the United States, with about 12,000 open at last count.[7] For those Karma Queens who don't have $150 to drop on a triple-oxygenated facial or hot stone massage, mainstream beauty products are making the Karma Queen aesthetic available at home. In 2005, Dove introduced a new Sensitive Essentials line, including a cleansing bar made with cucumber and green tea. Its Web site proudly proclaimed (in true Karma Queen language): "A new definition of beauty is needed. One not defined by unrealistic media images." Dove spurred this wider definition of beauty through what it called its "Campaign for Real Beauty," a campaign that included chat boards and personal reminiscences, as well as the use of "real-looking" models in their advertising. Smart marketers aiming for this C-Type would be wise to follow suit: Karma Queens welcome the opportunity to see realistic images of women who look their age, as opposed to the look of perpetually dewy adolescence peddled by Madison Avenue. At the same time, realistic needn't mean dowdy. Karma Queens are proof that women in their 40s and 50s can feel vibrant and sexy and very much alive.

> I never lie about my age. Never. I often tell younger women how old I am, especially those who express fear about aging. I feel a responsibility to show them that I'm proud of who I am and what I've achieved in my life.
>
> **Emily, in *Our Bodies, Ourselves***

Even when it comes to clothing, some of today's biggest retailers seem to be in agreement—natural is the new glamour. Recent flurries of interest in organic-looking sheepskin UGG Boots and hemp-based clothing are examples of high-fashion fads, but there is growing proof that the idea can and will be leveraged long term. Eileen Fisher, for one, parlayed a natural beauty mindset into a $144 million a year business in 2005.[8] Fisher could be the official Karma Queen designer, not only because her simple and wearable clothes (mostly made from natural fibers) fit the ethos of this C-Type, but because her corporate philosophy does not lose sight of her workers' individuality and humanity. Fisher's official company mission statement encourages individual growth, collaboration, and social consciousness. She gives her 400-plus employees a yearly $1,000 education benefit and a $1,000 wellness benefit, to be spent on rejuvenators such as massages, nutritional consultations, reflexology, spa visits, and gym equipment. The company even hosts free classes in yoga, tai chi, dance movement, and stress reduction. Fisher's explanation for why she does things differently? "We just want people to love this company," she says. So far, that approach has paid off, and in more than just office karma. Although women's apparel sales dipped by more than 6 percent in 2004, revenue at Eileen Fisher—which is privately held—was up 12 percent.[9]

> I want to buy clothes for my children, but I want to know they weren't made by somebody else's children. I think that's where people are heading.
>
> **Ali, *Los Angeles Times*, 3/28/05**

> I love fashion. I've always been interested in it and inspired by it, but I also have a passion for improving and maintaining our environment.
>
> **Camala, *San Jose Mercury News*, 8/22/04**

Smaller designers in the world of high fashion are also turning to the Karma Queen target as a profitable niche. Stella McCartney, who inherited a love of animals from her mom (the late A-list Karma Queen Linda McCartney), makes sure all of her clothes are animal-free. That includes her line of shoes, which, amazingly, even forgo polyvinyl chloride (PVC)-based plastics in favor of materials derived from plants. Canadian designer Linda Loudermilk recently launched a Luxury Eco line of green fashions, citing a growing desire for ecologically conscious manufacture and design. According to her figures, consumers in the United States and Canada spent $85 million for organic fashions in 2004.[10]

Inside the home, the Karma Queen aesthetic is also taking hold. A review of the 2005 International Interior Design Show in Toronto concluded, ". . . the 2005 show reflected the resurgence of natural materials. . . . In fact, nature's influence was everywhere at the show. Many exhibitors showcased products or ideas ripped from the natural world. Rounded, smooth river rock was caged in by a cube of raw metal fencing in a smart end table. Water was evident in interior waterfalls suitable for residential or commercial installations."[11] The natural look is also visible in mainstream retailers' inventories, such as Pottery Barn and Crate and Barrel. For its recent "The Art of the Quilt" line, Crate and Barrel commissioned fiber artist Denyse Schmidt to create the bedding line. In a nod to the authenticity beloved by Karma Queens, Schmidt paid Amish women in Minnesota to create an original model of each custom quilt for the factory to copy from.

There are a number of developers across the nation creating suburban communities in tune with Karma Queen principles and aesthetics. These developments are environmentally friendly (which includes being aware and respectful of local wildlife), built with healthy natural materials, and intentionally designed to foster community interaction. They're also within easy distance of the goods and services (e.g., health food stores, day spas, yoga centers) Karma Queens demand in everyday life. Civano, in Tucson, Arizona, is a great example. It's built around a central court where residents can mingle and celebrates its surroundings with landscaping that features plants native to the Sonoran Desert. There's no pretense that it's in a temperate climate—no lush green lawns that require water on an unsustainable scale. Another community, Summerset at Frick Park in Pittsburgh, offers buyers green options like bathrooms tiled with recycled glass, tankless water heaters, VOC-free paints, cabinets made from formaldehyde-free particleboard, energy-thrifty lighting, and foam insulation made from soybeans. Bloomfield, Colorado–based lifestyle marketer Gaiam may still be a small player in the home arena (a mere $111.4 million in annual revenue in 2004), but the company is squarely focused on the Karma Queen market, with a stated aim to provide choices that allow consumers to live a more natural and healthy life, with respect for the environment. Future growth for the brand can be expected, as its natural housewares and organic linens have recently been added to the shelves of Target; Bed, Bath & Beyond; and Linens 'n Things nationwide.

CRADLE TO CRADLE DESIGN

A new design paradigm takes the Karma Queen philosophy and runs with it. (*Time* magazine called it "a unified philosophy that—in demonstrable and practical ways—is changing the design of the world.") Instead of designing cradle-to-grave products that are dumped in landfills at the end of their useful life, products are designed to be recycled, and perpetually repurposed. Maintaining materials in closed loops maximizes their value without damaging the ecosystem.

Cradle to Cradle Design posits that merely minimizing toxic pollution and the waste of natural resources, though a nice idea, is not a strategy for real change. Designing industrial processes so they do not generate toxic pollution and "waste" in the first place is true change. Cradle to Cradle Design's strategy is rooted in the systems of the natural world, which are not efficient at all, but effective. Consider the cherry tree. Each spring it sheds thousands of blossoms, most of which fall to the ground and don't produce a new tree. Not very efficient. But the fallen blossoms do become food for other living things, contributing to the health of the thriving, interdependent system that is a forest.

There are already some examples of Cradle to Cradle Design in the market. Herman Miller's Mirra Chair is a high-performing, environmentally advanced piece that combines ergonomic comfort, aesthetics, sustainability, and a reasonable price in the midrange office seating market. Mirra was scrutinized from top to bottom to ensure that its material chemistry, recyclability, manufacturability, packaging, and ease of disassembly are environmentally friendly. In fact, Mirra is the first chair designed from the ground up to meet Herman Miller's stringent Design for the Environment (DfE) protocols, which focus on creating economic value while simultaneously protecting the natural environment for future generations. In 2003, Mirra received a Gold Award in the Best of NeoCon 2003 Competition, winning the Desk-Workstation-Task category.

Another example is Climatex®Lifecycle, an attractive and functional fabric that can safely be returned to the environment at the end of its useful life. It is so safe that scraps and trimmings can be used as mulch. Climatex Lifecycle combines free-range wool and ramie, selected for comfort and their moisture-wicking properties and because they could be safely abraded into the environment over the course of their use. The 38 chemical dyes, auxiliaries, and fixatives that are used meet performance criteria: They're not harmful to plants, animals, humans, or ecosystems. The resulting fabric has garnered gold medals and design awards and has proved to be tremendously successful in the marketplace. Climatex Lifecycle exemplifies what is possible with intelligent design, ecological soundness, social fairness, success in the marketplace: a design that is restorative rather than depletive.

KARMA QUEENS: FOOD AND DRINK

Eating and drinking are not mindless activities for Karma Queens. Members of this C-Type carefully consider which foods they will eat, and which they won't. While many (though not all) are vegetarian or vegetarian-leaning, it goes almost without saying that they prefer natural or organic varieties to processed products. Karma Queens were the pioneers of the green revolution, helping push sales of organic goods through the roof (retail sales of organic products have increased steadily from $3.6 billion in 1997 to $13.8 billion in 2005[12]) and bringing to the forefront ideas such as sustainability and the local-foods movement. Natural and/or organic packaged goods brands are now reaching more consumers than ever before, and even mainstream brands such as Healthy Choice and Lean Cuisine, two of the largest in the prepared foods category, continue to grow, based on their better-for-you, if not all-natural, halos.[13]

> I have not eaten meat for probably 25 or 30 years, because I believe in more sustainable food systems. I thought it was something that was worth doing.
>
> **Mary, age 58**

> "I try very hard to only have organic food," Ms. Varcher says. "The accumulation of chemicals and pesticides can be really hard on us, especially in small bodies. Sure, it is a financial sacrifice, but it is also expensive to eat processed food in restaurants. I'm not that strict about it, though. What we have at home is quality, so if Sasha wants to go to a birthday party and eat, that's OK. I believe the closer the food is to the original state, the better it is for us. That doesn't mean I don't eat out."
>
> **Catherine Varcher, 41,** *The Washington Times,* **7/6/03**

But despite this talk of halos and organics, Karma Queens are not Spartan in their relationship to food. Nor are they food disapprovers—quite the opposite. They relish what they perceive as the chance to connect with the glory and wonder of nature's bounty. And they're not averse to pampering themselves. Of course, their idea of decadence is more likely to be a steaming cup of (herbal) tea rather than a sumptuous meal at a trendy restaurant. In fact, helped along by Karma Queens, tea sales are up by more than $3.4 billion over the past decade. There are now 1,200 to 1,500 tea salons operating across the country, up from only 200 five years ago.[14]

When it comes to the other hot beverage, Karma Queens look to the Fair Trade Coffee cooperative, an international agency founded to guarantee coffee growers and harvesters a living wage. (Coffee is, after oil, the world's most valuable traded commodity.) Last year the Fair Trade governing agency certified only $208 million worth of coffee (out of a nearly $20 billion American coffee market), but Fair Trade sales have tripled in the past three years and constitute a growing slice of the booming $8.4 billion gourmet coffee market. Today Fair Trade coffee is imported and roasted by 280 U.S. companies and sold at 18,000 retail outlets.

The overall message of Karma Queens' relationship to what they ingest is that they see the world from the outside in, rather than the other way around. Which is to say, they don't see the food they eat as having been put on the planet just for them. They feel that they must place themselves and all humankind in the context of the natural order, to make sure there *is* a planet to bequeath to future generations. And they try (as best they can) to keep their own bodies in tune with the rhythms and organic processes of nature. When marketing food products to Karma Queens, stress any benefits that go beyond simple nutrition. Anything that leverages the source story of the ingredients will help them see a greater value in the product.

Newman's Own was one of the first brands to appeal to this C-Type by focusing attention on the charitable causes supported by the company's profits. This strategy has since been taken up by many brands, and very successfully. Toward the future, there may be an opportunity for forward-thinking brands to take this cause-and-effect marketing to the next level. A corporation that creates a program of devoting actual hours and energy to charitable organizations, rather than (or in addition to) simply giving financial support, would be likely to garner much positive attention from Karma Queen customers. Remember, Karma Queens make purchasing decisions with their brains *and* their souls.

> At dinnertime we have a ritual of saying something we
> appreciate about the day. We often recognize the farmer, the
> animal, the land, and the water for making it possible for us to
> have this nourishing food.
>
> **Jen, 43, mother of two**

FOCUS ON: CHOCOLATE

Everyone loves chocolate, but for Karma Queens the average Hershey bar just won't do. Fortunately for them, the chocolate market is in the middle of an artisanal boom, which means plenty of chocolate brands to choose from offering the kind of exotic, healthy, or globally conscious credentials they seek when indulging.

Cloud Nine
All natural, vegan, nonalkali, gourmet chocolate sweetened with unrefined, evaporated cane juice, from a company that supports Fair Trade practices and the preservation of the rain forests where their high-quality beans are grown. Cloud Nine bars are made without hydrogenated oils, artificial colors, artificial flavors, or synthetic ingredients. They do, however, have an abundance of natural berries, nuts, and fruits in six delicious varieties.

Vosges Haut-Chocolat
Haute chocolatier Katrina Markoff uses specially grown spices and flowers to infuse her "East meets West" chocolates with flavors from all over the globe. The truffles in the Aztec Collection are filled with Ancho chili and Ceylon cinnamon, and the Collection Italiano includes chocolates stuffed with either taleggio cheese, fennel pollen, olive oil, or balsamic vinegar.

Valrohna
This premium European chocolatier offers varieties from dark to milk, with names like Caraibe and Guanaja that make specific reference to their exotic origins and authentically international flavors.

Scharffen Berger
Berkeley-based Scharffen Berger prides itself on small-batch methods that produce superior, traditional chocolates primarily made from Fair Trade cacao.

Jacques Torres
This French baker may get a hefty paycheck from The Food Network, where he hosts a show, but his delicious artisanal chocolates, handmade in his two Manhattan stores, taste way too good for him to be considered a Karma Queen sellout.

MARKETPLACE EVIDENCE

Amy's

Launched in 1987 by husband and wife team Andy and Rachel Berliner, with just one product (a vegetable pot pie), Amy's has now grown to become the top-selling brand of natural and organic convenience foods in the nation. The brand has shown growth of 10 to 15 percent per year for the last five years, and 2004 sales were in the neighborhood of $150 million.[15] Besides a current product lineup that includes more than 80 items in virtually every section of the grocery store (from frozen meals and canned soups to jarred pasta sauces and salsas), the company is notable for remaining, even after 17 profitable years of growth, family-owned and run, and still true to the very Karma Queen philosophy it espoused when it launched. "All we wanted to do was create a business that would allow us to earn a living by providing convenient and tasty natural vegetarian meals for people like ourselves, who appreciated good food but were often too busy to cook 'from scratch.'"

KARMA QUEENS: CULTURE, SOCIETY, AND SPIRITUALITY

Karma Queens have been represented on some of today's most popular TV shows and movies, albeit sometimes in an exaggerated comic form. Phoebe Buffay, the vegetarian massage therapist cum folk singer on *Friends* (perhaps still, even in syndication, the most popular sitcom in America) made Karma Queens seem admirable as well as funny. Her views on every subject could be depended on to be "alternative," if not downright kooky. Barbra Streisand played a Karma Queen named Roz Focker in 2004's smash movie *Meet the Fockers*. An ex-hippie, free spirit, and sexual healer by trade, Roz managed to freak out her son's future in-laws with her candid conversation and exotic massage techniques. Amplified for comic effect, the character of Roz was still immediately understood by mass audiences as a recognizable type. A less ebullient example was featured on HBO's *Six Feet Under*. Lisa Fisher, wife of leading man Nate, was a classic Karma Queen: a Pacific Northwest, commune-living vegan chef. She even asked Nate to bury her, when she died, "directly in the ground, with nothing between me and the earth." While that might seem a bit gory to some, the show presented it as a reasonable and admirable sentiment. Score one for the Karma Queens.

☆ ☆ ☆ ☆ **A-List Karma Queens** ☆ ☆ ☆ ☆

Shirley MacLaine   *Christy Turlington*

Madonna   *Angelina Jolie*

Stella McCartney   *Goldie Hawn*

Gwyneth Paltrow

If there is any single media figure in recent years who exemplifies the growth of the Karma Queen ideal, and its transformation from the fringe "aging hippie" model to a cutting-edge, forward-thinking iconic status, it is Madonna. She has transformed herself from oversexed, hard-living rock star into an earth mother, spiritual diva, mostly through her embrace of Kaballah (a set of ancient Jewish mystical beliefs). Even if the current neo-Kaballah observed by Madonna (and many Karma Queens) is not true to the historical model, it is typical of the sort of spiritualism that has become commonplace among Karma Queens.

Karma Queens are eclectic when it comes to religious practices or spirituality, with many of them finding enlightenment in lessons that the modern world may have forgotten or bypassed. The 2001 American Religious Identification Survey, conducted with the aid of the Graduate Center for the City University of New York (with more than 50,000 respondents, it's the largest sample of its kind) found that nonstructured religious organizations were on the rise.

My home is a mixture of just about every religion! I have
Buddhist prints, Zuni fetishes, crosses . . . and of course lots of

candles and incense! It's fun to see the expression on guests'
faces when they come into my home for the first time. They
can't pigeonhole me according to what they see. . . . I have a
little Zen cat soap and Virgin Mary nightlight in the guest
bathroom.

Hope, 35, homemaker

The first survey in 1990 made no mention of paganism, but 11 years
later, researchers found 140,000 pagans in the United States. Wiccans,
who believe in a panoply of deities and practice witchcraft, increased
their numbers from 8,000 to 134,000. Alternative religious sites on the
Web are also a measure of a growing need to seek new sources of spirituality. World Pantheism's site, at pantheism.net (their motto: "Revering
the Universe, Caring for Nature, Celebrating Life") has had over
300,000 hits this year alone and has chapters in all 50 states and across
Europe.

Finally, female energy is being recognized, that has been
neglected for so long. I haven't given up on Jesus, but I
wouldn't say I am Christian. I would call myself eclectic . . . and
spiritual.

Michelle, *Salt Lake Tribune*, 3/12/05

A goddess does not have to be the big diva that we usually
think of. Being a goddess is honoring the feminine spirit within.
Sometimes it's just taking a walk and getting in touch with
yourself. Sometimes it's being with your best friends on the
front porch.

Maria, *Lansing State* Journal, 8/12/04

KARMA QUEENS: WHERE YOU LEAST EXPECT THEM

Obviously there are certain products and current categories where Karma Queens naturally make up a healthy chunk of the consumer target, but this C-Type has application far outside of the boundaries you might be tempted to set for it. The truth is, there are few categories where Karma Queens will *not* find their niche, and the product choices they make in these less obvious categories can prove revealing when it comes to sussing out their decision-making processes.

Karma Queens behind the Wheel

The automotive category is exhibit A in this regard. One's natural inclination is to think, "Karma Queens aren't interested in cars." Well, they may not think of cars with affection, but as citizens of the twenty-first century they need to drive and they do buy cars.

The VW Bug, with its retro 1960s style and its curvy as opposed to rectilinear (read: masculine) silhouette, is one car that has captured the heart and dollars of the Karma Queen. The built-in bud vase is one feature (completely incidental to the running of the car) which allows Karma Queens to carry around a bit of nature's beauty with them even when they are on the road.

A more interesting case is the Honda Element. Originally marketed to Generation X men, it's now more likely to be found cruising down a suburban street with a 45-year-old woman in the driver's seat. A quirky, funky cousin to the minivan, it was embraced by Karma Queens because it's completely wash 'n wear (so to speak). The whole thing can be easily opened up and hosed down (perfect for moms, pet lovers, home gardeners, and the like), and its no-nonsense shape completely suits the no-frills, no ostentation aesthetic Karma Queens are drawn to, especially in categories they deem utilitarian.

Karma Queens and Technology

When you imagine a store that sells high-end audiovisual equipment, you probably think of a bunch of guys drooling over the latest tech toy.

And while that may be accurate, Karma Queens are in the store too, just over to one side. What they might be ogling is the Tivoli radio. This retro-style radio has features which make it a piece of equipment that Karma Queens often gravitate toward. There's an admirable simplicity in the way it's designed. Its buttons are not decorated with obscure, indecipherable icons, and there's no hard-to-understand manual. It links back to the natural world (with a solid wood exterior) and to an earlier time perceived as warmer and less tech obsessed. The feel of a product—especially one in the technology arena—is of paramount importance when courting Karma Queens. The Tivoli's wood casing is humanizing, where a brushed metal finish would feel distancing.

This is an important consideration when designing a product you hope will appeal to this C-Type. Are there connections you can make between your product and the natural world? Is there any way to play up this connection or to enhance the consumer's perception of it? Does the product have an aura of warmth, or is it "cool"? Does it maximize the human interactive aspect or reduce a person to being a cog in a machine? Ergonomics are also very important. Although as a culture we have gained a greater ability than ever before to make household electronics bigger (TV screens) and/or smaller (keychain hard drives), the size of human beings hasn't changed (well, not much). Human-scaled products, and ones that are easy to use and that feel natural in the hand, will always win out for a Karma Queen. And a TV that dominates a room will lose out to a flat screen plasma TV that hangs on the wall unobtrusively. (It might surprise you to know that plasma TVs are embraced by Karma Queens.)

Green concerns, needless to say, rank high when Karma Queens are deciding between products. Many machines can be made more environmentally friendly. Compare the 10 gallons of water per load used by the Bosch Nexxt Premium front-loading washing machine versus the 20+ used by a standard washer. Many big name makers are now offering greener washers, like Whirlpool's Calypso or GE's Profile Harmony. (The names of these models alone are a sign they are designed to appeal to Karma Queens.) They're energy efficient, as well as water conserving, but still as effective as a standard machine. And that's important because

Karma Queens are demanding consumers and won't accept second-rate quality just for the sake of the environment. They will, however, pay for the pleasure of getting it all. None of the models listed above would be featured in a bargain roundup of washers.

Obviously, not every product can be made 100 percent earth-friendly, but often at least some gesture can be made in the right direction. Harmful chemical by-products can be minimized, or the use of recycled materials in a product can be increased.

> ...you can be modern and mainstream and still help the environment. It is just a matter of researching before buying. Little things make a big difference...Imagine if all manufacturers sold appliances that were energy-efficient.
>
> **Alice, on homemakers.com**

> ...we as human beings are predisposed to have our senses engaged...choose natural materials, like stone, art glass and wood—anything with warmth and texture.
>
> **Rosalyn, in *The Washington Times*, 10/6/04**

Karma Queens in Other Categories

Financial services are taking advantage of the Web as a way of reaching out to women (since many women feel that they are overlooked or talked down to in banks and financial service offices) with very Karma Queen–type strategies. Citibank, whose 2005–2006 advertising campaign "Live richly" had a very Karma Queen feel (with slogans like, "Be independently happy," and, "Don't wait until someone says, 'Your money or your life' to remember that they are two different things") and has a feature on its Web site called Women & Co.—Addressing Women's Needs. This service offers members the resources to help them work toward financial objectives, a way to connect with other women to share money strategies and frustrations, and a promise that it will help consumers "Live life your way." What Karma Queen could resist?

If women tend to leave the hard spirits to men, the vineyard is very much a place where Karma Queens feel at home. The important differences between whisky and wine? Karma Queens see wine as a subtle, small batch product, with strong links to place and individuals (and, in many cases, to families, since many vineyards remain family-owned and operated). Additionally, it helps that wine is a sipper's drink and is mostly free of the partying associations that beer and cocktails have. Karma Queens never "party the night away" or think to themselves, "It's the weekend! Let's get drunk!"

There is an association of "handmade" that goes along with wine, and Karma Queens are in favor of handmade. Even when price is an issue, they are more likely to gravitate to a product they perceive of as handmade. Any sort of hand processing, if not actual hand assembly, beats a product made completely on an assembly line. The idea that handmade labor imparts some character of individuality to a finished product is deeply embedded in the Karma Queen psyche.

Finally, when it comes to communicating with Karma Queens, whenever possible make it woman to woman. The historical tradition of oral history passed from mother to daughter translates into the twenty-first century call to sisterhood. Corporations should highlight the women at the top of their businesses and stress the input women have in the development and decision-making process leading to the final product. And in terms of advertising directed toward Karma Queens, always try to forge an emotional connection, no matter the category. The emphasis can be placed on a service's ability to lessen consumer stress or create a sense of emotional fulfillment rather than solely on product intrinsics. When it comes to your Karma Queen consumer, appeal to her heart.

MARKETING TO KARMA QUEENS: A CHECKLIST

☑ Present your brand with simplicity, not marketing hype.

☑ Karma Queens are tactile: warm = embracing, cold = distancing.

☑ Be environmentally sound, or at least environmentally friendly.

☑ Natural and/or organic will always beat artificial; handcrafted trumps machine made.

☑ Emphasize woman-to-woman communication.

☑ Be sophisticated, but not flashy.

☑ Leverage the three S's as part of your communication: Sensuality, Spirituality, Success.

☑ "Every person is an individual, but we are all connected"; no woman is an island.

☑ Think lifelong growth and/or maintenance versus momentary benefits.

☑ "Bring out the essential you" versus "make yourself better; change yourself."

☑ Multigenerational messaging and imagery will resonate.

☑ Encourage women to take time to nurture themselves as well as others.

☑ Emphasize a sense of place and/or origins (locally produced or exotically foreign).

☑ Acknowledge the wisdom that comes with experience.

DIG A LITTLE DEEPER
FURTHER RESOURCES ON KARMA QUEENS

Karma Queens in Print
Check out your local magazine store or local book shop. You might be surprised at the variety of titles targeted to this C-Type!

Spirituality & Health magazine
Body + Soul magazine
Yoga Journal magazine
Karma Queens can keep abreast of the latest yoga practices, expert opinions on diet and spirituality, and resources for keeping mind and body in balance with any of these (among many) monthlies devoted to the Karma Queen lifestyle.

Women's Bodies, Women's Wisdom: Creating Physical and Emotional Health and Healing by Christiane Northrup, MD
This comprehensive and popular book (one of Amazon.com's top sellers) is the self-help reference of choice for Karma Queens. Positing a holistic view of wellness and healing, the book covers the treatment of many physical concerns, among them PMS, menstrual cramps, breast cancer, depression, childbirth, and menopause, and explains how many of these physical problems have roots in emotional upsets and outlook.

Alternative Cures: The Most Effective Natural Home Remedies for 160 Health Problems by Bill Gottlieb
A bible of sorts for ailing Karma Queens (and their families). Non-medical remedies are offered for everything from serious ailments (HIV and AIDS, stroke, and cancer) to more pesky afflictions (oily hair, acne, nightmares, and wrinkles).

Heaven and Earth by James Van Praagh
Celebrity medium Van Praagh follows up his bestsellers *Talking to Heaven* and *Reaching to Heaven* with this step-by-step course designed to help interested Karma Queens develop their psychic abilities.

Becoming a Goddess of Inner Poise by Donna Freitas
Mother God: The Feminine Principle to Our Creator by Sylvia Browne

The Power of Intention: Learn to Co-Create Your World Your Way by Wayne W. Dyer

These books all speak to Karma Queen readers, and they all pretty much say the same things: tap into a universal source of energy . . . have a more authentic, joyful, and spiritually fulfilling life . . . oh, and women rule. There's a whole section of any bookstore devoted to telling Karma Queens what they want to hear about the universe and their place in it.

Bergdorf Blondes: A Novel by Plum Sykes

In this popular chick-lit book, two super rich sisters move downtown to the Bowery to open a spa and a holistic food shop. They exemplify the aspirations and perhaps self-absorption (if not the average income) of true Karma Queens.

Karma Queens Online

EckhartTolle.com

The home page of noted spiritualist Eckhart Tolle offers the keys to "The Flowering of Human Consciousness," plus easy links to buy his books, CDs, and products.

Hayhouse.com

This California-based transformational publishing company puts out books, audio, and video in the areas of self-help, new age, sociology, philosophy, psychology, alternative health, women's issues, environmental issues, astrology, and more. Check out the selection; you can be sure some Karma Queens are browsing there, too.

Goddessmoon.org

An online resource for alternative spirituality seekers, with links for nonreligious parenting, alternative wedding and officiant listings, midwife and doula listings, and more!

Sacredcirclechurch.com

An online church of Earth-centered spirituality offering a monthly full moon ceremony called MoonCraft Full Moons, and clergy services like baby blessings, and services honoring rites of passage such as Menarche. All profits over operating costs go toward a Sacred Earth Fund.

Dermae.com

Aveda.com

Origins.com

BodyShop.com

More and more specialty personal care and beauty stores and brands are targeting Karma Queens—and the little bit of Karma Queen inside all of us—with an emphasis on natural elements, purity of ingredients, and minimal, simply designed packaging.

Alaskanessences.com

The Web home of the Alaskan Flower Essence Project—the only system of "vibrational remedies based on the co-creative relationship between the plant, mineral, and elemental kingdoms."

KARMA QUEENS: ASPIRATIONAL ICONS

Dr. Jean Houston

A protégé of Margaret Mead and colleague of the late mythologist Joseph Campbell, Houston is a scholar, researcher, and author who inspires women throughout the world through her work in exploring and explaining latent human abilities. She's also founder of the Mystery School—a program of cross-cultural studies dedicated to the many dimensions of our human potential.

Deepak Chopra

Time magazine called him "the poet-prophet of alternative medicine." We call him an honorary Karma Queen.

NOTES

1. *American Demographics*, 1/01.

2. National Association of Holistic Aromatherapy.

3. Yoga Education and Research Center.

4. *Alternative Medicine Review*, 8/1/03.

5. National Nutritional Foods Association Northwest Region, 8/03.

6. *The New York Times*, 2/16/03.

7. *The San Luis Obispo Tribune*, 5/15/05.

8. *Advertising Age*, 5/1/05.

9. *Advertising Age*, 5/1/05.

10. *Apparel*, 5/1/05.

11. *London Free Press*, 4/16/05.

12. CNN.com, 11/9/06

13. Frozen Food Age, 4/05.

14. Tea Council of the USA.

15. Amys.com.

PARENTOCRATS

Parenting [has become] the most competitive adult sport. We're trying to professionalize childhood.

Alvin Rosenfeld, psychiatrist and author of *The Over-Scheduled Child*

More than ever, for many parents, raising children has become life's main preoccupation.

"Early Pangs of Empty Nest Syndrome," *The New York Times*, 9/4/05

Statistics consistently show that we live in probably the safest time and civilization for children in recorded history, and yet we have never been more worried about their welfare.

Jay Teitel, in *Today's Parent*

t's a scary and competitive world, no doubt about it. But there are certain parents for whom worry seems to have gotten the better of them. These parents obsess over their kids' safety and are determined to see that their kids succeed no matter what the cost. We call them Parentocrats.

The first thing that needs to be said, and which cannot be stressed enough, is that Parentocrats act out of love. While many of them do pursue high-status prizes for their kids (e.g., attendance at a top-ranked college), they are genuinely motivated by their concern for their offspring. Parentocrats truly believe that certain socially accepted markers of success will ensure their kids a lifetime of security and happiness. In this quest, however, they often deny their children some of the classical joys of childhood—the ability to experiment and fail and the freedom to waste time and be carefree.

The Parentocrat impulse manifests itself in two distinct, if related, ways: first, the need to protect their kids from all threats, and second, the desire to ensure that their kids excel in every way. A kind of familial narcissism permeates the thoughts of this C-Type. Not only do Parentocrats believe that their children are special, they believe that their children are important to the world. Therefore, they must shield these special creatures from any outside influence that might harm them and see that they get the opportunities to surpass their peers.

Parentocrats have always existed, but it is a type that is most definitely on the rise. Broadly speaking, members of this C-Type come from the middle and upper-middle classes, the large swath of the population that requires two incomes to support the family, but has a large enough combined income to afford music lessons, sports trainers, computers, and the like. Parentocrats usually have small numbers of children, or a single child—all the better to lavish time and resources on them. This makes sense, since parents with many offspring often reach a point where they are so relaxed, or just so plain sleep-deprived, they can't muster the energy it takes to micromanage like a Parentocrat. Additionally, the older consumers are when they begin to reproduce, the more likely it is that they will fall into this C-Type. Couples who procreate in the second half of their thirties or early forties, especially if they have had problems conceiving their "miracle babies," often become Parentocrats. But it's important to note that Parentocrats can fit into almost any age demographic, since their kids can range in age from one week to college age.

NEW PARENTOCRATS

It's never too early to become a Parentocrat. The arrival, or imminent arrival, of a baby can turn previously sane adults into obsessive creatures scouring the marketplace for any product or service that will raise him or her above the common horde. Lately it has become fashionable to rent an ultrasound machine for the entire duration of pregnancy, the better to constantly monitor the development of a child before it has even entered the world. There is little these new or expectant parents won't worry about. According to a recent BabyCenter.com survey, more than 52 percent of expectant parents believe the choice of the "correct" name contributes to a child's future success in life. (This is up from 40 percent in a survey from 2000.)

Baby Einstein
Baby Einstein offers videos and toys that help a baby or toddler learn about music, astronomy, theater, and a variety of other "adult" topics. Since being acquired by the Walt Disney Co., the company has grown by leaps and bounds, from $25 million in sales in 2001 to $200 million in 2005.[1] This despite the fact that the Mozart Effect, the belief that listening to classical music somehow enhances academic performance, has basically been debunked by researchers at Stanford University.[2]

Itsy-Bitsy Yoga
Itsy-Bitsy Yoga classes (offered at certified venues around the country) are designed for infants who still measure their age in months (participants must bring along a caregiver). Organizers claim the class can help a child develop a healthy body, happy confident awareness, and creative spirit. Certainly you don't have to be a Parentocrat to want that for your child.

Diaper-Free Babies

The buzz in all the mommy chat rooms is a new movement (no pun intended) that encourages the introduction of potty training to—believe it or not—infants! Followers of the not-for-profit DiaperFreeBaby (www.diaperfreebaby.org) movement say that babies too young to talk, or even crawl, are able to be trained to use the toilet. As of 2005, 77 local groups had been formed in 35 states, while upward of 50,000 copies of a how-to book describing the process had been sold to interested Parentocrats.[3]

The growth of this C-Type can be partly ascribed to economic realities faced by all families today. We live in an era of two working parent households. As a result, there seems to be less time to practice the hands-on parenting that was the norm in earlier generations. Feeling guilty over this, Parentocrats overcompensate.

It's also true that we live in an increasingly numbers-driven world, one where it's easy for parents to get caught up in benchmarking their kids at every stage of development. From a newborn's Apgar score, assigned just moments after birth to the SATs (or the LSATs or the medical boards, and on and on), it's inevitable that some parents let the numbers do the talking for them. Comparative rankings, if the news is good, offer the opportunity for parental pride, thus Parentocrats never stop checking and assessing. The marketing implications of this are key. Parentocrats may be the rare breed of consumer who actually *wants* to see charts and statistics detailing the efficacy of a product, or a detailed ranking of a competitive set. They will actually pore over a detailed ad or visit a linked Web site that offers more information. Parentocrats like to do research and dig deep before making important purchase decisions. So offer them the opportunity.

BY THE NUMBERS

So what, exactly, are Parentocrats so afraid of? For the record, here are some commonly expressed parental fears and their actual probabilities of occurring in the real world (in any given year).

Probability that a child will . . .

Die from meningitis: 1 in 588,7091[a]

Die in a motor vehicle accident: 1 in 25,6722[b]

Die in any accident: 1 in 14,2863[c]

Die from poisoning: 1 in 60,2534[d]

Drown: 1 in 71,9015[e]

All figures are based on statistics for children aged 0–14, unless otherwise indicated (see footnotes) from the *Centers for Disease Control and Prevention's National Center for Health Statistics* and *America's Children: Key National Indicators of Well-Being 2005* by The Forum on Child and Family Stats.

a. Estimated figure based on 2003 data
b. Estimated figure based on 2003 data
c. Estimated figure based on 2003 data for children ages 5–14
d. Estimated figure based on 2003 data
e. Estimated figure based on 2003 data

As pride drives the Parentocrat, so too does fear, whether the threat is real or perceived. The current state of the world certainly adds fuel to this particular fire. While 9/11 can't be held solely responsible, it has intensified many parental fears (especially the fear of being out of touch with their children at any time). When targeting this C-Type, remember that any marketing efforts should engender confidence in consumers, and boost their sense of stability and security. When addressing Parentocrat fears, the tone and manner of advertising should be straightforward.

Parentocrats often react to their fears with an attempt to "circle the wagons," almost as if they wish to cut their families off from the harmful world outside the front door. In practice this can mean keeping kids under constant surveillance, as well as monitoring every cultural influence (e.g., TV, the Internet) that might lead kids astray. As we discuss later in this chapter, home schooling is popular among Parentocrats, as are any aids and devices that allow them to mediate between mass culture and their children's minds. Parentocrats really trust only themselves to safeguard their children, physically and mentally, and this can lead to all sorts of issues. It can lead to the feeling among Parentocrats that they always have to "go it alone" if they encounter problems at home, even when there are societal mechanisms in place to help them. Parentocrats fear that outsiders will not understand and might even (heaven forbid!) see problems as a sign of weakness.

> If a child is caught doing something...like drinking and driving...the last thing [protective parents] will do is call on anyone outside the family to help, like the local police or the school. They don't want anything on their child's record that could hinder their quest for achievement some day.
>
> **William Damon, director of the Stanford University Center for the Study of Adolescence**

PARENTOCRATS AND EDUCATION

There is no topic more likely to engage Parentocrats than education. Parentocrats of the littlest students often turn to the HIPPY program (the name stands for Home Instruction for Parents of Preschool Youngsters). It's designed to help parents to (according to the company's Web site) "begin their child's learning process and prepare the child for school." There were (as of 2004) 157 HIPPY programs in 26 states, and the average curriculum for 3- to 5-year-olds included 27 books and 90 (!) weekly activity packets.[4] For Parentocrats living in New York City, the obsession is with getting into the right school—and it starts uncomfortably early. According to a 2006 *New York Times* article,[5] the competition for entry into the top private preschools in Manhattan is so competitive, it resembles a kiddie version of the reality television show *The Apprentice*. Rich, urban Parentocrats may spend upwards of $50,000 on their child's education before the child reaches grammar school!

As mentioned earlier, home schooling is popular among this C-Type, since it means that every aspect of a child's curriculum is under parental control (and, as an added benefit, it severely decreases the polluting effects of peer pressure). While there are other segments of the population that favor home schooling (like families on both the far left and far right of the political and social spectrum, and those with religious beliefs at odds with the public schools in their area), Parentocrats are a definite part of home schooling's slow rise. According to 2003 figures (the most recent available at press time) from the National Center for Education Statistics, the number of home-schooled kids had grown to 1.1 million by the spring of 2003, up from 850,000 in 1999. That's one in every 45 students.[6]

The majority of Parentocrats do allow their children to attend schools. That doesn't, however, imply that they have a laissez-faire attitude about education. Parentocrats take an active role—much more active than teachers and administrators might like—in the day-to-day schooling of their kids. They'll go to any lengths to see that their kids excel and earn the ultimate reward: acceptance into a prestigious college. Some Parentocrats are even encouraging their prep school students to repeat entire school years, buying them extra time for the all-important extracurricular activities, as well as a second attempt at a higher GPA.[7]

> The books that I buy him are more advanced forms of literature. I want to prepare him to read advanced lit so that he is prepared well for taking A.P. courses in high school. For example, his books include *The Plague, Lady Chatterley's Lover, Madame Bovary, Rhinoceros,* and so many other books.
>
> **Katherine, parent of 11-year-old boy on parents.com message board**

> I have a friend who will cry when she gets a B on a math quiz. A lot of the parents think that other people see them as higher up if their kids do better. They can brag about their kids.
>
> **Cassie, *Marin Independent Journal*, 7/25/06**

There is disagreement about how good all this parental involvement is for kids. According to a study by Eva Pomerantz, a University of Illinois psychology professor (reported in *Child Development*), children who struggled in school performed better when parents took a hands-off, positive approach rather than a critical, controlling one. Still, controlling behavior continues to thrive, continuing even when kids enter college. Parentocrats will step in to argue with a professor over a grade or to demand a better class schedule for their grown kids. At this level, at least, some schools are stepping in to curb the trend. Overinvolved moms and dads, called "helicopter parents" by school administrators across the country, proved to be such a problem at the University of Vermont that the school was forced to train some students as "parent bouncers." These students removed helicopter parents from events like class registration, gently explaining they're not welcome.

> We certainly have parents calling about everything. I mean, everything from who will be doing the laundry for my son or daughter, to if they have to miss a few weeks of class, can I come in and sit in on the class and take notes for them.
>
> **Annie Stevens, University of Vermont, on ABC News *20/20*, 10/21/05**

> We have a generation of parents who are heavily involved in their students' lives, and it causes all sorts of problems.
>
> **Dean Adam Weinberg of Colgate University, quoted on University Wire, 9/2/05**

> A mother in Salt Lake City flies to Cambridge, Mass., to argue with a Harvard University professor about her daughter's biology grade. Changes in transportation and technology, from cell phones—nicknamed "the world's longest umbilical cord" by one Georgia university administrator—to e-mail, give parents an almost split-second way to be involved.
>
> **The Arizona Republic (Phoenix), 10/1/05**

Parentocrats' educational obsessions extend beyond the school system. In fact, Parentocrats are anxious to find educational opportunities outside of school, the better to give their offspring a chance to move ahead of their peers. Driven by go-getter Parentocrats, tutoring has grown into a $4 billion industry, with for-profit tutoring centers now opening at an unprecedented rate across the country.[8] Eduventures, a market research firm for the education industry, estimated that the amount of money spent on supplemental educational services in 2005 was $879 million and that the figure would grow to $1.3 billion by 2009.[9] The biggest of the learning services companies, Educate Inc., which includes both Sylvan Learning Center and Catapult Learning, posted $330 million in 2005 alone, up from $273 million the previous year.[10]

Most Parentocrats learn about these types of programs from fellow Parentocrats. When these C-Types uncover a new product or service, they like to spread the word. And they're as quick to latch onto someone else's good deal as they are to proselytize about their own. Which makes a grassroots, word-of-mouth campaign an effective marketing strategy when targeting them. If you can, try using community organizations, like school booster programs, to help get your message out.

There has been an explosion of summer camps that allow Parentocrats to be sure that their kids are making good use of their summer vacations. College admission prep camps, like those offered by Academic Study Associates and Musiker Teen tours, are a good example. They offer essay writing, admission interview skills, and other counseling that they claim will give these students a leg up on their campus-aspiring competition.

These days, kids attend camps that offer instruction and internships in professions like veterinary medicine, sports management and photojournalism. At the same time, children who normally stopped going to camp at 15—the traditional cutoff age—are continuing to attend until they're 18, thanks to the specialty camps that excite them or offer pre-career programs.

The Philadelphia Inquirer, 4/23/05

MARKETPLACE EVIDENCE

Kumon

The Kumon system is a head-start educational program for young students. Parents can enroll kids as early as preschool, and they can continue through their early teens. Originating in Japan over 30 years ago, the Kumon "self-motivated learning" system has now spread to this country, where it has been embraced as a way to give kids an advantage before the first school bell has rung. Today, there are more than 100,000 students enrolled at more than 1,400 Kumon centers across North America alone. At about $100 per subject per month it's not cheap, but devotees swear by its efficacy.[11]

MARKETPLACE EVIDENCE

Ivy Wise

For a $30,000 flat fee, Ivy Wise will spend two years helping Parentocrats and their high schooler learn what it takes to get into a good school (meaning, basically, the Ivy League) and holding their hands through the application process.

PARENTOCRATS AND TECHNOLOGY

Technology proves challenging for this type. On the one hand, technology allows Parentocrats to constantly monitor and assess their children. On the other hand, it can be an uncontrollable conduit for the outside world to enter into their children's lives.

> I recently caught my 14-year-old daughter chatting on line with someone who was using inappropriate language, and when I asked who the boy was, she replied "a friend." I wanted to respect her privacy, but was concerned about who she was talking to, so I searched the Internet for IM monitoring programs.
>
> **Omegaedu on the Education World message board**

> I don't let them go on the Internet without me in the room. No
> chat rooms. She isn't allowed to have her own password. She
> isn't allowed to open mail from screen names she doesn't
> know. I periodically do check her sent and old mail. . . . I
> explained to both my kids that the First Amendment is
> overruled by parental privilege.
>
> **Unnamed mom quoted in *New York Magazine*, 5/04**

Despite the Internet filtering and/or spying software that's currently available (see sidebar "Internet Spy Software"), it's virtually impossible for Parentocrats to censor what their child sees and reads (or even, more frighteningly, whom they communicate with) on the Web. Nevertheless, Parentocrat households usually have stringent rules restricting children's Internet usage. Of the 20 million American children who currently have access at home to the Internet, about 50 percent are being protected by some sort of Web safety software. (For 75 percent that means filtering software, and for the other 25 percent it's spy software.)[12] This is not to say that Parentocrats are anti-Internet. Far from it. They see the educational value of the Web clearly and would never dream of denying their kids access to this increasingly necessary medium. Additionally, the Internet provides Parentocrats themselves with great opportunity (once the kids are asleep) to harness the Web's informational power to their own uses. As noted, peer recommendations tend to carry great weight with this C-Type, so they often look to parents' message boards, blogs, and the like for advice and information regarding upcoming Parentocrat purchases.

> I caught my 12-year-old son looking at the adult cartoon sites
> online several months ago. . . . I know, now that he's already
> been there, he'll continue to go. The curiosity will probably be
> too much. The only thing I can think of as a punishment right
> now is to completely take computer access away from him. (I'm
> thinking for the rest of the year!)
>
> **Blank65 on parents.com message board**

I feel that we as parents have to monitor what our children do on the computer, and take the appropriate steps to insure their safety. The computer in our living room is the only one with Internet access.

Melanie, on parents.com message board

I have friends that have banned their kids from MySpace and even Internet at home, but I feel like kids will find a way, and even though I find myself struggling with it and some of their content and choices, I am more glad that I know what they are doing and that they know I know.

Mom on NetFamilyNews.org

INTERNET SPY SOFTWARE

There are numerous programs designed to help Parentocrats monitor what goes on in cyberspace while their backs might be turned.

IamBigBrother specializes in recording all incoming and outgoing instant messages.

SpyAgent records all correspondence, whether it be instant messages, e-mails, or chat room exchanges.

eBlaster immediately forwards incoming and outgoing e-mails to parents as they are sent.

Xanovia offers the ability to spy on webcam activity as well as to capture and compress screen shots.

Net Nanny is a software package that provides Parentocrats with a broad set of Web safety tools, allowing them control over everything that comes into and goes out of their homes through their Internet connection.

Keeping tabs on kids is a major Parentocrat activity, and here technology is very much a friend. Any place that can have a webcam directed at it can now be under constant surveillance. Using various Internet businesses (often local), working parents of small children can, from the office, literally see how the kids are doing at day care or check up on them at home. Using a relatively new service, Bunk1.com, Parentocrats can even keep tabs on kids when they're at sleep-away camp, with the live feed from the Web site's cam.

> My 9 year old is going to overnight summer camp for the first time. I'm in a panic now wondering why i ever agreed to send him. i don't think i'll be able to breathe while he is away, worrying about him. i won't completely relax until he's home safe in his bed.
>
> **shelbyrd on parents.com message board**

While the phrase "global positioning system" usually calls to mind a car, the same technology is actually being put to use to keep track of straying young 'uns. The Wheels of Zeus tagging system, developed by Apple Computer cofounder Steve Wozniak, has developed small and completely portable GPSs which can be incorporated in products specifically designed for parents. Another device is the Wherify Wireless bracelet (at $400 a pop, only for upper crust Parentocrats) which places the mini-GPS on a child's wrist—and once locked there it can be unlocked only by a parent's key.

> If I could, I would have [a GPS device] permanently put on my child like a tattoo or planted in them like tubes in their ears, or a chip under their skin. I would pay a lot of money for this.
>
> **rworden, on parenting.com message board**

> I have the right to know where my daughter is. Yes asking her is good enough for some kids but with 1 out of every 5 kids between 12 and 14 already having sex and only 1 in 3 parents of those kids knowing their child is acting in such a risky way, I'm

gonna do everything I can not to be the parent that didn't know what was up with their kid.

Kim, 47

Beyond GPS, modern technology has provided Parentocrats with the means to keep in constant contact with their flock. The cell phone has made it easy for mom to pick up the phone when Junior is a minute past his curfew, and has rendered null the excuse, "I didn't call home because I wasn't near a phone." In the wake of 9/11, with its attendant fear of being separated during a crisis, many parents are giving even young children their own phones. For children too young to use a phone, wireless phone service providers have created features that turn regular cell phones into glorified walkie-talkies (like Nextel Push-to-Talk Services, or the hot button on Cingular's Wireless GoPhone), so Parentocrats can connect in an instant.

No matter what the cost of any of the above devices, Parentocrats are willing to pay the price. Given the pace of technological change, it seems certain that by the time this book goes to print, there will be new marvels for Parentocrats to use in their quest to track and protect their offspring, as well as new technological bogeymen for them to fear. It's important to note that all these technologies can also be very useful to marketers. After all, any device that can send a message can also receive one, and mobile phones, Blackberries, and the like, can make excellent channels for advertising and marketing campaigns. Going forward, these channels are likely to become even more important as they also become more flexible and ubiquitous.

MARKETPLACE EVIDENCE

Teen Arrive Alive
Much like the GPS bracelet described above, this service allows Parentocrats to locate their teens and older kids wherever they might be on the globe. The Teen Arrive Alive software works in conjunction with any Nextel phone enabled with global positioning satellite technology, and in addition to letting parents see *where* the teen is, it can tell them roughly how fast their teen is driving.[13] And this info is transmitted in real time, which means if mom calls to say "slow down!" she can see right away if her baby listens!

Parentocrats and Culture and Society

There is a big area of overlap between this section and the last, mainly because most of today's arts media are inextricably linked with technology, for example, Web casts, iPods, MP3s, portable DVD players, and so on. Of course there are some old, relatively low-tech pastimes that still matter to Parentocrats, like broadcast TV and movies, as well as genuine low-tech entertainment like books and live performances. The "appropriateness" of any of these is a *big* issue with Parentocrats, perhaps only second to concerns about education. Luckily for them, there's a plethora of goods and services addressing these concerns.

The Parents Television Council (PTC), which now has over 860,000 members (many of them, needless to say, Parentocrats) aims to influence the content of shows on TV. They run ParentsTV.org, a Web site that lists recent examples of what the PTC found offensive, plus a list of companies that purchased advertising time during these shows, for easy boycotting. Their attitude seems to be if it isn't fit for a child's eyes, it shouldn't be on TV.

> I work with kids at a daycare center and it seems like once a child enters junior high, all the shows available to them are consisting of nothing but violence, sex and who knows what else.... I grew up on Disney and whatnot until high school.
>
> **Ulisa, on parents.com message board**

> Television is pretty bad. What's worse is that they go to school and everybody is talking about the latest trash TV that they sneaked and watched.
>
> **Angie on Parenting Club message board**

Parentocrats themselves are visible on TV . . . as characters, that is. Bree, who started out as a pent-up perfectionist mom on ABC's *Desperate*

Housewives was a prime example until the rules of soap-opera land decreed a change in her personality. Greg and Kim on *Yes, Dear* (now in syndication) remained good examples for the entire run of their show. This sitcom contrasts the neurotic parenting style of this couple with that of Kim's down-to-earth sister Christine and her downright slob of a husband, Jimmy.

There is *some* TV programming that more than meets the approval of Parentocrats, because it is programming designed for and by them. The aptly named Alpha Mom TV launched in May 2004 (on digital cable), the brainchild of Isabel Kallman, a chic former Wall Street executive who traded in her high-powered career when she had a baby. Alpha Mom TV touts itself as crucial for the "new breed of go-to moms who are constantly looking to be ahead of the curve on the newest innovations, hippest trends and research breakthroughs."[14]

One of those hip trends appears to be children's museums. If there was a time that kids were expected to stroll through a regular old museum, quietly and politely, that's a time Parentocrats believe is long past. They want their kids to be cultured, but heaven forbid they should be bored! And, from a Parentocrat perspective, time spent visiting a museum is time they don't need to worry their kids are playing in the street. (When selling any service or activity to this C-Type, just make a connection to education or safety, and you can never go wrong.) There were a paltry 38 children's museums in 1975 in the United States. That jumped to nearly 120 by1990 and to over 220 by 2005. Sixty-five more are in the planning phase.[15] And, according to a 2005 Association of Children's Museums survey, more than 30 million children and families now visit children's museums annually. That's a lot of museum visits, although it still can't begin to compare to a TV ratings champ like *SpongeBob SquarePants* (Nickelodeon) which draws over 56 million viewers every month.[16]

One type of entertainment available to this generation, which is mostly alien to their parents, is interactive video games. While 61 percent of parents believe video games are a positive part of their children's lives, 92 percent of them say that they do monitor the content of all the games their children play.[17] Parentocrats are especially alert to the violence content in these games. While the industry self-regulates and has a ratings code (like the film industry), there is a general perception that the games are too bloody, especially after certain games were linked in the popular imagination with tragedies like the Columbine school shootings.

PARENTOCRATS AND HEALTH AND WELLNESS

When it comes to anything that can affect the health of their kids, Parentocrats are careful about what they do and do not allow and that no potential health risk be given a chance to develop. The typical Parentocrat home has a lock on the liquor cabinet and handle locks on any cabinet with household cleaners. The thermometer in a Parentocrat medicine chest doesn't gather dust—it's used regularly, just to be sure junior doesn't have a fever. And Parentocrats make up a good portion of the callers who wake up pediatricians in the middle of the night with concerns . . . and not just once in a while, either.

Because of the level of their concerns, this C-Type is perfectly positioned to respond to endorsements. Having your product recommended by a pediatrician, or an opinion leader with a high credibility quotient, will resonate with Parentocrats, and do far more than a slick TV commercial or memorable tagline. This endorsement strategy holds true beyond health and wellness but is especially pertinent in this arena because the stakes are so high and the parental impulse to nurture and protect is so primal.

As far as food goes, Parentocrats aspire to serve their kids the most wholesome products available. It's easier said than done, since busy schedules often get in the way of nutritious, home-cooked meals, but Parentocrats do believe that good nutrition will have a positive impact on the health and physical performance of their little ones. Soda is usually a rare treat because sugar-filled treats are closely monitored and/or regulated. Organic food is preferred, especially when it comes to the youngest eaters. Sales of organic baby food jumped nearly 18 percent over 2004–2005, double the overall growth of organic food sales, according to ACNielsen.

Erin O'Neal has two daughters and a fridge stocked with organic cheese, milk, fruits and vegetables. "The pesticide issue just scares me—it wigs me out to think about the amount of chemicals that might be going into my kids," said O'Neal.

The Associated Press, 11/2/05

When buying snack foods for my 22 month old, when there is a sugar-free option to choose from I choose it. . . . I would never give a small child artificial sweeteners! Most of them are only tested in animals and grown-ups.

Enya, on parents.com message board

I [like] the new tamper seals on bakery items in the grocery store. You can tell if your bag has been opened already by checking the paper tab. I am glad that someone is finally taking the food safety issue seriously.

DutchGirl, on parents.com message board

Of course, there is only so much a parent can control over what kids eat outside the house, though some Parentocrats are trying to alter that. One possible sign of the future is MealPay, an Internet-linked school cafeteria checkout system that lets parents check their kids' lunch choices online. MealPay is still expanding—as of 2005 it was used in 75 school districts in 21 states.[18] The system is fairly straightforward: parents electronically place money in a MealPay account, and the student receives a MealPay card (like a debit card) with which to pay for food in the school cafeteria. Because the transaction requires students to enter a PIN, the system can log a record of the items purchased, which parents can review by visiting www.mealpay.com (records of purchases are kept for 30 days).

There is a $2 service charge for [MealPay] deposits made by credit card, but as fifth-grader Keily Geekian's dad says, "It's not too much to pay for more control over Keily and her sister."

USA Today, 10/4/05

In September 2004 my daughter started Primary School.... We were disturbed by the fact that the school cannot provide basic safe and healthy conditions for children to grow and learn in. This relates to children's poor nutrition at school and their regular but unacceptable exposure to midday sun.

Julia Volkova, on her Web site, volkovs.com

One enabler of parental health concerns is the Internet. Parentocrats often go online to self-diagnose (or sometimes misdiagnose) their kids. Too much information often leads to a situation where Parentocrats look for the signs that their kids have certain health problems rather than looking at symptoms (if there are any symptoms) and then trying to decide what the problem might be.

One particular health preoccupation among Parentocrats is allergies. To be fair, allergy rates do appear to be climbing. Studies of peanut, tree nut, fish, and shellfish allergies suggest that 11.4 million Americans, or about 4 percent of the population, now have food allergies, according to the Food Allergy & Anaphylaxis Network. Ten years ago, scientists believed that less than 1 percent of the population was affected. Though many kids outgrow allergies as they mature, that doesn't allay parental concerns in the here and now.[19] There is a boom in stores and on Web sites offering products to alleviate allergic distress, from microbe-zapping air filters and antiallergen duvet covers, to any number of exotic and expensive products that counter dust, dander, and pollen. But even the threat that an allergy will be life-threatening (which only a very few are) gives Parentocrats something big to worry about. Many launch full-force campaigns to rid their children's schools of any offending allergen.

[My 12-year-old kid] could die from a nut. If someone put a gun on the table and there was a potentially deadly situation, everybody would scream, "Oh my God!" But that doesn't happen with nuts.

Janine, *The Lowell Sun*, 9/24/2005

MARKETPLACE EVIDENCE

Psychemedics

This company, originated to test workers for drug use in corporations, government agencies, and schools, has set its cap for the Parentocrat market. Now Parentocrats can settle their minds about whether or not their kids have tried illegal substances. All they have to do is snip off a lock of their child's hair, send it to the Psychemedics laboratory, and then phone in for the results.

PARENTOCRATS AND THE OVERSCHEDULING EPIDEMIC

No pickup games of stickball in the vacant lot for the kids of Parentocrats. This type prefers the regimented and supervised play of organized sports leagues. They believe that every moment of their kids' lives can and should be planned for and filled up. From even a young age, they work to arrange not only outings, field trips, and activities, but simple play dates for their kids. There are no hard-and-fast data as to when the formal "play date" replaced the old-fashioned "going over to a friend's house," but it seems as though it happened over the course of the 1980s, the decade during which (coincidentally or not) the urban myth about razor blades in Halloween candy became a favorite of the mainstream media. Parentocrats now feel an obligation to vet the households of all potential playmates and make sure an adult will be carefully monitoring playtime.

As free playtime has diminished, competitive sports have catapulted to the forefront of the Parentocrat mindset. If their kids just express an interest in, or (especially) show an aptitude for a particular sport, Parentocrats will encourage them to refine their skills with a personal trainer or private coach. This obsessive behavior can backfire, however. According to some physicians, overuse injuries are a growing problem among kids. "It's all about doing too much, too soon, too fast," says Dr. Eric Small, director of the Sports Medicine Center for Young Athletes at Blythedale Children's Hospital in Valhalla, New York.[20] Torn knee ligaments, or ACL tears, have reportedly reached epidemic levels in high schools and colleges. Even if no one is injured, some psychologists see the focus on achievement that leads to overtraining as harmful in itself. For the kids of these sports-obsessed Parentocrats, there's precious little fun left in after-school sports and playground activities.

> Our parents think we're insane because we're flying all over the place... But I feel it's part of my job, my obligation, to expose my children to the arts, sports, various activities.
>
> **Angela, mother of 4**

> My kids were involved with many, many activities... ice skating, hockey, soccer, ballet, tap dancing, chess lessons, Spanish lessons, Chinese lessons, piano lessons, violin lessons, swimming lessons, lacrosse.... You want your child to have everything you never had.
>
> **Marjorie, a stay-at-home mom**

One recent study found a dramatic rise in the "overscheduling" of children since the 1970s. Children ages 3 to 12 lost 12 hours per week of overall free time, including a 25 percent drop in playtime and a 50 percent drop in unstructured outdoor activities.[21] There are many possible causes of this. Some of it is simple: keeping up with the Joneses. Or, as noted earlier, it may stem from working parents' attempts to make the most of the limited time they have to spend with their kids.

> There's so much pressure, like if your kids aren't involved in something, what's wrong with you?
>
> **Teri, *Arizona Republic*, 8/17/06**

Overscheduling is an epidemic in America. Parents are overscheduled and parents overschedule their kids.

Charles Fay, school psychologist/parenting consultant

If you live in a neighborhood of overachieving parents raising overachieving, overscheduled kids, you're going to feel pressure to be that way and guilt if you're not.

Cathi Hanauer, author of "The Bitch in the House," in the *Chicago Tribune*, 12/21/04

But some of the need to schedule and supervise can also be put down to the culture of litigation and liability we live in, which seems to especially permeate the suburbs. There is a vicious circle at work, an insidious logic to the creation of some of these suburban Parentocrats. Since parents often must sign waivers for even innocuous activities, they then think that these activities must be more dangerous than they imagined. Therefore, they demand more safety precautions, which make the institutions react to protect themselves by making parents sign more waivers. Sometimes the children lose out completely, when school and playground administrators decide that the only course is to simply bar kids from climbing on the jungle gym unsupervised or from participating at all in whatever the activity was. In those cases it's up to mom to plan another play date or trip to the children's museum.

It's too dangerous [for children to be unsupervised]. I can spend five minutes and take [my daughter] to school, rather than wonder if she's ok. . . . I always tell her, 'If you're going to fall and hurt yourself, I want to see it.'

Victoria, in *Modesto Bee*, 8/12/06

Of course, scheduling all of these various activities and balancing different family members' desires and commitments is a full-time job (see sidebar Chairman of the Brood). In marketing to this C-Type, always highlight any time-saving elements — whatever the category, the most efficient product or service will likely win out. But there is one caveat to this advice. You need to always be sensitive to the tone of your advertising when mentioning speed or simplicity. No Parentocrat wants to be perceived as rushing through his or her parental duties. By its nature, "Parentocrat" is a double-edged term, and you need to ensure that your product's positioning casts a positive light on Parentocrat attitudes and behaviors. This C-Type doesn't want to be seen as overzealous, just involved. Not as overprotective, but prudent.

CHAIRMAN OF THE BROOD

Today's moms are taking the techniques they've learned in the workplace and using them to great effect in the home. Moms are now using high-tech tools like Personal Digital Assistants and computer spreadsheets to run their homes efficiently.

Stacy DeBroff, president of Mom Central, Inc.

Many Parentocrat mothers manage their homes as if they were corporations. In fact, of the 100 moms who took part in Whirlpool's 2004 State of the Home survey, a full 40 percent said they try to run their home like a business. Though that isn't perhaps the warmest model for family life, it makes perfect sense . . . especially since many of these women gave up their high-powered careers to become parents. While the majority of moms have not traded in the 9 to 5 to stay at home, there is still a price they often pay in terms of a lowered chance of advancement to the upper echelons of corporate power.

Based on the results of the survey quoted above, Whirlpool has begun using the term CHO (meaning chief home officer). The term was coined by noted author and parenting commentator Jody Lynn in 1996. The CHO is a new mom paradigm (CHOs are rarely dads), since the key components of the role are delegating tasks and assigning responsibility. Of the moms surveyed, 95 percent said they delegated household tasks, while 58 percent admitted to keeping to-do lists for themselves and each family member, clearly assigning responsibility for specific chores.

For those moms who don't naturally fall into this role, there are a multitude of books and products to help them learn the ropes. *The Organized Mom Workbook: Management for Moms* by Amy A. Dwyer and Terri Rose White is a great primer in how to apply the scheduling and organizational strategies used by large businesses to the busy lifestyles of today's families. *Mom Central: The Ultimate Family Organizer* by Stacy Debroff and Marsha Feinberg simplifies mom's role by giving her a plethora of spiral-bound charts and schedules all ready to be filled in.

A chairman of the brood tends to be on the tech-savvy side of the spectrum and likes to be able to put the skills she has honed on the job to good use. She will frequently turn to the Internet to find solutions or strategies to help manage her awesome workload or just to connect with other like-minded Moms. (Perhaps it's also because the Internet is "always open" and the only free time busy Moms have is after the rest of the world has gone to sleep!) Chat boards on Organized-Mom.com, OrganizeTips.com, and OrganizedHome.com are good examples of the helping hand model, while ClubMom.com and BlueSuitMom.com (specifically a resource for working CHOs) offer good places for women to commiserate and empathize with each other.

Lest anyone doubt a chairman of the brood's reliance on the Internet, just check out the new LG Side-by-Side Refrigerator with LCD display and Internet access. It allows her to go online without leaving the kitchen. The message is clear: if you want to sell appliances to today's all-business Mom, make them smart and make them multitask as much as she does.

It's no surprise that, despite their best wishes, Parentocrats often create stressed kids. Caught in these pressure-to-succeed traps, and continually shepherded from activity to activity (carefully supervised!), these children often will have a difficult time adapting to college or post-collegiate life. (Assuming their Parentocrats let go of them when they turn 21!) In some cases, a lifetime of shielding and hovering (see "helicopter parents" above) can result in adults who remain dependent on their parents, exactly the opposite result parents were hoping to achieve. It can also take a physical toll. In 2002, 11 million antidepressant prescriptions were written for children and adolescents in the United States. Doctors recommended the drugs primarily to treat depression, but also for other emotional problems, from anxiety to shyness to obsessive-compulsive disorder.[22]

> [We ask ourselves] Are they getting enough sleep? Do they have enough time to be kids? Are we robbing them of developing their imaginations because we're enrolling them in so many after-school activities?
>
> **Eric and Eileen, *Arizona Republic*, 8/17/06**

> Children are not naturally fearful. They learn it from parents' expectations. Somehow we have instilled in them the desperately sad idea that the world is not safe enough for them to run free
>
> **Anne Atkins, author of *Child Rearing for Fun*, quoted in the *Daily Record*, 5/25/04**

> A teacher at a Tennessee elementary school slips on her kid gloves each morning as she contends with parents who insist, in writing, that their children are never to be reprimanded or even corrected. "We've given [kids] this cotton-candy sense of self with no basis in reality. We don't emphasize what's best for the greater good of society or even the classroom."
>
> *Time*, 2/21/05

MARKETPLACE EVIDENCE

Mom's Calendar

A true Parentocrat mom needs a calendar that does more than merely tell her the day of the month. Mom's Calendar is a super-large calendar that helps manage a family's overbooked schedule. It consists of a large grid with vertical column headings (one for Mom, one for Dad, plus three for kids) up top and horizontal rows for each day of the month. And it's a bestseller at Web retailers like Amazon.com.

MARKETING TO PARENTOCRATS: A CHECKLIST

☑ Appeal to parental pride and competitiveness.

☑ Stress safety, but don't provoke fear or anxiety.

☑ Customization is always a plus (because Parentocrats' kids are never run of the mill).

☑ As David Ogilvy said, "Do not regard advertising as entertainment or an art form but as a medium of information." Stats, facts, figures, and studies—the more the better.

☑ The world is tough . . . every little advantage counts. Parentocrats believe this.

☑ Authority figures (e.g., nutritionists; physicians; teachers, etc.) have clout; leverage them as much as possible.

☑ Parentocrats are willing to pay a premium for the good of their children.

☑ Be empathetic in tone and manner. Parentocrats want to feel understood. Even though others see them as often overzealous or overly cautious, they are trying to do the best they can for their kids.

☑ Parentocrats are big on multitasking. Give them products and services that do the same.

☑ Get 'em while they're young; the Parentocrat mindset often begins before a baby is even born.

DIG A LITTLE DEEPER

FURTHER RESOURCES ON PARENTOCRATS

Parentocrats in Print
Check out your local magazine store or local bookshop. You might be surprised at the variety of titles targeted to this C-Type!

The Culture of Fear: Why Americans Are Afraid of the Wrong Things
by Barry Glassner
This book, popularized in Michael Moore's Oscar-winning documentary *Bowling for Columbine*, deflates virtually every high-profile "scourge" supposedly plaguing modern society, underscoring that life today is far safer than it was in the past, particularly for upwardly mobile, middle-class, educated people—exactly the kind of people, ironically, most likely to be gripped by fear.

The Over-Scheduled Child: Avoiding the Hyper-Parenting Trap by
Alvin Rosenfeld and Nicole Wise
Chapter by chapter, this book examines everything from parents' reliance on "expert" opinions to the huge impact of media messages on parent behavior. The authors encourage parents to look inward and ask themselves what messages they are sending—not with their words, but with their behavior.

Little Children by Tom Perrotta
This very funny, darkly comic novel reveals a number of types currently inhabiting the great American exurbia . . . including Parentocrat Mary Ann, an uptight supermom who schedules sex with her husband every Tuesday at 9 and already has her well-drilled 4-year-old on the inside track to Harvard.

Cookie magazine
"When Fairchild Publications held its "idea day" last year, no fewer than five employees posed the same question: where was the magazine for affluent parents who want sophisticated things for their children?"[23] Enter *Cookie*, a magazine about children's products that is clearly for Parentocrats.

ON PARENTOCRATS' BEDSIDE TABLES

The titles of all these books pretty much speak for themselves—and clearly indicate that the publishing world has its finger on the pulse of what Parentocrats want to read.

Raising Safety-Smart Kids/Teaching Your Kids to Protect Themselves When They Are at School, Between Home and School, at Play, or Home Alone by S. Rutherford McDill, Jr., Ph.D., and Ronald D. Stephens, Ed.D.

The Other Parent: The Inside Story of the Media's Effect on Our Children by James P. Steyer

Keeping Kids Safe: Effective and Easy Steps to Protect Your Kids Against Crime by Richard W. Eaves and Richard L. Bloom

Who Is Looking After Our Kids?: A Guide for Parents to Protect Their Children from Environmental Chemicals by Harold Buttram and Richard Piccola

Smart Parents, Safe Kids: Everything You Need to Protect Your Family in the Modern World by Robert Stuber and Jeff Bradley

Parentocrats Online

ProtectKids.com
Parentocrats who worry about the dangers of the Internet are sure to find this comprehensive Web site an invaluable resource. The site is sponsored by Enough is Enough, a national nonprofit educational organization whose mission is to make the Internet safer for children and families.

ScreenIt.com
ScreenIt makes it easy to monitor what kids are watching on television or at the movies, with listings on every curse word, violent or sexual act, or even every cigarette that makes its way into the media.

Safekids.com
Parentocrats can find all sorts of child-rearing guidelines on this site, including how to control kids' Internet and cell phone usage.

DrGreene.com
Dr. Greene, a San Francisco–based pediatrician, holds online question-and-answer sessions and answers specific questions e-mailed in by worried Parentocrats.

www.commonsensemedia.org
This nonpartisan media-watchdog group helps keep parents informed about the child-friendliness of media of all types: TV, movies, music, Internet, and video games.

NOTES

1. *The Atlanta Journal-Constitution,* 4/15/05

2. *BusinessWeek,* 4/18/05

3. *The New York Times,* 10/9/05

4. *The Dallas Morning News,* 12/8/05

5. *The New York Times,* 3/3/06

6. *Orlando Sentinel,* 6/12/05

7. *The New York Times,* 12/6/05

8. *Fresno Bee,* 1/29/06

9. *The New York Times,* 2/12/06

10. *The New York Times,* 2/12/06

11. Kumon North America, Inc., 2004

12. *Christian Science Monitor,* 1/28/04

13. *The Houston Chronicle,* 1/3/05

14. *Austin American-Statesman,* 7/5/05

15. Association of Children's Museums, www.childrensmuseums.org

16. *USA Today,* 5/17/02

17. ESA (Entertainment Software Association), 5/04

18. *USA Today,* 10/4/05

19. *The Capital,* 7/16/06

20. *The New York Times,* 9/22/02

21. *Austin American-Statesman,* 7/15/06

22. *The New York Times,* 11/21/04

23. *The New York Times,* 2/28/05

DENIM DADS

Men don't want to be stick figures in their kids' lives . . .
They want to be very involved . . .

Jeff Csatari, executive editor of *Best Life* magazine (in *The Indianapolis Star*, 1/9/05)

There's been a shift in men's attitudes and aspirations so that now involvement with their children is part of their definition of success and counts as much as success in work.

James A. Levine, director of the Fatherhood Project at Families and Work Institute in New York City (in the *Boston Globe*, 10/4/04)

I n the early 1970s, feminism was in full force. Women were entering the workforce in droves, bursting into even the most traditionally male industries. *Ms. Magazine* began publication. Girls of the time were told they could grow up to be "anything they wanted to be." And the first generation of Denim Dads was taking it all in . . . as little boys.

Though they wouldn't technically belong to this C-Type for decades (after all, one can't be a Denim Dad without first fathering or adopting a child), the stage was already being set. A favorite children's album of the time—Marlo Thomas's *Free to Be . . . You and Me*, an infectious work that espoused feminist ideals, such as gender equality and sharing the housework, in catchy songs and comedy sketches—was aimed as much at boys as girls. In this album's carefree vision of a utopian future, hundreds of years of cultural baggage could be repacked, creating a generation of happy and centered grown-ups unconstrained by restrictive gender roles.

But the road to adulthood wasn't all rosy. For this was the group that, upon entering the workforce in the early 1990s, would become known as Generation X, and be derided as slackers and cynics. Cultural anthropologists blamed the many negative events that Xers witnessed during their coming-of-age years, including the Cold War, AIDS, a flagging economy, and rising divorce rates. Yet at least some of Generation X's influences, most notably feminism and having to fend for themselves as "latchkey children," inspired a social distinction that would finally earn this generation some praise. Generation X, having lived through what some called the "demise of the American family" (a full third of Xers had divorced parents), was determined to do things differently when they had their own kids.

Gen X moms certainly differ significantly from their counterparts in prior generations, but the arguably more interesting shift has occurred among Gen X dads, the group of 25- to 40-year-olds who largely makes up this C-Type. Forget the buttoned-down, three-piece-suit–wearing fathers of yesteryear, who arrived home from work just in time for dinner, and who left nurturing strictly to mom. When it comes to parenting, Denim Dads have a new style and a new attitude about what it means to be a man with kids. Without much soul-searching or critical thinking, they've made parenthood and the maintenance of a household their priorities. Denim Dads seek out a better work-life balance, because they believe they can get more satisfaction at home than they can on the job. Creating a happy home life takes precedence over acquiring toys (a stereotypical vice of this age cohort). Having enough flexibility in their work schedules to allow for this increased familial involvement means more to them than climbing the corporate ladder to the very top.

> The "ideal worker model," where the employee is supposed to put workplace as the first priority, and kids/family come second, is not a healthy model for kids, for moms or for dads.
>
> **Chip, 34-year-old father of 2**

The fact that many men are delaying fatherhood may be increasing the maturity and wisdom they are bringing to the role of father. Today, the average American man is marrying a full five years later (at age 28 versus 23) than he did in 1950, which means that most Denim Dads are probably starting families closer to age 30.[1] And they recognize that a strong paternal presence can have a beneficial impact on their kids.

> My motivation to be a stay-at-home dad came a lot from being a Big Brother with Big Brothers/Big Sisters for 7 years. Most of the kids in that program have little or no contact with their fathers, and I really got to see the consequences of that.
>
> **Riggs, on Dadstayshome.com**

> I think older Dads are more likely to stay at home than younger ones.
>
> **Dave, Rebeldad.com**

Changes in society have also played a part in the creation of the Denim Dad. Technology has made it easier for Denim Dads to work from home, full-time or via flex-time schedules. The stigma of the stay-at-home dad (think Michael Keaton's character in the 1983 film *Mr. Mom*) has been shed, and continued advances toward gender equality have meant less pressure on men to be the primary breadwinner.

> The only people that hassle me anymore are older women who assume I'm playing "Mr. Mom" and giving Mom a break. They don't even bother me anymore since I realize they're making assumptions based on their experience growing up and raising kids.
>
> **SGTDad, at parents.com**

All of this translates into more face time with the kids, more influence on the kids and on their upbringing, and an entirely new definition of fatherhood. Kids, say hello to the Denim Dad.

DENIM DADS AND RELATIONSHIP TO FAMILY

> I grew up in a single parent home. My dad was never there for me. I want to be there for her.
>
> **George in the *Miami Herald*, 6/19/05**

While today's moms spend about the same amount of time doing things with and taking care of their kids as moms of 25 years ago did, modern-day dads spend twice as much time with their kids as dads of 25 years ago according to a study, "Generation and Gender in the Workplace," by the Families and Work Institute. Generation X dads, when asked, also report spending more time on child rearing than Baby Boomer dads, who are just a generation away. According to the study, 48 percent of Generation X fathers say they spend three to six hours per day on child rearing, compared to 39 percent of Baby Boomer fathers. And 47 percent of Xer fathers wish they could spend more time with their kids, while only 36 percent of Boomer fathers express the same wish.[2]

As a dad, I can't imagine not seeing my 23-month-old daughter every day. I can't understand dads who can't be bothered seeing their kids.

Daddymummydaddy, *Parenting* message board

Our daughter has a special smile just for Daddy. He sings her songs and has a million nicknames for her.

Shari, iVillage.com Just For Dads message board

All of this extra time spent with kids means a shifting of roles and responsibilities in the family. Involvement goes further than just a commitment to the quantity of time. Their own childhood experiences, combined with a post-9/11 world, have given Denim Dads the perspective that life can be too short to miss the special moments and opportunities to connect with your children. According to a *Best Life* magazine poll, 84 percent of men said that spending time with their family was the number one element that defines a balanced life. So the time they spend must be "quality" time.

On a more tactical level, whether inspired by a sense of egalitarianism, or precipitated by realities such as having a wife who works (earning as much, or more, as they do themselves), Denim Dads are more likely to share in housework. They are often the primary, if not a significant, caregiver to the kids, and that includes cooking, cleaning, changing diapers, playing nurse, and even acting as psychologist. If you want to reach Denim Dads, you need to start viewing men as being interested in categories and products that are primarily used in caring for the kids and the home. Denim Dads care about household cleaners and baby food. They read labels and view ads through the lens of the family. If you want to market to Denim Dads, put them in the picture, literally and figuratively. In your advertising, show him as a caregiver, with a baby on his hip, not just behind the wheel of the car. Be empathetic about the stress he feels as he tries to balance home and work—present family-focused brands with warm and fuzzy cues that both men and women can relate to.

DENIM DADS, NEW ROLES—
WHAT SETS THEM APART

Postwar Pops	Biggest responsibility: *earning a paycheck for the family* Discipline style: *spanking is okay* Friend or parent? *Parent*
80s Boomers	Biggest responsibility: *raising good kids* Discipline style: *household is a democracy* Friend or parent? *Friend*
Denim Dads	Biggest responsibility: *being there for their kids* Discipline style: *parents as authority; kids need boundaries* Friend or parent? *Friendly parent*

These days Denim Dads can be found in all of the places tradition-ally inhabited only by moms: *the PTA meeting, the playground or soccer field after school, the kitchen table at lunchtime on a weekday.* What's re-markably evident is just how comfortable the Denim Dad is in these scenarios.

> I've noticed my husband has no problem "talking kids" with other dads whenever he gets the chance.
>
> **Lea, commenting on Daddytypes.com**

> I think another long-term influence has been changing sex roles. It fell to the father to get more involved in the day-to-day life of their kids. Coming with this has been an involved father taking pleasure and delight with his kids and an open depth of affection.
>
> **Jim Hasenauer, professor at Cal State Northridge**
> **(in the *Chicago Tribune*, 2/12/06)**

Either I never got funny looks, or I'm not particularly observant. Probably both. But whatever the case, since I knew years in advance that I would take on this role and am pretty comfortable with it, it never bothered me much.

Silviomossa, at Dadstayshome.com

Unlike our other parental C-Type—Parentocrats—Denim Dads have a more relaxed attitude toward child rearing, blended with a healthy respect for old-fashioned parental authority. They make it a point to be "in the moment" with their kids, whether playing with them or reading to them. They are liberal with their affection—not afraid to hug or kiss their children, even in public—but they encourage a household with rules and standards, and believe parents should set boundaries for their children.

My son is so much better around me than he is around my wife. I get way fewer tantrums than she does. Seriously, all it takes is just a slight look and the kid straightens up and flies right.

Flavobean, commenting on Daddytypes.com

"When I grew up, there were no spankings. We'd get a talking to, and reasoning was used to show us right from wrong," she says. "I do think my parents were more lenient, and my husband and I have talked about it. I think we'll be more strict."

Lynne, in the *Argus Leader* (Sioux Falls, South Dakota), 4/7/06

Perhaps this level of engagement with their offspring is responsible for another Denim Dad phenomenon (though it could have a little something to do with the latest technologies, too)—the lack of a compelling generation gap. Denim Dads might be the first group to not fight with their children over what's played on the car radio or what to wear. You never hear a Denim Dad saying, ". . . and get a haircut!" On the contrary, we've noticed Denim Dads and their children sharing styles and fashions like Diesel jeans, Chucks (Converse sneakers), and North Face jackets. In April 2006, *New York Magazine* had a cover article specifically discussing this new generation's proclivity to stay "Forever Young"—terming male parents "alternadads," and arguing that their behavior might reflect a desire to raise children that are "perfect Mr. Potato Head versions of themselves." This is something definitely worth bearing in mind if you are portraying fathers with their family in your advertising. What is your dad wearing? How close is his look to that of his teenage son?

> I've got a baby carrier called a Babyhawk. I face the silly design part in so it's all jet black on the outside. Just 'cause I'm a dad I still wanna look cool.
>
> **Tsquared, on Dadstayshome.com**

Musically speaking, it's clear that there is a lot more crossover between generations as well. Thanks to the family computer's new role as an MP3 music library, dad can sample the music his kids are listening to in just the time it takes to update an iPod playlist. (And it works the other way, too. Kids often download tracks from their parents' playlists, learning to appreciate "old folks" music.) Exposure seems to translate naturally into acceptance, or more.

Digital devices are also allowing Denim Dads new ways to indulge their love of gadgets while broadcasting their sensitive sides. Now they can create video home movies complete with soundtracks and captions, create Web pages devoted to each kid, or a blog to detail every passing musing they have on what it means to be a father. They can even carry around a digital slide show of family photos on their iPods, ready to show every friend, coworker, or casual acquaintance who'll stand still long enough.

> I don't keep photos in my wallet. Now it seems there's a digital solution that I can get behind... the iPod Photo. Before I had a

kid I never would have cared about this, but now it seems like a great idea. I already carry my iPod around with me most places I go; now I can have pictures of my daughter with me as well.

Post on moderndaydad.com, 10/04/05

DADS WHO BLOG

Ben MacNeill, author of the blog Trixie Update (www.trixieupdate .com), has logged every detail of his toddler daughter's life—from minutes napped to diapers changed. Jay Allen, author of Zero Boss (www.zeroboss.com), chronicles life with his four young children. Laid-Off Dad (http://laidoffdad.typepad.com) is the blog of a 40-year-old New York City man who writes anonymously about day-to-day dealings with his wife and preschool-age son.

Blogging on all subjects has reached stratospheric levels of popularity, and parents seem to take special pleasure in airing their musings and grievances in this forum. Technorati, a San Francisco company that tracks blogs, reports that there are approximately 125,000 parenting blogs on the Web. The majority are written by moms, yet dads who blog have a lot to say as well and offer some of the most telling insights about the Denim Dad C-Type. "I love to write, and I love being a Dad," says Laid-Off Dad. It is absolutely important that dads have a voice in the blogging world."[3]

For an extended list of Dad blogs, visit the blog list in the "Dig a Little Deeper" section at the end of this chapter.

Denim Dads are confident about their lifestyle choice and are happy to share their experiences. It's worth considering having your brand sponsor a dad blog, or align with local PTAs or youth sports organizations to create a "dad caregiver" appreciation day.

Denim Dads as Primary Caregivers

The numbers (of young men) willing to do this are stunningly high.... Fifteen years ago, women took time off for the children. It was the accepted assumption. Now, among students, there is no assumption. Young men and women are saying decisions will be based on individual circumstances.

Stephanie Coontz, author and professor (*Detroit News*, 6/19/05)

Not all Denim Dads are stay-at-home dads, but virtually all of today's stay-at-home dads are Denim Dads. Stay-at-home dads, in fact, represent the leading edge among this C-Type.

In the typically unapologetic Denim Dad fashion, Denim Dads who are the primary caregiver to their children speak of their position loudly and proudly, even if the decision was made out of convenience rather than desire. A recent Careerbuilder.com survey found that 40 percent of working fathers would give up their jobs to be stay-at-home dads if their spouse earned enough money for their family to live comfortably.[4]

I think, as recently as five years ago, if you were a stay-at-home dad, you maybe didn't want to talk about it. But my wife has a great job, with great benefits, making great money, so why should she give that up? . . . It's about what's best for the family.

Mark, in the *Palm Beach Post* (6/19/05)

One of the most aggravating stereotypes out there is the idea that dads are somehow not equipped to parent as well as moms—that there is something intrinsic to motherhood alone that makes for good parenting. But I've always argued that all parents have the capacity to be great caretakers, and it is simply a matter of doing the job.

Posting on Rebeldad.com, 4/26/06

I gotta admit I was a little self-conscious at first. I usually limited the outdoors/stroller time to early AM to reduce chances of being spotted by others. But one day it just dawned on me that it's not really that "mom-ish"; society just seems to want you to think that way. Go to the country fairs, parades, etc., and you see Dads pushing strollers quite a bit. Now it doesn't bother me at all.

Spk, at Dadstayshome.com

Though there are no concrete statistics on how many men would consider themselves stay-at-home dads, the best estimates put the number in the United States at around 2 million. The statistics are complicated by the fact that stay-at-home dads can take many forms. There are those whose wife is the sole breadwinner, but also those who work full-time in a position that allows them to work at home. Some stay-at-homes work part time, or merely have a more flexible job than their partner and therefore play the larger role in child rearing within the household.

Just as stay-at-home moms look to other stay-at-home moms for support, advice, and just some plain old adult stimulation, so too do stay-at-home dads. Some dads' groups, such as The Dads' League in North Carolina or Watch D.O.G.S. (Dads of Great Students) are modeled after moms' groups and offer Denim Dads the opportunity to discuss sports, spanking, or violence in schools. Others, like the Grateful Dads, a dad's hiking group with local chapters all over the country, inject a little more brawn by being part support group and part activity group. And for those Denim Dads who want to gripe or get advice anonymously, there are cyber support groups all over the Web.

AT-HOME DADS CONVENTION

For more than a decade, At-Home Dads have been convening in a different American city each year for a day-long event intended to cultivate a sense of community, spark discussion, and offer informative seminars. Some past sessions have included seminars on topics such as forming your own dads' group, injecting creativity into parenting, and stretching the household budget. For more information on this year's event, visit www.athomedadconvention.com.

Though stay-at-home Denim Dads are usually responsible for the housekeeping chores, they definitely don't take the job as seriously as most stay-at-home moms. This is a substantial difference—a crucial one if you happen to be marketing household appliances or cleaning supplies—and one that points up one of the key attributes of stay-at-home dads. They consider their stay-at-home role to be "dad" and not a male version of a housewife. Anecdotal evidence shows that stay-at-home Denim Dads are not really interested in keeping a "perfect" house. They prefer to concentrate on daddy duties like helping with homework rather than vacuuming or stripping the beds. And they suffer none of the guilt moms often feel when their house doesn't pass the white glove test or measure up to the neighbors' houses.

> There are no manuals on how to be a GOOD dad, it should come naturally, so i make the most of the time i do have with him. We read, do puzzles and i help him with his homework, spellings, etc.
>
> Singledad, Parenting.com messageboard

> When I'm the one at home, I'm worrying about laundry, and dinner, and gee, I really should get out there and weed those beds. I think women in general have this need to strive for perfection in everything. . . . Mark is more likely to say, "Oh gosh,

we forgot the extra diapers. Oh, well, the world won't come to an end." And that's really nice because then the kids don't feel stressed, either.

Julie and Nika, in *The Palm Beach Post,* 6/19/05

Some psychologists think that this more laid-back approach to housework may actually have a positive effect on kids, keeping them calmer. Certainly it gives these kids a unique amount of bonding time with their male parent, strengthening emotional father-child ties even as it loosens general household hygiene. But, as ever, modern technology is there to take advantage of this newly opened window of opportunity. The first generation of robotic cleaners would seem to be aimed squarely at stay-at-home Denim Dads, combining as they do an aura of futuristic, R2-D2 cool with the ease and simplicity that comes from letting someone else do the work. Roomba, a self-propelling mobile vacuum bot, and Scooba, a hard floor–washing version (both from iRobot), are perfect examples. While these cleaning bots dodge clutter and bounce off walls as they make their way over the entire floor surface, dad can sit peacefully with the kids reading a book or go out in the yard for a game of catch.

MAMMA MIA! DENIM DADS IN ITALY

Sharing the housework has never been much of an issue in Italy; cooking and cleaning were simply the woman's role. But now, even in this traditionally macho country, "househusbands" are emerging from almost every corner of the boot. The Association of Househusbands in Italy boasts 4,000 members (huge for that country!) who exchange recipes, sew, and share ironing tips. Some of the members claim to have never done housework before in their lives!

There is a growing subset of the stay-at-home Denim Dad, and that is the temporarily-staying-at-home new father. Even men who have no intention of becoming full-time or semipermanent stay-at-homes might take up to a full year off from their careers in order to spend quality time with their babies and to lessen the massive burden that falls on new mothers. While this option is not available to the majority of working fathers, among those who can make the choice, it is growing in popularity. (All dads must juggle family responsibilities with work, but Denim Dads are wont to prioritize in a way that puts the family, rather than the job, first.) When Denim Dad Heath Ledger's girlfriend, Michelle Williams, gave birth to their daughter, Heath promptly announced he would take a year off from acting to take care of his girls. Actor Rick Moranis also made the decision to retire and stay home (permanently), though in his case it was a choice that came about after the death of his wife. He decided that parenting was a job he didn't want to delegate, and he appears not to have any regrets: "It got to the point where I was doing a lot of films with kids—really nice kids, but not my kids. So, I was like, 'You know what? I'm tired of talking to my kids from a hotel room. I'm going home.' . . . [and] I didn't miss the work, I didn't miss the travel, I didn't miss the people. I didn't miss any of it."[5]

Denim Dads who don't have a movie star income are forced to rely on the generosity of their companies, and thankfully, for them, many companies are rising to the occasion. About 16 percent of U.S. companies (including biggies like Microsoft, IBM, and Eli Lilly) offer paid paternity leave, according to a survey conducted by the Society for Human Resource Management (SHRM) released in the summer of 2005. That's up one percentage point from 2004. The state of California, in 2002, passed the Paid Family Leave Act, which allows both male and female employees in California to take up to six weeks of paid leave to spend time with newborns. As Denim Dads continue to take advantage of the benefits, and as more companies try to entice better workers with work-life resources, paternity leave options are expected to grow.

Paternity leave is something employers are going to have to take into account as a recruiting and retention tool.

Jen Jorgensen, the Society for Human Resource Management

...there's a golden rule of HR: To motivate a baby boomer, offer him a bonus. To motivate a Generation Xer, offer him a day off.

"Forever Youngish" by Adam Sternbergh, *New York Magazine*, 4/3/06

Marketing to the stay-at-home dad means thinking about him as a new opinion leader, not at the watercooler but in the car pool. Stay-at-home dads are still relatively novel in most suburban communities, but they can be great brand ambassadors to stay-at-home moms. Imagine the intrigue that a company like Procter & Gamble could create if it were to use BzzAgent or Tremor to seed a laundry care product with stay-at-home dads rather than moms.

VIDEO VISION: *HOMEDADDY*

Homedaddy is a documentary by filmmaker Kent Ayyidiz that reveals the darker side of the stay-at-home Denim Dad reality—the disdain stay-at-home dads can encounter, and the loneliness and trauma it can cause. While not sugarcoating the problems, the documentary takes a basically positive view of the changing face of fatherhood and features a number of at-home fathers enjoying their time with their kids.

DENIM DADS AND NEWBORNS

It is difficult to believe that, not so many decades ago, fathers were (perhaps willingly) banned from the hospital delivery room. Denim Dads would never stand for such banishment. When it comes to everything involved with having a baby, Denim Dads not only want a front-row seat; they prefer to tackle as much of the heavy lifting (no pun intended) of pregnancy as they are biologically able, especially when that baby is a first child. Have you heard modern-day couples say, "*We're* pregnant?" Denim Dads take this statement very seriously. Pregnancy is an event that happens to both of them, and though mom carries the fetus to delivery, the Denim Dad plays a very important and, as always, involved role as well.

This involvement can even begin before conception. Would-be Denim Dads who have not yet procreated are joining women in hearing (and fearing) the sounds of their biological clocks. As they age, these men are beginning to consider whether their sperm will continue to be viable until it is finally required and are embracing options like freezing and storing their sperm until needed. The increasing consumer demand has also led to the world's first over-the-counter male fertility test, introduced in the United Kingdom in early 2006. Created at the University of Birmingham in collaboration with London-based Genosis, the Fertell Male Fertility Tester measures the number of active sperm in a man's semen. "Normal" sperm is indicated through a red line in the sample. The makers claim the test is about 95 percent accurate; results take just about an hour, and it's available over the counter, specifically for home use.

Moving past conception, and assuming a safe and healthy pregnancy, the Denim Dad faces the challenges of dealing with a newborn. As usual, each dad deals with every step in his own fresh and unique way: Denim Dads are much more likely than their old-school counterparts to groggily arise from interrupted slumber to feed a hungry, crying infant. Even Denim Dads with breast-feeding wives don't escape this chore. In most Denim Dad households there are bottles filled with pumped breast milk in the refrigerator for this very occasion. For Denim Dads who are *really* in touch with their nurturing sides, there is also a host of new breast-feeding simulators on the market. These devices usually consist of feeding tubes that can be taped to the chest so the feeder can know what it is like to have a baby suckling at his nipples!

> Our baby likes to play with my husband's beard; she tugs at it and just giggles. He is just so sweet and tender with our daughter. So endearing.
>
> **Shari, iVillage.com Just for Dads messageboard**

Eager Denim Dads have a resource for basic training in infant care. Boot Camp for New Dads, started in 1990, offers support and education for fathers of newborns, including hands-on workshops in communities across the country. More than 120,000 fathers have participated during the past decade. To see what sort of information Denim Dads are looking for, visit the program's site at www.bcnd.org.

BOYS WILL BE BOYS: HIGH-TECH BABY GADGETS

Denim Dads may play a momlike role, but don't try to market to them like you do to moms. Dads still favor their gadgets. Take a look at some of the baby products that have done a good job appealing to Denim Dads' tech-happy sides.

Delphi Intelligent Child Restraint
Though not yet on the market at press time, this car seat monitor will give high-tech support to the type of Denim Dad who doesn't like to ask for help installing his child's car seat. Child seats are installed incorrectly 80 percent of the time, but this built-in monitor senses whether the belts are tight and the seat is correctly positioned and, if there is something wrong, a red light signals the Denim Dad in which of the four zones the problem lies. Also in the works for Delphi are high-tech crib sensors that can do things like detect motion and breathing irregularities.

Lullabub Self-Rocking Cradle
Denim Dads of newborns want to care for their baby the best way they know how, but it's often exhausting and Denim Dads certainly won't turn away a helping hand. Babyhugs' Lullabub gives them just that. The Australian company has come up with a remote-controlled crib-rocker which lulls your infant to sleep. The Lullabub modules are motorized cups you place under the legs of a crib that produce a gentle motion that's a lot like the vibration of a moving car (and what kid doesn't fall asleep in the car?). The product has four settings and an automatic timer, so it can be shut off after a certain amount of time. Visit www.lullabub.com to find out more.

The DadGear Diaper Vest
In recent years, new designers have emerged with hip, funky fashionable diaper bags—perfect for the *en vogue* mom, but never for the

Denim Dad (or any dad, for that matter). Denim Dads, nevertheless, have the same transporting needs that moms have, and that's where the DadGear Diaper Vest comes in. It's got large pockets for spare diapers, tall pockets for bottles, chest pockets for gadgets like an MP3 player and a cell phone, and a special travel wipe pocket for unexpected cleanups. For more info, visit www.dadgear.com

---

Of course, Denim Dads' stereotypically male tendency to enjoy cars, gadgets, and sports points up a real opportunity to create new trappings around categories and products traditionally marketed to males with a Denim Dad sensibility. What could a new digital camera do to be more Denim Dad relevant in terms of online photo sharing or even scrapbooking? How could a kids' athletic equipment brand engage Denim Dads? Perhaps by not emphasizing winning but by addressing teaching and skill-building. Imagine new cars that offer high-tech ways to make on-the-go-eating easier. Or a new, father-focused PDA or calendaring technology, for example, a program that enables team coaches or teachers to update the parental calendars with just a click? Denim Dads may be the point person within the family you need to target with these kinds of bells and whistles, but the Denim Dad mindset will help you create ideas that will resonate with both Denim Dads *and* moms.

DENIM DADS AND SOCIETY

Dads today are doing a lot more than their fathers, even if they still lag moms. I see this as half-full and getting fuller.

Brian Reid, founder of rebeldad.com, quoted on washingtonpost.com, 4/6/06

It's a chicken-or-the-egg scenario. Changes in the larger society may be at least partly responsible for the Denim Dad, but it's impossible to discount the way Denim Dads are in turn changing society. While the cultural stereotype of the bumbling dad who can't handle the kids is alive and well in entertainment, the reality is that diaper-changing tables are appearing in men's rooms, acknowledging that men change diapers, too, and new mass market parenting magazines are appearing that are aimed at men.

Denim Dad Greg Allen, author of the daddytypes.com blog, specifically wondered about the diaper-changing table in public restrooms question. And, while his results show that there is still a great distance to go (his interactive map of Manhattan, on his site daddytypes.com, listed only about 30 fully equipped restrooms), there is also anecdotal evidence that progress is being made. Home Depot, that bastion of power tools and riding mowers, now has changing tables in the men's room, and most airports and highway rest stops do as well.

Beyond paternity leave (discussed above), corporate culture in America is also becoming more dad-friendly. It's a slow process to be sure, but some major players are rising to the challenges of competing for employees in a Denim Dad world. IBM offers tips, on CDs or in pamphlets, on such topics as becoming a dad and what infants need from fathers, while Ernst & Young now sponsors regular "Dad Group" meetings for employees with kids. Greeting card giant Hallmark has noticed the change as well. While it still produces cards with pictures of the traditional briefcase-toting dad, it now also offers cards that portray fathers changing diapers. According to Ali Nicolle, associate product manager for Hallmark, the new cards are for "the wife thanking the husband for his help with raising the kids."[6]

PERIODICAL CHART

When you hear "men's magazine," certain images come to mind. But when it comes to the mags Denim Dads have stashed by the toilet or bookmarked on their Web browser (as with periodicals in any category, many mags for dad have migrated online where printing and postage costs are nil), you're more likely to find an article on the latest stroller than the pics of the latest TV starlet in a bikini. Here's a small sample:

FQ is the UK's first men's magazine developed entirely for the "family-oriented man" devoted to celebrating the lifestyle changes that come along with fatherhood. In 2006 it celebrated three years of "Cool Britannia" dads.

iDad (Interactive Dad), an online, subscription-only magazine, claims to offer what today's fathers want from a parenting magazine: "insightful, original articles on family and money matters."

Fathermag.com which declares, "Fatherhood is man's most important work," is available in two distinct versions: the Family Life edition (for happy dads) and the Family Strife edition (for dads dealing with divorce, custody, and child support issues—who just might need it more).

Denim Dads not only help kids with their homework, but they are also more involved with the teachers and schools. The National PTA, for example, although it doesn't keep formal records, reports an increase in both male members and male presidents across the country.[7] In addition to providing school associations with more varied points of view, this is good for the kids as well. A 2001 U.S. Department of Education report determined that having an involved father increased a student's likelihood of getting mostly As. Perhaps in recognition of this, some school districts are trying to teach boys just on the cusp of manhood how to be Denim Dads. Albuquerque's Independence High School now offers such a class, called GRADS Dads, as part of New Mexico's statewide effort to encourage involvement from fathers. The class was originally intended for teen fathers, but is now open to all boys (students receive a health class credit for the course).

Denim Dads are also becoming more of a presence in traditionally female causes and organizations. In 2005, Mothers Against Drunk Driving (MADD) got its first male national president, Glynn Birch, whose toddler was killed by a drunk driver. Birch became president after more than 15 years as a volunteer with the group, and his presidency, according to those involved with the organization, is expected to help MADD spread the message that its services aren't just for mothers.

People say, "Oh, there are men in MADD?" Predominantly, the organization is a lot of females, but there are men, as well. We have constantly put that message out, but Glynn can now bring it out even more.

Cynthia Roark, MADD's national chairwoman (from *The Chronicle of Philanthropy*, 8/18/05)

SURF DADS

Meet the perfect Denim Dad metaphor: cool, laid back, wading out into the thick of things, and riding big waves and small. As a sport, surfing, like fatherhood, combines fear and excitement in equal measure and demands a dedication of body and a delicate balance of mind and spirit. Surfing is also something that can be shared between father and child, an expertise passed with love from one generation to the next. Many first forays into the turbulent sea occur wrapped in the arms, or under the watchful eye, of a doting dad.

Jack Johnson, popular musician and surfer, is a paragon of the type. Johnson's father was a surfer, too, and now the pastime (or is it really a way of life?) is the source of some of his best-known riffs. Now a father himself, Johnson created the music for the film *Curious George*, in part as a gift to his young son. "I'm going to be, in a way, the voice of Curious George, because he doesn't talk. It's perfect timing 'cause all I do right now is sit around writing songs trying to make my kid laugh."[8]

Despite their beach bum image, many of surfdom's top stars are devoted fathers as well. Glenn Tanner, of James Island, has a respected reputation as a surfer, but is better known among his neighbors for his rock-solid family life. A surfer since early childhood, the sport is something he now shares with his 15-year-old daughter Kristin, already a competitive surfer in her own right, and son Evan, who first skimmed the waves as a two-year-old. "A lot of surfers are devil-may-care types," says Folsom, codirector of the Southern South Carolina District of the Eastern Surf Association. "But Glenn is a true family man."[9]

As you contemplate this type, stop for a moment and ask yourself: how is your business, brand, or company treating male employees with kids? The process of successfully marketing to Denim Dads starts by acknowledging that they exist within the rank and file of your own organization. Are you giving men the same latitude to work from home when a child is sick as you would a working mom, without judgment? Are you creating any family outings and activities focused around dads?

Creating a different sensibility for your brand or business as you go forward can lay the groundwork for future relevance with this generation of Denim Dads and the next. If you do it right, you may create awareness in today's 10-year-old boy (who will at some point be the dad in his own family) who will see it as more relevant because it was his dad who once-upon-a-time introduced it to him.

TV TIMELINE

It's interesting to note that although Denim Dads are a recent phenomenon, examples of the fathers with some very Denim Dad-ish characteristics have existed in TV land for decades. Could it be that yesterday's fantasy Dad is today's real-life Dad?

Ward Cleaver of *Leave It to Beaver*—Ward not only brought home the bacon, but he always seemed to be around the house—and always had just the right parental advice for Wally and the Beav.

Mike Brady on *The Brady Bunch*—Adding three stepkids to your family is no problem when you have a sensitive, let's-talk-this-through Denim Dad like Mike Brady!

Ted Kramer in *Kramer vs. Kramer*—Ok, it's a movie not a TV show, but this character, played by Dustin Hoffman, became a cultural flashpoint when the movie was released. Ted Kramer not only learned to play mom to his only son, but he also fought to gain custody of the boy—unheard of at the time.

Steven Keaton of *Family Ties*—He was a hippie liberal before having kids, so it's no surprise that Steven Keaton (played by Michael Gross) was a peace-loving, nurturing dad to his brood.

Cliff Huxtable of *The Cosby Show* — This 80s version of a Renaissance man was not only a doctor by profession, but he also played serious psychologist to his many TV children.

Danny, Jesse, and Joey of *Full House* — Three guys bringing up three girls — need we say more?

Tom Scavo on *Desperate Housewives* — The show is a satire, yet it portrays a realistic view of the modern parent partnership, with Tom and his wife Lynette playing musical chairs as to which one works and which one stays at home with their pack of hyperactive offspring.

MARKETING TO DENIM DADS: A CHECKLIST

☑ No dad bashing! Yesterday's teasing is today's condescension.

☑ Denim Dads = Blogging Dads.

☑ Show dads together with their kids in your advertising without tugging at heartstrings.

☑ Men have a sense of humor when it comes to parenting; use it to your advantage.

☑ Denim Dads want equipment and gadgets that help make the household run smoothly.

☑ Be masculine and playful versus feminine and nurturing.

☑ Denim Dads share music, sports, and more with their kids. Think generation rap, not generation gap.

☑ Youthful energy; youthful outlook; youthful appearance—Denim Dads are not stodgy.

☑ Balancing work and home is a key consideration for Denim Dads.

☑ Society at large may not have fully caught up to the leading edge. Helping stay-at-home Denim Dads feel less marginalized can create a lasting brand bond.

☑ Foster links between Denim Dads and their sons.

DIG A LITTLE DEEPER
FURTHER RESOURCES ON DENIM DADS

Denim Dads in Print

Parenting Partners: How to Encourage Dads to Participate in the Daily Lives of Their Children by Robert Frank and Kathryn E. Livingston

At first glance this book might seem like an attack on men. But, in the end, Frank's argument that fathers and mothers should be on an equal footing just sounds like common sense—and could be a Denim Dad credo. *Parenting Partners* states that everyone benefits when dads play a major role in bringing up kids, and it offers specific tips on how men should be involved with kids of every age and in every situation.

Stay-At-Home Dads: The Essential Guide to Creating the New Family by Libby Gill

Media executive and working mother Libby Gill shows readers wanting to switch to a stay-at-home dad model how to do it, with minimum disruption and maximum satisfaction. She profiles many families that have happily done just that.

Finding Time for Fatherhood by Bruce Linton

Linton wants to help men become better fathers and better men. In brief, essaylike chapters he discusses the ways being a better husband and better person can make a man a better parent, and one who just happens to be male.

The 7 Secrets of Effective Fathers by Ken R. Canfield

Drawing on thousands of interviews with real fathers, this book provides a practical blueprint for successful fathering in the real world.

Dad Duty Seattle: Dad-tested Kid-approved Adventures That Won't Bore Your Socks Off by Ean Vent

Here's the author's philosophy (verbatim): "Avoid the 'riums' and 'seums' such as aquarium, planetarium, museum, auditorium . . . ad nauseum! . . . Don't worry, your kids will get cultured, but you can concentrate on adventures that knock your kids' socks off—or, at least get something useful done like a trip to the dump." A very male outlook permeates this useful book on how working fathers can maximize the time they spend with their (Seattle-based) kids.

Fatherneed: Why Father Care Is as Essential as Mother Care for Your Child by Kyle Pruett
Yale child psychiatrist Pruett explores the way fathering affects both children and men. "Men are the single greatest untapped resource in the lives of American children," he contends, and, "the mutually dependent relationship," which he calls "fatherneed," plays a vital role in both child development and the emotional and physical well-being of men.

The Way We Really Are: Coming to Terms with America's Changing Families by Stephanie Coontz
What's Coontz's book about? Ask her: "With 50 percent of American children living in something other than a married-couple family with both biological parents present, and with the tremendous variety of male and female responsibilities in today's different families, the time for abstract pronouncements about good or bad family structures and correct or incorrect parental roles is past." To see how the Denim Dad fits into the picture, you'll have to read the book.

Denim Dads Online
Slowlane.com
An online reference, resource, and network for stay-at-home dads (SAHD) and their families. It also has a useful collection of links to sites for all fathering issues, including local and international dad organizations, single dads, Denim Dads, divorced dads, custody issues, personal stories, and places to connect to other dads.

Dadstayshome.com
An online meetinghouse for stay-at-home Denim Dads. Coming from all walks of life, these Denim Dads can post on this site to gain validation, learn how to cope, or just let off steam.

Fatherville.com
The Web site of the Fatherville organization, a resource for fathers ". . . by fathers and about fathers." Read the posted articles, or post in an online forum. The important thing is to connect to other dads.

Fathersforum.com
A great site for "pregnant" Denim Dads. The site offers detailed essays on what to expect month by month during pregnancy, and then as your newborn grows into a child.

Fathers.com
A site created by the National Center for Fathering, which provides tips and resources, "Helping you become a better dad." Founded in 1990, the National Center for Fathering believes that every child deserves to have an involved father figure.

Babygadget.net
Subtitled "Contemporary finds for modern tots," this site allows Denim Dads to get cool things that are good for baby and fun for dad. Users can purchase innovative and fun products for offspring, or read up on what designers have in mind for the future.

Dad Blogs
daddytypes.com
theblogfathers.com
defectiveyeti.com
snowdeal.org
laidoffdad.typepad.com
moderndaydad.com
morediapers.com
thingamababy.com
rebeldad.com
All of the above sites are incredibly idiosyncratic and very similar at the same time. Looking for a day-by-day, blow-by-blow rundown on life in the Denim Dad trenches? Just check out any of these online fatherhood diaries. (Each one lists links to other blogs as well, so once you get started, you may never finish!)

DENIM DADS ONSTAGE: "IT'S A DAD THING!"

When five Aussie fathers come together to build a playground for a local school, there are plenty of laughs and lots to learn about Denim Dads. That's the premise of the comedic play *It's a Dad Thing* now showing at playhouses down under. The play examines parenthood from a modern-day Denim Dad perspective and covers topics such as childbirth, alcohol, and pizza! If you aren't in Australia, you're out of luck, but plans are afoot for an American production.

DENIM DAD ROLE MODEL: PITTSBURGH STEELER LARRY FOOTE

Denim Dads take their fatherly responsibility very seriously, and no one in the public eye personifies that better than Pittsburgh Steeler linebacker Larry Foote. In 2004, Foote was a carefree single 24-year-old enjoying life in the pros when he got the shock of his life—he found out about an 8-year-old son he had fathered back in high school. Rather than shirk his responsibilities or merely offer child support, Foote asked for, and got, legal custody of the child. Knowing nothing about fatherhood, Foote began a new life with young Treyveion, a move he calls "tougher than football."

NOTES

1. *The Washington Times*, 9/7/06
2. "Generation X: From Grunge to Grown Up" a study by Reach Advisors of Boston, quoted in the *Christian Science Monitor*, 7/21/04
3. *The Washington Times*, 5/22/05
4. *St. Petersburgh Times*, 4/17/06
5. *The Independent*, 5/16/06
6. *San Jose Mercury News*, 6/19/05
7. *Philadelphia Inquirer*, 5/8/05
8. *Salt Lake Tribune*, 8/27/04
9. *The Post and Courier*, 4/24/04

Ms. Independents

"

I'm a very happy single woman. I'm dedicated to my career. I have a high-power executive job. I own my home. I travel all the time. I'm a mentor to a girl in the Big Brothers/Big Sisters program. I have many friends and really don't want the messy trappings of a relationship, although I enjoy male company. I'm confident, sexy and attractive. I have a fulfilling sex life, and when I don't have a partner, I take care of my own needs. My friends have a hard time believing that I want to be single. They're always trying to convince me that I'm not being truthful with myself. I disagree.

Brooke, quoted in the *Chicago Tribune*, 7/8/05

Many of my male friends have expressed frustration with "independent" women in our age group. The guys say they need to be needed. After so many years of making my own decisions and relying on myself, I'm not sure I even know how to need someone else.

Posting on WashingtonPost.com

"

I n the same way that the zeitgeist of the 70s and 80s influenced the boys who would become the Denim Dads described in the last chapter, the environmental influences and popular movements of those decades also had a lasting effect on the girls who would become Ms. Independents. These strong, unmarried women, ranging in age from their mid-twenties to late thirties, are, without question, a product of the times they grew up in, but sometimes unpredictably. If they eventually marry, they do so later, certainly, than their mothers and grandmothers did, unwilling to risk becoming trapped in the "comfortable concentration camp," as Betty Friedan described suburban home life in *The Feminine Mystique*. But they also resist the feminist label and reject the strident tone of activists like Gloria Steinem and Naomi Wolf. They take their jobs seriously, but don't embrace the "power woman" ideal of the ladder-climbing eighties. Ms. Independents have no desire to become indistinguishable from their male peers. But they are adamant that women be free to pursue work at the expense of family and to explore fields like finance, or science, often dominated by men. Resisting any label that might pigeonhole them, these women do what *they* like and make *their own* rules. Neither completely embracingn nor rejecting previous models of femininity, they feel free to pick and choose from all the options our modern world has to offer.

We live in a time when women in general are amassing more power than ever before and are renegotiating the rules of marriage, career, and motherhood. Ms. Independents are certainly part of this. They're powerful females, but ones that would rather just get on with their lives than take the time to define exactly who they are as a group, or organize into a feminist movement like the women of previous generations. Ms. Independents are too busy starting businesses and taking trips, buying homes, and celebrating personal achievements and milestones with indulgent, high-priced gifts—to themselves. By living well, they feel they are committing their own unspoken act of rebellion and making the strongest statement of all.

Though not inherently averse to marriage or relationships, Ms. Independents who marry often do so past the age of 30. What's more, they refuse to view their lives before marriage as somehow incomplete. Ms. Independents aren't sitting at home waiting for Mr. Right. In fact, they're not waiting for much of anything. Whether in a committed relationship or not, they look for fulfillment in building a career, enjoying leisure time with their usually large network of friends, pursuing hobbies or educational interests, or traveling. This C-Type came of age in a more liberal era than their mothers, and this means that, as far as they're concerned, things like sex, home buying, and even having and raising children can take place outside of a marriage.

> My life is so expansive, and the people I know are so diverse. I have such a full life in that respect.
>
> **Joanne, in the *Pittsburgh Tribune Review*, 8/22/06**

> It absolutely kills some men to think that women today are self-sufficient enough that they can make it just fine without a man.
>
> **Aleigh, AOL Money & Finance Message Board**

Though the description above might conjure up images of upscale, fashion-conscious, *Sex and the City*-like urbanites, the surprising truth is that this C-Type is easily found outside cities, in America's expanding exurbia. Even in suburban communities in the middle of the country, Ms. Independents are building their own totally independent lives.

WHAT DO YOU CALL A MS. INDEPENDENT IN JAPAN?

It sounds like an insult, but to young women in Japan, the name Loser Dog is actually a compliment. Loser Dogs are women who say they'd rather focus on their careers than marriage. It has its origin in the title of a bestselling book, *Howl of the Loser Dogs*, a chronicle of the Japanese dating scene written by thirtysomething writer Junko Sakai.

Ms. Independents: Love, Sex, and Marriage

Remember the *Newsweek* article back in 1986 claiming that a 40-year-old, single, college-educated woman was more likely to be killed by a terrorist than marry? The magazine eventually retracted the article, saying the findings weren't valid, but Ms. Independents had never been bothered by it anyway. (In truth, this generation of Ms. Independents was most likely too young to have been upset by that particular faulty statistic, but the attitude behind it, that all women must want to get married, continues to manifest itself in our culture in myriad ways.)

Ms. Independents just don't define themselves by their lack of a husband or partner. The older edge of this C-Type cohort grew up as part of the generation that saw the divorce rate rise to 40 percent. Not surprisingly, this caused them to become more skeptical of marriage and to think that waiting to make the commitment is wise. (According to the U.S. Census Bureau's 2003 figures, the proportion of never-married women between 30- and 34-years-old is triple what it was in 1970.)

Why do you think 50% of American marriages end in divorce? Getting married right out of college, you are still growing and learning things about yourself.

Densel, on feministe.us/blog

Just because someone isn't ready for marriage doesn't mean they lack maturity or need to "grow up."

Winter Storm, on the Quarterlifecrisis.com message board

It definitely takes years after college to find yourself and grow as a person. I'm 27, finishing up my masters, and changing careers within the next year, and I don't see myself settling down until my early 30s. Take your 20s to have fun!

Undercover, on the Quarterlifecrisis.com message board

Ms. Independents are also freer to make the choice to delay, or eschew, marriage because the single life no longer means a life of celibacy. Today's "nice girls" can, and do, have sex lives. In fact, this C-Type enjoys what is probably the most liberal, free, and uninhibited sexuality of any generation of women to date. They have an unrivaled sexual confidence; for them sex can be pure pleasure, with no guilt. Whether in the context of an ongoing casual relationship, a one-night stand, or a romp between "friends with benefits," Ms. Independents have far less sexual baggage than the single women who came before them. Ms. Independents are not afraid of their sexuality. They will unashamedly get a Brazilian bikini wax, buy and use sex toys, read spicy literature, and/or enroll in pole dancing classes.

SHOPPING HABITS OF THE SEXUAL MS. INDEPENDENT

How do you satisfy a Ms. Independent if you're a sex shop? Treat her the way she's used to being treated when she shops for clothes or jewelry. These sex stores around the country get it right.

Kiki du Montparnasse: This recently opened, women-focused boutique in New York peddles upscale sex toys, from a platinum travel vibrator to a hand-sculpted obsidian diletto.

Myla: Located on Manhattan's ritzy Madison Avenue, Myla's sex toys come with a hefty price tag. That's acceptable to Ms. Independents because the products fit into their lifestyle so well.

Early to Bed: Chicago women can find beautiful, and sometimes edible, lingerie here, along with a wide range of sex toys. The store also offers products online (www.early2bed.com), but a true, uninhibited Ms. Independent prefers a more hands-on buying experience.

Just as Ms. Independents can be more aggressive in the boardroom and on the street, they feel free to be aggressive in bed (not stopping until *they're* satisfied). To show they're in control, and also because they're not embarrassed by their sexuality, Ms. Independents will often take the initiative by buying and carrying their own condoms. The recent FDA approval of the "morning after" contraceptive pill (marketed under the name "Plan B") for over-the-counter sale was a great triumph for this C-Type. As long as safe sex is practiced (and most of these women wouldn't consider sex any other way), Ms. Independents find it perfectly acceptable to rack up more than a few lovers before marriage (assuming they're planning to ever marry).

Because they're more sexually empowered, they are also likely to take the initiative sexually. Remember the 1994 Diet Coke commercial in which a group of working women ogled a shirtless and hunky construction worker? The ad, with its implication that females might enjoy objectifying men as much as vice versa, caught many by surprise. Today there's no excuse for underestimating the power of the unclad male form to sell products to (especially younger) women. It's true that women usually have more of a sense of humor about such overt appeals than men, but treated with the right dose of Gen X irony, a reverse objectification ad is always a good bet when targeting this C-Type. At the very least, make sure your advertising shows a man as a peer, not as the knight on a white horse sweeping in to "save" the damsel. And many Ms. Independents enjoy hanging with the boys, doing "boy" things (drinking beer, watching football, playing pool, etc.). Consider images and marketing messages that level the playing field, that unite instead of make distinctions between the sexes.

Technology further empowers Ms. Independents sexually. E-mail allows for a less intimate way of testing the romantic waters or scheduling booty calls. Online dating sites like match.com, lavalife.com, and others give Ms. Independents access not only to hordes of men, but hordes of men they might not have otherwise met in real life. An estimated 21 million Americans—a quarter of all single people in this country—visited online dating sites in a single month in 2003, according to Nielsen NetRatings. Sites like craigslist.com even include searchable categories, such as "Casual Encounters," in which Ms. Independents looking for sex with no commitment are able to find like-minded partners in an instant.

It's an empowering thing for women.... Before I did Internet dating, I always felt a bit helpless ... you are the one in control of your life. Shouldn't that be true for your dating life as well?

Cherie Burbach on her Web site thedifferencenow.com, 5/21/06

Online dating is an empowering experience for many women because they feel more confident flirting and asking for what they need in cyberspace than in face-to-face situations.

From a 2006 article on the dating site pocado.com

So, to whom can we credit this new flowering of sexual confidence? Its roots lie back in the 70s, when female authors like Erica Jong and Nancy Friday called upon women to satisfy their sexual desires and explore their erotic selves. But today's young single women probably can thank four women who came onto the scene a little later: Carrie, Samantha, Miranda, and Charlotte. These girlfriends, the lead female characters in the HBO series *Sex and the City*, showed women everywhere that it was perfectly normal to have lots of relationships, be sexually selfish and, most importantly, discuss the most intimate details of your romantic entanglements, loudly and often. Midway through the landmark show's six-season run, Candace Bushnell (the creator of the *Sex and the City* characters, and perhaps greatest modern-day hero to single women) left the single ranks to marry her boyfriend. In true Ms. Independent fashion, she did what she wanted, when she wanted, and in the process affirmed that it's possible to celebrate the single, independent woman and simultaneously embrace marriage as an institution.

WHEN IT COMES TO MS. INDEPENDENT SEX . . . WHAT'S IN?

☑ Masturbating (and not being afraid to admit it)

☑ Vibrators (for use alone or with a partner)

- ✓ Sex shops just for her/at-home sex-toy sales parties
- ✓ Erotic chick lit
- ✓ Locker room talk among gal pals
- ✓ Casual romantic encounters
- ✓ Friends with benefits
- ✓ Sex skills classes

MARKETPLACE EVIDENCE

Mama Gena's "Womanly Arts Mastery Program"
Regena Thomashauer (aka Mama Gena) is a New York author and sexual empowerment guru who considers all women goddesses and thinks they're the planet's greatest untapped natural resource (a belief few Ms. Independents would argue with). To help them unleash their inner goddess and join the "pleasure revolution," Thomashauer offers a course called "The Womanly Arts Mastery Program," in which goddesses-in-training learn to be more comfortable with their bodies and sexuality (those embarrassed by nudity need not apply) and reach new levels of sexual excitement.

MARKETPLACE EVIDENCE

Passion Parties
Move over, Tupperware. Single women who wouldn't be caught dead at a party devoted to housewares think nothing of inviting some friends over to meet with a sex expert who demonstrates and sells her wares. According to a 2005 article in the *Charlotte Observer*, two companies, Passion Parties and Pure Romance, are the most popular, with Pure Romance posting sales of more than $46 million in 2004!

Ms. Independents: Home

For many young, single men, independence is signified by *not* owning a home; being free of the responsibility of a mortgage allows them to feel rootless and carefree. Ms. Independents, on the other hand, find home ownership empowering. And they're indulging this desire more and more. According to the National Association of Realtors, 21 percent of new home purchases in 2005 were made by single women (versus only 9 percent by single men).

Though unmarried men tend to buy a home only when on the verge of settling down, single Ms. Independents are eager to buy a home whenever they've amassed the cash. In their estimation, finding Mr. Right has relatively little to do with owning a home. Ms. Independents know it's not only a good investment but it's also good for their psyche; there is no better proof of all they've accomplished than a set of keys to their own front door. Owning a home also proves they can take care of themselves, no matter what.

> I bought my own house. What do I like about living on my own? Freedom. I can come and go as I please. I can do the things I want to do. A lot of my female friends have done the same and love it.
>
> **Nicki, commenting on the CNN News site**

> I bought a place on my own last year. It gives you personal security and it's nice to have an investment when you're working hard.
>
> **Lexie, commenting on the CNN News site**

There are some distinctions that can be made when women buy homes for themselves, and buy alone. The National Association of Realtors data found single women tend to favor condominiums. Forty percent of condo buyers in 2005 were single women, partly because of amenities such as maintenance and security that come with condo liv-

ing. Marketers, take note! Ms. Independents are willing to pay for services that help them feel secure, happy, and confident. That can mean
the convenience of having service people on call, or a place to find emotional support when going through the sometimes rough process of buying a first home. Chrysalis, a nonprofit women's center in Minneapolis,
now offers home buyer classes for women. They got the idea when one
of their counselors witnessed a single woman so stressed about whether
she was doing the right thing that she cried while signing the purchase
and sales agreement. Ms. Independents have embraced the classes en-
thusiastically. Unlike many men, they're not afraid to get help or admit
what they don't know.

Also stepping in to support house-buying Ms. Independents is the
home repair industry. Building supply giants like Home Depot, Lowe's,
and Ace Hardware can't have helped noticing how many of their customers are female homeowners (with DIY inclinations!). By some accounts, women now make up half of the shoppers in home improvement
stores. They also comprise 40 percent of all sales in the home repair and
improvement market.[1] Needless to say, not all these female shoppers are
Ms. Independents. Still, Home Depot is anxious to court this influential and profitable C-Type. It currently offers a "Do-It-Herself" workshop,
aimed primarily at women without husbands at home, and the chain
claims it has attracted hundreds of thousands of women.

> I consider myself to be very independent. Financially,
> professionally—I've even learned to do stuff around the house!
>
> **Carrie, on myspace.com**

Not all women, however (Ms. Independents or otherwise,) need the
instruction. A study by Sears, Roebuck and Company finds that 83 percent of women believe working with tools makes them feel "independent." Various other studies show that more than 80 percent of women
own, at the very least, a basic set of hand tools, along with a few power
tools. One in five women owns an extensive collection of hand and
power tools. A number of brands are introducing home tool kits specifically with this C-Type in mind, appealing to their sensibilities and ca-

pabilities, with tools that are lightweight, easier to grip, and come in appealing colors and textures. Lynda Lyday, a former carpenter and host on the DIY Network, now sells her own red-and-white coordinated tool belt and tool set. Kellie Reamer, a self-taught contractor, dreamed up a product line that would appeal to women by being . . . well, the name says it all: Pink Tool Belt.

HANDYMAN? HANDY WOMAN

A survey of 1,000 women conducted by ACE Hardware found that more than 50 percent of them had repaired a running toilet, 46 percent had fixed a leaky faucet, and 38 percent say they'd installed a light fixture themselves.

Ensconced in their own homes, Ms. Independents can now turn their attention to hobbies. Surprisingly, they are engaging in the sorts of domestic activities their grandmothers would have understood and admired. Knitting, crocheting, sewing—these crafts are all back and are favorites of many Ms. Independents. It's big business, too. The craft category had retail sales of more than $30 billion last year, according to the Craft and Hobby Association. Web sites are proliferating that make it easy for interested women to explore their options. Just one site, the multicraft mecca craftster.org, has over 50,000 registered members and gets 300,000 visits a month.[2] Craftster.org's site motto is "No tea cozies without irony," which is a pretty good indication that its target audience is more Ms. Independent than June Cleaver. In the noncyber realm, weekly knitting circles, called "Stitch 'n' Bitch," are now being offered at various locales around the country (craft stores, community centers, and bars). Once considered stuffy, knitting and crocheting are now seen as hip, creative, and challenging. Of course it doesn't hurt that knitting is a favorite activity of movie stars. Julia Roberts is an avid knitter, as are Sarah Jessica Parker and Scarlett Johansson (who likes to have a project to pick up for the time in between takes).

Women who embrace what I call the new domesticity are not traditional women...most of them, I think, consider themselves third-wave feminists. They're independent, earn their own living, but also come to appreciate doing things by hand.

Jean Railla, founder of GetCrafty.com

"The young generation's interest in crafting is a reverse rebellion," says Jane Saks, director of the Institute for the Study of Women and Gender in the Arts and Media. "The modern woman can approach crafts with a healthy dose of irreverence."

Chicago Tribune, 12/14/05

The TV networks have most definitely noticed this new interest in crafts. And, more importantly, they've understood that today's crafters are not as wholesome and sincere as the knitters of yesteryear. Thus we now have crafts served up with a healthy dollop of postmodern humor and irony. The Style Network's *Craft Corner Deathmatch* is but one example of the new programming. This tongue-in-cheek competition takes its cues from the super-charged showdown style of Food Network's *Iron Chef*. Armed with limited supplies (Tyvek envelopes, duct tape, and scissors, for instance), challengers battle to see who can create the most impressive product before time runs out. The DIY Network's entry (and please note that the very existence of the DIY and Style Networks is, in and of itself, a good indication of crafting's new cultural cachet) is called *Stylelicious*. The show's stars are eight members of the Austin Craft Mafia, a Texas-based collective as notoriously crafty as their name suggests. On each episode they walk viewers through cool, modern projects of all kinds.

Though it may seem as though all these homemaking Ms. Independents are turning their backs on feminism by embracing domesticity, the truth is that the freedom to choose is at the heart of feminism. It's important to note that Ms. Independents indulge in these domestic activities because they *want* to, not because they *have* to. Knitting, crocheting, embroidering, and the like are not about making a new pillow cover or a scarf to keep warm in the winter. The projects this C-Type chooses are about experimentation, the joy of creation, and the pleasure of nurturing a new skill. Domestic tasks that don't bring this sort of enjoyment or fulfillment tend to be summarily rejected by Ms. Independents. Housecleaning, for example. If she finds no satisfaction in making her kitchen floor shine herself (and most don't), she'll hire someone else to do it and consider it money well spent. Ms. Independents are among the increasing numbers of busy professionals responsible for the growth of the home cleaning business. According to the Association of Residential Cleaning Professionals, the home cleaning industry is growing by 15 to 20 percent a year. Same story with cooking. Those who love it become weekend gourmet chefs. Nonenthusiasts look instead to role models like the Food Network's Rachael Ray, queen of the 30-minute meal, for inspiration. Or they just order in meals from the local trendy eatery.

Ms. Independents and Children

Ms. Independents recognize that raising children is a challenging endeavor, no matter how rewarding. Thus they plan not to have children until they're good and ready. In other words, they want to feel adequately fulfilled and satisfied with their premothering lives, or to have reached a certain level of career accomplishment, before splitting their focus between their own needs and the demands of a baby. Some Ms. Independents decide they don't want kids to be a part of their future at all. Others decide they do want a child, but don't want a marriage. For them, sperm banks and adoption agencies are ready to lend a hand. What's important is that, for this C-Type, childbearing is a personal choice for an individual, and no single choice is the "right one."

> I don't think that a woman is incomplete if she does not bear children in her lifetime. I feel that children should only be brought into life if the living environment is healthy.
>
> **Unfazed, Femalethiink.com message board**

[My husband and I] plan to do the stay-at-home-mom/breadwinner model for a while too, but this is by choice—and a really, really tightly planned budget—not societal expectation or not "needing" to work because I'm female.

Marian, on former Feministe.com

When it comes to having and rearing kids, Ms. Independents tend to fall within one of the following thought camps.

Voluntarily Becoming Single Moms

Among those Ms. Independents who do want to have children, having a husband (or being partnered with the father of the children) is becoming less and less a prerequisite. According to the National Center for Health Statistics there was an almost 17 percent jump between 1999 and 2003 in the number of babies born to older unmarried women, those between the ages of 30 and 44. Single Mothers by Choice, a 25-year-old support group, claims its 2005 membership was double what it was the decade prior. And in a YouGov Omnibus survey, two-thirds of the women surveyed said it was okay for a financially secure single woman to deliberately set out to have a child by herself.

Some single Ms. Independents who find themselves ready to take the plunge into motherhood call on friends or former boyfriends to impregnate them with no strings attached. Others turn to artificial insemination, which is on the rise among single women. (The California Cryobank, the largest sperm bank in the country, drew a third of its customers in 2005 from the single women pool.) Adoption, too, is gaining ground as a choice for solo Ms. Independents. Although currently only about 5 percent of adoptions are initiated by single people, some experts in the field call single-parent adoption the category's fastest-growing trend.[3]

Taking Charge of Their Fertility

For many Ms. Independents, their twenties and early thirties are for figuring themselves out, establishing their careers, and finding what their true purpose is in life. At that point, they aren't even thinking of settling down and starting a family. Many of these Ms. Independents do assume they will one day have a family, but they aren't in a rush. Unfortunately, biological clocks can be put on hold for only so long. Luckily for this C-Type, some new technologies and strategies have come along in the recent past to help give them the freedom to postpone pregnancy for a good long while.

Assisted fertility has now become a booming business, especially in urban areas. Since the early days of "test tube babies," advances in treatment, including IVF (in vitro fertilization) and drugs that stimulate ovulation, have led to the conception of more than a million children worldwide. Yet despite all the advances in the fertility area, economist Sylvia Ann Hewlett still put a damper on take-charge Ms. Independents back in 2002, when she published a book *Creating a Life: Professional Women and the Quest for Children*, which argued that today's career women were sacrificing their fertility for career advancement.

Rather than change behavior, though, the book suffered a backlash from Ms. Independents who decried Hewlett's "scare tactics." It helped that, right around that time, a new weapon in the modern woman's fertility arsenal was developed: oocyte cryopreservation, otherwise known as egg freezing. Until recently, egg freezing was offered only to young women facing chemotherapy or suffering from illnesses that might compromise their fertility. Today, the process is available to any woman who's short on time, but rich in cash.

> Nobody can know but you what is truly important to you and how you want to make that happen. When I decided I was going to do it, and was in the process of it, I talked very openly to people about it as it was happening.... At the coffee shop... how are you today? I'm great! I'm freezing my eggs! Because I found the experience totally empowering.
>
> **Alexandra, 34-year-old pharmaceutical representative on www.extendfertility.com**

Remaining Childfree and Happy

Some Ms. Independents choose to forgo parenthood entirely. The Census Bureau reports that one-fifth of U.S. women reach the end of their childbearing years (approximately age 44) without having kids—twice as many as in the 70s and 80s. The reasons are as many and as varied as Ms. Independents themselves. Some claim to lack a nurturing ability, others balk at the expense of kids, and still others say they would rather focus efforts on career and their own personal pursuits than on raising children.

This attitude toward children is something that is still not completely acceptable to society at large. Ms. Independents who choose not to procreate often feel like a pariah around extended family, or feel pressure to rethink their plans. It should be no surprise that they sometimes need a little positive reinforcement from other women who have the same attitudes. As usual, the Internet makes it easy for like-minded individuals to find each other. Ms. Independents who have chosen to live their lives without kids can create bonds with other women like themselves via online communities like Happily Childfree (happilychildfree.com), Childfree by Choice (www.childfreebychoice.com), and Childfree (childfree.net). This last site's description of itself says it all: "We choose to call ourselves "childfree" rather than "childless," because we feel the term "childless" implies that we're missing something we want—and we aren't. We consider ourselves childFREE—free of the loss of personal freedom, money, time, and energy that having children requires."

MARKETPLACE EVIDENCE

Extend Fertility
Ms. Independents who may want to delay child rearing beyond their naturally fertile years can turn to Extend Fertility, a nationwide network of egg-freezing centers. Costs differ according to the center used, but on average, run about $15,000 per depositor, not including storage fees and other associated costs. The company reports the biggest interest is from women in urban areas, who are more likely to delay marriage and children. Extend Fertility currently has clinics in Los Angeles, Dallas, and New York. The good news for Ms. Independents who are considering oocyte cryopreservation? Researchers at the University of Southern California Keck School of Medicine reported an unprecedented pregnancy success rate of 63 percent using frozen eggs.

Ms. Independents: Work

From very early, the girls who have grown into Ms. Independents were groomed to succeed. Their mothers' generation was the hard-line feminists of the 60s and 70s who believed that women's place was in the boardroom, not in the kitchen, and they often pushed their daughters to continue their educations and go for the brass ring. Whatever they did worked. Today it's women, in fact, who are more likely than their male peers to go to college. Department of Education statistics show that men, regardless of race or socioeconomic group, are less likely than women to earn their bachelor's degrees. (The report also stresses that men, on average, study less, take longer to earn their degrees, and have measurably lower GPAs.) The proliferation of campus organizations specifically targeted to females (whether preprofessional networking, or primarily social) can be a boon to marketers, collecting in one place the women most likely to become Ms. Independents. While sororities were long seen as the breeding ground for the next generation of American homemakers, a group like Women in Mathematics (WIM) at the University of Maryland is concerned with tomorrow's female entrepreneurs and thought leaders. Seeding new product samples through organizations like this, or using its network as the basis for a stealth grassroots campaign, could prove more than fruitful. It's important to remember, though, that you need to speak to these women the way they speak to one another. Don't rely on traditional notions of the way "ladies" are supposed to talk. When Ms. Independents talk to or cyber-communicate with each other, they can be as ribald and hard-edged as "guys" and will respond better to marketing that does the same.

Not that all the education news is good. Although women are more educated, bulldoze past men in college, and set themselves up in the highest-paid professions, the sad truth is that full-time working women with college degrees still earn about 30 percent less than similarly educated men.

How long do women have to wait to crash the glass ceiling in numbers that truly represent our talents, experience, and abilities? When that happens, the business world and politics, etc., would see a real change rather than just a "tinkering" around the edges.

Laix, on the www.women.com message board

Down with all the people against career women; maybe they just want dolls.

Mind Curry, commenting on the Within/Without feminist blog

To be sure, the figures are changing, but slowly. Since 2000, female college graduates have increased their full-time workforce participation at more than twice the rate of men, and their income level (though still lower) is rising faster than men's. In fact, over the past five years, full-time working women aged 25 to 64 have seen their median income (adjusted for inflation) rise by 4 percent compared with a 3 percent decrease for men.[4] Female entrepreneurs are also the fastest growing segment of entrepreneurs. Women now own some 10.6 million firms—nearly half of the privately held businesses in the country, according to the Center for Women's Business Research. (And women's companies tend to be more profitable than those run by men!) There's another, more subtle difference here, too: 73 percent of women who own firms with $1 million-plus in annual sales *founded* their businesses, as opposed to buying or inheriting them. That's versus 60 percent of men who run their own companies.[5]

One reason Ms. Independents can anticipate a bright career future is that they've finally learned it's okay for a woman to take charge and do things *her* way in the work world. Networking is one such example.

WOMEN ON TOP

These powerful CEOs, power brokers, and thought leaders are inspirations and role models to Ms. Independents everywhere. What would be the effect of using one of them—or a woman like them—as a spokesperson, or endorser, for your product or brand? Ms. Independents respect a woman of accomplishment in a way they don't a woman of mere good looks or peppy personality.

Muriel Siebert ("The First Woman of Finance"): President of the New York Stock Exchange brokerage firm Muriel Siebert & Co., Inc.
Condoleeza Rice: U.S. Secretary of State
Meg Whitman: CEO, eBay
Anna Wintour: Editor in Chief, *American Vogue*
Dawn Hudson: CEO, PepsiCo North America
Mary Kay Ash: Founder of Mary Kay Cosmetics
Shelly Lazarus: Chairman and CEO, Ogilvy & Mather
Katie Couric: Anchor and Managing Editor of CBS Evening News
Anne Mulcahy: Chairman and CEO, Xerox
Particia Russo: Chairman and CEO, Lucent

Previous generations of non-golf-playing women may have suffered because the golf course is one of men's favorite networking venues. Today's successful woman, though, rather than forgo the networking opportunity, has simply redone it to suit her lifestyle. Women's networking can and does take place at a girls' night out, as part of a book discussion or a hobby group. Online organizations for women are also popping up, like WorldWIT.org, a 30,000+ online networking group that allows women to virtually congregate with women who either live near them or share the same career interests or pursuits. As with the college organizations mentioned above, these women's organizations can be a useful tool in spreading a marketing campaign or creating awareness among this C-Type.

MARKETPLACE EVIDENCE

CapitalistChicks.com
This business site for business women has a little bit of everything: news, feature stories, community boards, and even products for sale. What it doesn't do is take itself too seriously. CapitalistChicks's founders are two young women who hope to change the face of capitalism—making it just a bit more feminine. In their mission statement, they call on the "productive women of the up and coming generation" to show they are just as ambitious and hardworking as men and that they believe in capitalism. Check it out at www.capitalistchicks.com.

MARKETPLACE EVIDENCE

Citibank's Women & Co.

Ms. Independents who earn a good living and are successful at their jobs believe they should be equally successful at managing their money. Citibank offers a new service just for them. Women & Co. was established to "help women pursue multiple financial goals, prepare for the unexpected and live life their way." Open to women with all levels of financial knowledge, the service offers financial education (including seminars and online newsletters), personal advice (for managing money, handling life events, buying or selling a home, etc.), as well as special offers and discounts. At press time, users paid a $125 annual fee. See womenandco.com.

MS. INDEPENDENTS: POWER PURCHASING

As women earn more and advance in their careers, their spending habits change. In part because they can afford it and in part because they believe they deserve it and would like to reward themselves, Ms. Independents are spending more, and on bigger ticket items, than ever before. Although purchasing a home more likely represents a demonstration of independence or a smart investment opportunity, "power purchasing" represents something different. These buys are more frivolous and more lavish and include everything from spa treatments to shoes, jewelry, expensive face creams, and even cars and gadgets. These purchases represent the level of wealth Ms. Independents have acquired, all on their own, and they are all about personal pleasure.

BUILDING AN INDEPENDENT NEST EGG

I'm a woman who wants to ensure that I will always be financially secure, as I do not want to depend on anyone else to take care of my financial needs.

M. Kushner, Amazon.com review

Financial consultant Suze Orman has become the go-to woman among a generation of today's young women who want to take control of their finances and make the most of their dollars. After all, you can't spend it if you don't have it! Orman is the author of several books with big appeal for this C-Type: *The Money Book for the Young, Fabulous & Broke* and *9 Steps to Financial Freedom* among them. She also hosts a CNBC program about money planning and is a frequent lecturer to women's groups. "You don't have to be good with numbers to be good with money," she says. "You have to learn to listen with your own gut. What does your gut tell you that you really should be doing? If you do that, financial advisers can't take advantage of you."[6]

Of course there are exceptions but, generally speaking, the easiest way to spot a Ms. Independent is by the clothing she purchases. Styles may vary from individual to individual, but whatever she's wearing, it isn't cheap. Ms. Independents are among the rare women who will shop for couture or au courant designers such as Marc Jacobs, Catherine Malandrino, and Michael Kors. And they pay retail. Why wait for end-of-season sales? Barneys, Neiman Marcus, Fred Segal (in L.A.), Jeffrey (New York and Atlanta) and other high-end boutiques are their shopping meccas.

A Ms. Independent's wardrobe is defined by the choices she makes about three key items: her jeans, shoes, and handbag. Forget Levi 501s. Ms. Independents prefer their jeans in the $150 to $250 designer range, from brands such as Hudson, Paper Denim & Cloth, and Rock & Republic. A pair of her shoes, from brands like Jimmy Choo, Manolo Blahnik, and Prada, can get even pricier. Like Carrie Bradshaw, Sarah Jessica Parker's character on *Sex and the City*, many Ms. Independents rationalize their lavish shoe purchases by considering their shoes a "collection." At the top end of the price spectrum, Ms. Independents who want to carry a Balenciaga, Kooba, or Chloé on their arm can drop more than $1,000 for a single bag.

Jewelry purchasing by women for themselves is also on the rise. This can partly be attributed to a savvy campaign for the "right hand ring" by diamond marketer DeBeers. The campaign pushed to convince single women to buy diamond rings for the fourth finger of their right hands, instead of waiting for a man to buy one for her. Ms. Independents have embraced the movement and decided that buying diamonds or other jewelry for themselves is a great way to reward themselves and express their personalities. During the first half of 2004, according to the Diamond Information Center, the number of women buying diamonds for themselves increased by 11 percent.

No matter your category, bringing a style and design sensibility to your product or brand will attract the attention of this C-Type. Ms. Independents are inevitably attracted to design-forward packaging and product formats even in everyday categories like housewares and cleaning supplies. (Look at Method dishwashing soap. A cool bottle made the mundane seem sexy.) If it's luxury products or services you're marketing, consider creating an über-premium offering that many women would consider almost too self-indulgent. Ms. Independents have disposable income and no one to spend it on but themselves. If you create a nail polish that retails for $50 or a custom-made bra for $500, a goodly portion of the women who will consider your product will be Ms. Independents. As they buy more, and infiltrate almost every luxury consumer goods market, even those previously dominated by men, marketers are finally taking notice and recognizing that Ms. Independents need, and deserve, to be targeted in different and innovative ways.

Travel, both domestic and international, is one of Ms. Independent's favorite pastimes. Ms. Independents like to take adventure and/or relaxation trips, not simply because they can afford to, but because such travels offer an unparalleled opportunity for them to decompress, explore new lands and cultures, and otherwise enrich their lives. Ms. Independents are most likely to travel with female friends, but not having a designated travel partner certainly won't stop them from taking a trip. Instead of waiting around for a significant other to share such experiences with, Ms. Independent recognizes the need to take advantage of her untethered "freedom years." She may, in fact, travel half the world on her own before settling down (if she does plan to settle down) with a husband and family.

There was another person inside of me wanting to get out. That person was fun-loving, self-assured, confident in her abilities, not afraid to take chances and willing to show the world who she really was.

M., on AdventureWomen.com

The plethora of vacation outfitters for the single traveler makes it easy for Ms. Independents to plan holidays and travel alone to even the most exotic locales. Journeywoman (www.journeywoman.com), an on-line travel resource for women, gets more than 2,500 hits a day and has more than 150 women-oriented travel advertisers.[7] And a 2005 survey by Impulse Research in Los Angeles found that nearly 50 percent of women surveyed had taken an all-female vacation in the past three years and that 88 percent of those had plans for another. Whether alone or in a group, European jaunts, spa vacations, and bike or other active trips top this C-Type's must-do list.

WILD WOMEN

Most travel experts agree that women represent the most important segment of the adventure travel industry. The following are just some of the outfitters Ms. Independents turn to when planning adventurous vacation days from work.

Adventures in Good Company: This Baltimore-based company offers African journeys, all-female trips to spas and vineyards, and pilgrimages to sacred sites. One sample trip is a two-week African adventure that includes a climb up Mount Kilimanjaro. (www.adventuresingoodcompany.com)

AdventureWomen: One of the oldest adventure travel companies for active women over 30, Adventure Women takes small groups of women (of all abilities) on adventure trips that suit their interests—from swimming with the dolphins, to kayaking, hiking, and more. (www.adventurewomen.com)

Call of the Wild: Call of the Wild caters to Ms. Independents of any type—whether they're looking to combine comfort and action, or are seeking a hardcore "in the wild" experience. (www.callwild.com)

Gutsy Women Travel: Despite the intimidating name, Gutsy Women Travel offers more than just action and adventure trips. Women can also choose from cultural vacations, dining trips, and garden tours. (www.gutsywomentravel.com)

MARKETING TO MS. INDEPENDENTS: A CHECKLIST

☑ Aesthetics matter.

☑ Ms. Independents don't want to be treated as "one of the guys." At the same time, they don't want products created "just for women."

☑ Ms. Independents are willing to spend more for premium goods and services and have the income to do so.

☑ Turnabout is fair play; objectifying the male body in your advertising will turn Ms. Independents on.

☑ Ms. Independents look to fellow Ms. Independents for product and other guidance. Take advantage of this critical viral marketing opportunity.

☑ Teach, don't preach. Ms. Independents want to feel supported, not patronized.

☑ Extended warranties, service contracts, and "relationship selling" will appeal to Ms. Independents.

☑ Real-world role models (from single mothers to careerists) will resonate with Ms. Independents.

☑ Create new professional networking opportunities built around Ms. Independent activities (e.g., book groups, craft circles, exercise groups).

DIG A LITTLE DEEPER

FURTHER RESOURCES ON
MS. INDEPENDENTS

Ms. Independents in Print
Check out your local magazine store or bookshop. You might be surprised at the variety of titles targeted to this C-Type!

Buying a Home When You're Single by Donna G. Albrecht
Buying a home as a couple can be overwhelming, but singles face unique challenges when dealing with banks, real estate agents, and sellers. This well-organized step-by-step guide is ideal for singles on the hunt for the perfect house, condo, or co-op.

Nesting: It's a Chick Thing by Ame Mahler Beanland and Emily Miles Terry
Tips on the "four pillars of nesting": decorating, entertaining, cooking, and gardening, from two women who encourage readers to stop worrying about Martha-esque perfection and instead spend more time actually enjoying the great spaces and great meals they make.

MS. INDEPENDENT'S MAGAZINE RACK

Ms. Independents who are setting up their first home tend to prefer a low-maintenance casual chic style of decorating. Several magazines provide just the right amount of guidance and panache.

Blueprint: Designed to be a bible for busy, stylish thirtysomethings, Martha Stewart's latest publication offers easily digestible blurbs on everything that can enhance their lives, including quick-to-implement decorating ideas.

Domino: Affordable chic is the order of the day in this attractive mag that offers up home decorating tips and great products, along with purchase information, for the home.

Real Simple: For Ms.Independents whose idea of decorating resembles organizing more than anything else, there's no better source than *Real Simple*, which offers countless tips on whipping home spaces into shape.

The New Single Woman by E. Kay Trimberger

Singled Out: How Singles Are Stereotyped, Stigmatized, and Ignored, and Still Live Happily Ever After by Bella DePaulo
Both of the titles above seek to address the caricatures of dopey, sad singles in both popular culture and academia. DePaulo, a Ph.D. in psychology from Harvard, and Trimburger, a professor at Berkeley, dispel some of the myths about the sorry state of singledom and affirm the full and satisfying lives single women can live in the face of societal assumptions about the loneliness of the unmarried.

The Single Woman's Guide to a Happy Pregnancy by Mari Gallion
This guide covers how to get organized, stay positive, and keep finances in order while going through pregnancy solo.

Dare to Repair: A Do-it-Herself Guide to Fixing (Almost) Anything in the Home by Julie Sussman and Stephanie Glakas-Tenet
Dare to Repair Your Car: A Do-it-Herself Guide to Maintenance, Safety, Minor Fix-Its, and Talking Shop by Julie Sussman and Stephanie Glakas-Tenet
Written by two women whose CIA-employed husbands weren't always around when things went wrong around the house, the "Dare to Repair" guides are a must-have for any woman, single or partnered. Easy-to-follow instructions on everything from how to light a pilot light to how to change brake fluid.

Money, A Memoir: Women, Emotions, and Cash by Liz Perle
One part memoir, one part financial advice tome, an account of one woman's transition from financial ambivalence to financial independence following divorce. Includes commentary from experts in fields from finance to sociology on the subject of how to empower women to be more engaged when it comes to the money issue.

Stitch 'N Bitch: The Knitter's Handbook by Debbie Stoller
The basics are covered, casting on, knitting, purling, and so on, in this handbook by *Bust* magazine's editor in chief. But it's Stoller's writing style (headings include "Knit Happens") and selection of projects, the Ribbed-for-Her-Pleasure Scarf, for example, that really make it ideal for sassy twenty- and thirtysomethings that have taken up the hobby.

Get Crafty: Hip Home Ec by Jean Railla
Get Crafty the book has the same embrace of new domesticity as Railla's Web site getcrafty.com. Projects for knitters, sewers, home decorating fiends, and just about anyone else interested in making things with their own hands.

GREAT MOMENTS IN MS. INDEPENDENT PUBLISHING

Sex and the Single Girl by Helen Gurley Brown

When it was published in 1962, *Sex and the Single Girl* was perhaps the first, and certainly the most provocative, guide for modern women living on their own, dating whom they pleased, entertaining friends, and having the most fun possible in the process. The book may seem a bit outmoded today, but you can bet that some of its dating tips are probably just as true today as they were then!

Ms. Independents Online

Quirkyalone.net
One needn't be single to be a quirkyalone, but you're more likely to be single if you are one. What differentiates quirkyalones from the rest of the pack is that they don't see themselves as fundamentally one half of an incomplete unit or make romantic relationships their main focus in life. They're happy, maybe even happier, and more fulfilled on their own. According to Quirkyalone author, they're open to partnership but have "no patience for dating just for the sake of not being alone."

bwni.com (Business Women's Network)
A valuable source of news and information for professional women in all industries. Also useful for college-aged women just getting started in the working world.

DailyCandy.com
With a well-developed "service" section and endless updates on the latest shops, *boîtes,* and spas in large urban centers from coast to

coast, DailyCandy is the optimal resource for the Ms. Independent who likes to indulge.

craftster.org
getcrafty.com
etsy.com
supernaturale.com
Multiple sites of the indie craft revolution, offering project how-tos, business advice from established craft vendors, and two thriving bulletin board communities.

NOTES

1. *Pittsburgh Tribune Review*, 7/9/05

2. *Chicago Tribune*, 12/14/05

3. National Adoption Information Clearinghouse statistics, quoted in *The Post-Crescent*, 6/19/05

4. *Advertising Age*, 1/2/06

5. Center for Women's Business Research

6. *The News Journal*, 2/23/06

7. *The Baltimore Sun*, 8/11/05

INNERPRENEURS

The research is clear: after a certain point, money doesn't make us happy. So you need to decide what gives you energy and excitement and what drains those things from you.

Cecile Andrews, author of *The Circle of Simplicity: Return to the Good Life*

Traditional entrepreneurs are known for having a vision of something outside themselves—a new product, new store, or new way of offering a service to consumers. As the label would suggest, the Innerpreneur's focus is on the internal self: his or her peace of mind, feelings, spiritual self, and overall self-satisfaction.

Before you are tempted to write off the Innerpreneur as a hippie or a Benedictine monk, however, consider the characteristics that the Innerpreneur has in common with the entrepreneur: the willingness to take risks; a high need for achievement; and an obsession with opportunity. Innerpreneurs recognize themselves as the CEOs of their own lives and the chief managers of their own "brand." And, as such, they want to make sure that they are realizing their full potential, achieving measurable successes, and constantly evolving and improving with the times.

Innerpreneurs cross all demographics. They are equally likely to be male or female, may be barely out of their teens, or may be late in middle age. (Many discover or embrace their Innerpreneurialism only *after* trying to hew to more conventional societal expectations, and failing.) Success for this group is not always defined in dollars and cents. It's measured in warmer, fuzzier, more esoteric terms—again, by peace of mind, self-satisfaction, and contentment. The struggle for work-life balance is simple for this C-Type; they need to be doing their life's work in order to find balance.

To Innerpreneurs, life's journey should be an adventure. Innerpreneurs take risks. They challenge norms. They're open to new ideas and to the people they encounter along the way. And they're constantly learning, discovering, and creating. The Innerpreneurial spirit is intrinsically linked to the creative impulse. This isn't meant to suggest that all Innerpreneurs are budding Picassos or Beethovens, although they may be. It just means that Innerpreneurs have the impulse to *make things different*. Innerpreneurs have the creativity to see the world in different ways, and in the long run they often change the way many of us view it too.

THE CREATIVITY QUOTIENT

As noted, Innerpreneurs are intrinsically creative, and this creative impulse can alter the world in measurable ways. Currently, our society is in the midst of a creative revolution, where new ways of thinking are increasingly prized, and there is a new emphasis on the inner life of the individual. This, indeed, is a story that encompasses more than just Innerpreneurs, although they are definitely a part of it. It is a movement that has come to the world's attention through the groundbreaking work of some top thinkers and cultural analysts. For a deeper look at how the "new creativity" is altering our world, we suggest you start by consulting either of the following works:

The Cultural Creatives: How 50 Million People Are Changing the World by Paul H. Ray and Sherry Ruth Anderson
This pivotal work gives shape to the shared impulses that join 50 million Americans in a social movement to use human creativity to ensure a sane, sustainable future for all mankind. These cultural creatives share a social conscience, a concern for the environment and the use of natural resources, and a willingness to explore all the cultures and communities that make up the human family, and they care deeply about their own psychological and spiritual development.

The Rise of the Creative Class . . . and how it's transforming work, leisure, community & everyday life by Richard Florida
This best seller looks at the increasing number of Americans (38 million, according to the author, a renowned urban studies theorist) who are beginning to work and live the way artists and other creative professionals have always done. It paints a portrait of a society undergoing a major shift, moving away from the rigidity of corporate culture and toward a more broadly accepting culture, one which celebrates the experience and defends the rights of minorities, misfits, and all those once thought of disparagingly as "different."

MARKETPLACE EVIDENCE

Apple iLife Suite

Apple iLife Suite, which *Fortune* magazine called "a complete mul-timedia machine" is a creative Innerpreneur's dream come true. The Suite includes a number of programs that together offer users a complete home studio: everything they need to create professional caliber movies, digital slide shows, newsletters, and more. The favorite application is GarageBand, which wanna-be composers can use to make and mix their own music.

With the United States firmly settled in the Information Age and the transition from a manufacturing to a service economy complete, a great deal of creative control has been placed in the hands of everyday consumers. Paradigms are shifting, and our world is being reshaped from the bottom up as much as from the top down. Easy-to-use software makes it simple for a novice to make a movie. At the same time, though, we are bombarded by media from all sides and in all forms. In some ways, the more we are connected, the more alike we have become. Though the Internet has made it easy for unique subsegments of society to have a voice, it has also made it easier for mass-market trends to overwhelm everything else. And that's what makes the Innerpreneur interesting; in a time when it's easy to see what everyone else is doing, wearing, and thinking, this C-Type either ignores a trend and swims upstream of it, or is truly unaware that there is a trend at all. Innerpreneurs let their moral compass and passion for exploration guide their lives. Innerpreneurs have an inborn need to be creative, challenge assumptions, seek new pathways, and define new horizons.

As marketers, you'll want to pay attention to these "sleeper" C-Types. Their creativity and quest to alter the world for their own sake becomes, in the end, a vehicle to alter the world for all of our sakes. In an era in which so much market research and insight mining is outwardly directed—"let's quantify that" or "the focus groups said . . ."—it is critical that you identify Innerpreneurs around your brand category and business. Innepreneurs take the risks that fly in the face of the mainstream and change the status quo. They have an organic desire to learn more, to do more, and often to give something back to the world.

This desire to give back has led to one of the most visible signs of Innerpreneur impact thus far: the widespread embrace of cause marketing, especially by credit card companies. There are countless numbers of "affinity" cards which donate a percentage of a consumer's balance to a charity to which he or she has emotional ties. In fact, Visa International estimated that in 2003, *half* of all credit cards issued worldwide were affinity or co-brand cards, with public education, crime, the environment, animals, and children's causes most popular.[1] (Banks appreciate affinity card customers because they're loyal, preferring to stick with their cause rather than switch to a card with a lower interest rate or higher credit limit.) This sort of charitable giving can also be seen outside the financial services sector. GoodSearch.com, an online search engine, gives half of the advertising revenue it earns to each registered user's favorite specified charity. And the Newman's Own line of snacks and foods shows how easily cause marketing can be adapted to any product in the supermarket. None of this is new, of course, but Innerpreneurs have helped make the thinking behind cause marketing commonplace: that everything we do, every gesture we make somehow reverberates in the universe and leads to a better world.

COMMUNITIES OF INNERPRENEURS

Some leading-edge Innerpreneurs can be found living in alternative, communal living situations. Not only do these "communities of Innerpreneurs" allow individual Innerpreneurs to spend their daily lives with those who share their attitudes, but they appeal to this C-Type's sense of experimentation and exploration. Sometimes these planned communities are organized around an ideal or philosophy (such as lessening humans' environmental impact); other times they consist of people of similar ages or backgrounds. The important thing is that these communities are founded and inhabited by people who subscribe to the notion that a way of life is something that can be shaped, not something that must just be accepted as is.

Most Innerpreneur communities are founded by visionaries who identified a need within themselves. They're filled, in turn, by fellow Innerpreneurs who share the same housing aspirations. A desire to foster community spirit, social interaction, and interpersonal proximity is a common thread, as well as a willingness to challenge the American norm, to reject a sterile exurban sprawl of bloated McMansions.

New Urbanism is an Innerpreneurial social movement. At its core, it is a revolt against the growth of suburbanism, and stems from a desire to re-create a way of life that has largely disappeared in the age of the automobile. Houses in New Urbanist communities tend to be close together. Streets have sidewalks and bike lanes. And there's a mix of residential, office, and retail buildings.

Many New Urbanist developments are located in suburban communities like Plano, Texas, but the movement's influence is increasingly showing up in small cities like Portland, Oregon, and Denver, Colorado, as well. Glenwood Park, a development near downtown Atlanta, Georgia, is a good example. Established by Charles Brewer, founder of the Internet company Mindspring and Green Street Properties, Brewer set to work creating the kind of community he envisioned. He bought a 28-acre former concrete recycling plant near downtown and renamed it Glenwood Park. It has now become an idyllic community with more than 300 townhouses and condominiums, filled with a mix of inhabitants. It's near the city center, but a world removed from Atlanta's traffic congestion and sprawl. Communities like Glenwood Park are important to understand because they are living, breathing examples of this type as it exists in the larger world.

Another Innerpreneur community, Glacier Circle in Davis, California, was the country's first self-planned housing development for the elderly. It was conceived and designed by its elderly residents themselves. They found and bought land together, hired an architect together, ironed out insurance together, and lobbied for zoning changes together. To help foster close ties in the community, there is even a designated "common house," which has a living room, large kitchen, and dining room for communal dinners. More cooperative housing developments for the elderly are on their way. In Abingdon, Virginia, there is ElderSpirit, a small development of about 40 seniors led by a 76-year-old former nun, Dene Peterson. "I just thought there had to be a better way for older people to live," said Ms. Peterson—a classic Innerpreneur comment.[2] And, as of early 2006, six more ElderSpirit communities were in planning stages, with financing from the Chicago-based Retirement Research Foundation.

INNERPRENEURS: CAREERS, SECOND CAREERS, AND SABBATICALS

On the individual level, one of the basic ways for Innerpreneurs to achieve personal growth and fulfillment is through the way they make a living. Of all the C-Types, Innerpreneurs are the ones where you're most likely to find a deep connection between lifestyle and career choice. While Geek Gods or Karma Queens, for example, may be able to separate their 9-to-5 from their nights and weekends, most Innerpreneurs can't. Finding fulfillment and satisfaction *through* work is a large part of what makes an Innerpreneur an Innerpreneur.

Work and life are inextricably tied together for this C-Type. The formula is simple: follow your passion. Although there are would-be Innerpreneurs who have not figured out what they want to do or lack the gumption to risk a career change, true Innerpreneurs have recognized that which makes their heart sing and have followed its siren song. By translating that passion into a career, they are able to not only earn money but also to spend the better portion of their day doing what they love most and spreading the message of their mission to others.

As the C-Type who absolutely must find meaning in what they do for a living, Innerpreneurs often have unusual twists and turnarounds in their working lives. Realizing that they're not completely satisfied with their careers (often in spite of a big paycheck), many Innerpreneurs change careers, moving into industries that have a social conscience or whose mission is to create connections between people. Or they alter-nate periods of reflection and/or adventure between periods of career focus, using the model of the academic sabbatical.

As a marketer, if you're looking to speak with consumers who are passionate about what they do, "second careerists" will be of special interest. It's as simple as this: while a first career choice is often made at the urging of someone else, second career choices almost never are.

> I felt like I could reinvent myself. I didn't have to be one thing as an adult. I had been a book-publishing person, and that was great, but now I was going to do something different. I didn't worry about getting hired at my age when I got my degree—I figured if I'm good at what I do and I care about it passionately, I'll get a job. If I choose to go back to grad school again at 65, I'll have a similar attitude then.
>
> **Isabel, age 45**

> People ask me a lot about changing careers. I tell them that I didn't know what I wanted to do but I knew what I hated. Life is too short for that kind of conflict.
>
> **Soyoung, San Francisco**

No other industry, it seems, calls to more second-career seekers than the food industry. A 2005 article in the *Pittsburgh Tribune Review* explained that "second career" chefs often leave high-paying, sometimes glamorous jobs to take entry-level cooking positions that might start at little more than minimum wage. The article also reported that 15 percent of the student body in The Culinary Institute of America are "career changers." The National Restaurant Association's Cornerstone Initiative summarizes it this way: "There is a place for everyone in the restaurant industry."

> A good sabbatical, like a good book, has the power to change one's life.
>
> **Kenneth Zahorsky, author of "The Sabbatical Mentor,"**
> **in the *McGill Reporter*, 10/21/99**

When it comes to sabbaticals, they are mostly the choice of Innerpreneurs who can't change careers completely. These breaks can afford Innerpreneurs the time to refill their spiritual tanks or to explore sides of their personalities not tapped by their jobs. Many companies are catching on to the vibe (and recognize the value of having Innerpreneurs on their teams). These firms allow employees time off to pursue their Innerpreneurial desires (again, anything from a physical challenge to an intellectual pursuit). The hope is the employee will come back a new and better person (and worker).

> Employees are saying, "I want control of my career destiny and if I feel like I need a break, I'm going to take one." There's less punishment today for having a gap on your resume. You can fill it in with contract work or consulting. Even if you backpack off to Nepal, that's considered valuable international experience.
>
> **Roger Herman, CEO of The Herman Group, a workplace consultancy**

> Employers who invest time in providing opportunities for their fast trackers to explore how society works and get engaged in the wider world will hang on to their talent. Those who don't and who force young managers to choose between work and making a difference won't.
>
> **Julia Middleton, founder of Common Purpose**

Through their career choices, Innerpreneurs demonstrate that they are successful, busy, highly engaged, and sophisticated consumers. Take note of their sophistication, however, if you plan to target them. Keep your message real, without hyperbole. To an Innerpreneur, hype is never hip.

Not a group to ever rest on their laurels, Innerpreneurs' constant striving for knowledge and experience often leads them to new insights. For marketers this characteristic can prove invaluable. Leverage their creativity and you can find some great ideas. Why not include an Innerpreneur in your next brainstorming session? Or look to an interesting publication like *E* (an environmental magazine), *Utne Reader,* or

Fast Company to learn about how Innerpreneurs in various professional disciplines with vocations or avocations are changing the rules. Often these publications and the Innerpreneur practices they highlight can be bellwethers of big change.

MARKETPLACE EVIDENCE

Teach for America

For the past few decades, one of the most popular choices for an Innerpreneurial sabbatical has been Teach for America. The program, which places qualified college graduates into year-long teaching positions at low-income schools, is a perfect life-growth experience, enriching both the students and the teacher. Teach for America received a record number of applicants in 2005 (many of them Ivy Leaguers), up by nearly 30 percent from the year before.[3]

Life Coach Counseling

Though life coaching is relatively new, both the practitioners and clients of this profession tend to belong to this C-Type. Emerging Innerpreneurs are often the ones seeking to find their life purpose, to make the most out of their talents, to realize their desires, while Innerpreneurs who have already found themselves make great coaches. The industry is definitely on the rise, with 10,000 life coaches, of various types and methods, currently working in the United States.[4] According to the International Coach Federation, this number has more than doubled from the fewer than 5,000 life coaches practicing in 2001.

> My experience working with Brenda was amazing and enlightening. I have never had anyone put me in such a focused direction and give me such astounding motivation.
>
> Sande, on Findyourcoach.com

> I was stuck, mired in the past. Coaching transformed my life.
>
> Lou, on Findyourcoach.com

Notable Innerpreneurs

The lesson to be learned from the following profiles is that you, the marketer, need to keep your eyes glued to those people who reject the straight path to success and begin to carve out interesting directions that at first seem illogical. Innerpreneurs are not driven by popular culture, but sometimes they themselves drive it. Understanding their passion and ideas can help you identify meaningful "down-the-road" opportunities. Your Innerpreneur radar needs to go off the moment you start thinking, "That's the dumbest idea I've ever heard of."

While focus groups can be invaluable in refining an idea, they aren't necessarily the best place to help identify truly breakthrough ones. In fact one could argue that focus groups cast a blanket of blandness over innovative thinking. In order to truly identify new ideas, marketers need to identify self-directed new thinkers and then challenge themselves to decide whether they are worth following. Identifying some Innerpreneurial consumers in your category, and then tracking their passions, can be the biggest help in identifying truly new and breakthrough business opportunities. For example, if you're a mainstream marketer of skin care products, you should talk to someone who uses only biodynamic or organic skin care treatments. Tap into Innerpreneurial consumers and you'll gain invaluable insight and identify potentially breakthrough opportunities.

Jamie Clarke
Adventurer-Lecturer

When lifelong athlete Jamie Clarke decided to attempt to scale Mount Everest, he knew the experience would change his life, but not in the way that it eventually did. After much training and two failed expeditions (including a brush with death on one of them), Jamie reached the summit. Upon his return, he turned his experience into a book and a motivational speech. Jamie remains an adventurer and is now one of the most in-demand speakers on the corporate circuit, as well as author of several books about his experiences. His hobby has become his career, and he is happier for it.

Nina Planck
Food Writer and Expert on Farmers Markets

Decades ago, when Nina Planck's parents followed their Innerpreneurial spirits, leaving their academia-centered life on the East Coast for a farm in Virginia, young Nina had no choice but to go along for the ride. After a childhood spent working the land and selling produce, Nina started the first modern farmers markets in London. Now a food-nutrition writer and staunch supporter of local farms, Nina is also an expert on farmers markets, helping create New York's famous Union Square Greenmarket. We think that certifies her as a second-generation Innerpreneur.

Dr. Joseph Helms
Medical Innovator

We may now think of acupuncture as commonplace. Perhaps your health insurance even covers this "alternative" therapy. Yet, if you flash back to 1978, you would have found Dr. Joseph Helms hosting workshops to teach medical acupuncture (Helms's own term) to American physicians. By 1980, Dr. Helms had created the Medical Acupuncture for Physicians program for the Office of Continuing Medical Education at the UCLA School of Medicine, over which he continues to preside. Believing in the power of acupuncture, Dr. Helms went on to author the most widely used professional textbook, *Acupuncture Energetics*, and conducted America's first controlled research study on medical acupuncture. By 2001, an estimated 2.1 million adults a year in the United States were being treated with acupuncture, according to the National Health Interview Survey, the largest survey of alternative medicine ever conducted in the nation.[5]

> Acupuncture has become white bread in American society. It's no longer something that's very unusual. It's something patients expect their physicians to be able to provide or refer to.

> **sciencedaily.com, 4/17/05**

In addition to his UCLA post, Dr. Helms was instrumental in organizing the National Center for Complementary and Alternative Medicine at the National Institutes of Health. In 2001, he presented to the
White House Commission on Complementary and Alternative Medicine Policy. And he continues to train and certify physicians to teach his
Medical Acupuncture for Physicians courses.

Gary Hirshberg
CE-Yo of Stonyfield Farm

Gary Hirshberg currently oversees the world's largest manufacturer of organic yogurt. He certainly didn't start out aiming to be that big, though.
Stonyfield began as just a seven-cow organic farming school in 1983, run
by a socially conscious guy with a good idea. But, by steadfastly insisting
on running the company according to his own social, environmental,
and financial missions, Hirshberg turned it into a $300 million a year
business. Now owned by Groupe Danone, 10 percent of profits are still
donated to environmental causes (one reason fans of the brand find the
yogurt so irresistible). Proof that social consciousness and business can
play well together, Hirshberg has moved on to a new challenge, founding a chain of healthy quick-service restaurants called O'Naturals.

John Walsh
Host, America's Most Wanted

In 1981, John Walsh was enjoying a successful career in the hotel management business. But then tragedy struck. His six-year-old son Adam
was abducted and later found dead. The event spurred him into action
and lit an Innerpreneurial fire within. Making it his mission not to let
Adam have died in vain, he began to fight for victims' rights nationally.
His fame became a symbol that ordinary people with integrity can become today's most popular consumer heroes. The Fox Network asked
him to become the host of its crime-fighting show *America's Most
Wanted*—a show that now, with him as host, can lay claim to having captured almost 1,000 fugitives to date. From ordinary man to popular television host, Walsh has said that he wanted to turn Adam's death into
something positive and that he still believes in finding the good in

people. Still going strong, his Innerpreneurial flame shows no sign of dimming.

Carlo Petrini
Founder of the Slow Food Movement

In 1986, Carlo Petrini had had enough of the industrialized and fast food operations that seemed to be taking over his small Italian town. With artisans and local producers on his side, Petrini formed the Slow Food Movement. According to its Web site, slowfood.com, the organization now has chapters in 100 countries, and more than 80,000 members worldwide. Known as the "gastronomic version of Greenpeace," Slow Food's mission is to promote the rediscovery of local food varieties and flavors, the protection of biodiversity, the preservation of artisanal processes, and the enjoyment of nonindustrial foods. By staying true to his values even as his society headed in another direction, Petrini has become an Innerpreneurial icon.

Jack Cogen
Environmental Financier

One Innerpreneur whose work is currently attempting to remake the world for the better is Jack Cogen (as of this writing, it's too soon to assess the final results). As president of Natsource LLC, an energy environmental commodity broker headquartered in New York City, Cogen and company are pioneering a brand new kind of environmental activism: the financial kind. The company is the first brokerage in the United States with an Environmental Action Desk devoted exclusively to the retail consumer market. Previously, only corporations could engage in emissions trading (classically a trade between a low-emissions company selling its "right to pollute" to another firm that would otherwise exceed its federal quota). The newer consumer model allows individuals to essentially "buy" harmful pollutants to ensure they never will be emitted by anyone at all. For less than the price of a movie ticket, a consumer can "retire" a ton of CO_2, the main cause of global warming. Sixty dollars buys a ton of sulfur dioxide (SO_2), the culprit in acid rain.

Using market forces to effect environmental and societal goals, Jack

Cogen is both a classic entrepreneur (making money from his newest business) and a classic Innerpreneur (changing the world to conform to his vision of a better future). The consumer trading desk at Natsource is relatively new, but already hundreds of trades have been made. We suspect this will become millions as the years go by. We can only hope that his dream of a world with lowered emissions comes to pass as well.

> Emissions trading is growing and companies are taking it seriously. Carbon is becoming an expense that is factored into [companies'] business decisions.
>
> **Glen, on Climateark.org**

Gary Erickson
Founder of Clif Bar

The concept for the first Clif Bar came about when its founder, exercise fanatic Gary Erickson, was on one of his typically long bike rides. Frustrated with how bad the energy bar he'd brought along tasted, he vowed to create his own. He named the bar after his father, and Clif is now one of the best-selling nutrition brands on the market. Erickson has grown the business all on his own, trusting his gut, because he remains the target consumer. As his success shows, there is simply no substitute for living your brand or category.

The marketing lesson learned? Innerpreneurs are quietly—and not so quietly—inspiring changes across nearly every category and cause. Innerpreneurs often head in directions traditional research might have said were too risky. But the Innerpreneur knows the validity of his or her idea, because it emerged out of a personal need or discovery.

PART-TIME INNERPRENEURS

Innerpreneurs are people constantly on a quest for personal growth. While many are able to combine this pursuit with making a living, others are not so lucky. Still, even these so-called part-time Innerpreneurs are always looking to get closer to their inner Renaissance man or woman, learn about new things, and explore the depths of their own psyches. Some of these part-timers may eventually blossom into full exemplars of this C-Type, while for others this Innerpreneurial avocation will be enough to sustain them indefinitely. The following are just a few ways in which this type of Innerpreneur pursues his or her quest.

Blogging

As stated earlier, the Innerpreneurial spirit is intrinsically creative. If Innerpreneurs cannot create in their professional life, they often make up this deficit in their spare time. Thankfully, technology is making it easier to indulge their creative sides. Wanna-be writers need only have Internet access in order to have their own blog. More than 80,000 new blogs pop up every day (about one every second), and one in every three Internet users is either writing, responding to, or reading blogs.[6] While some have higher aims, an estimated 70 to 80 percent of blogs are merely personal journals.[7] Some Innerpreneurs see their blogs as a way to share enlightenment or as a service to the community (i.e., blogs that compile links and news items of interest to a particular audience, for example, resources for new parents).

> We're not all "diarists" or "journalers"—some of us really have something of value to add to public discourse on important issues.
>
> **Anonymous, posting on a Pcmag.com forum**

Athletic Challenges

A recreational athlete we know, someone who competes in Iron Man triathlons (the triathlons include a 2.4-mile swim and 112-mile bike ride followed by a marathon), explained why he takes part in these events. "My life is too easy and convenient. I drive my car to work, then take the elevator up to my office. This is the only time I can really challenge myself physically." An increasing number of Innerpreneurial Americans feel the same way. Single-player sports (like running) have grown steadily in popularity over the years and are now at an all-time high. In 2005, an estimated 432,000 people completed marathons in the United States, up from 389,000 in 2000.[8] And 60,000 people joined USA Triathlon, the sport's governing organization in 2005. That number is nearly three times as many as in 2000.[9] Besides the physical challenges such activities provide, Innerpreneurs seek the mental and spiritual rewards associated with them as well. Innerpreneurs see wellness as a combination of both the physical and the mental, and testing the limits of their bodies helps them find the limitless natures of their souls.

> Completing a marathon was the best thing I ever did. I felt like if I could do that I could do anything, change the world.
>
> **roadrunner45, on marathonguide.com**

Volunteering

Through volunteer work, an Innerpreneur can satisfy his or her need for spiritual growth and fulfillment. There's also the self-satisfaction that comes from helping others. Americans, in general, are volunteering more, possibly looking for meaning or to make a difference in our post-9/11 world. A 2005 *USA Today* story reported that 64 million Americans did some sort of volunteer work the prior year, 4 million more than the year before. It's this impulse to "give something back" that underlies the myriad charitable-cause marketing campaigns discussed earlier.

> When your volunteering comes straight from the heart, you feel a pleasant sense of satisfaction that makes it easy to look forward to the day when you may give again.
>
> **Kevin, on Nitaleland.com**

> Other than the obvious gratification aspect of helping others, volunteering enabled me to make some lifelong friends whom I otherwise would not have met.
>
> **Asif, commenting on the Adhunika.org blog**

Vacations with Meaning

Innerpreneurs eschew typical no-think vacations filled with relaxation, mindless fun, and overly scheduled "leisure activities." Instead they have a completely different philosophy on vacationing. They're looking for vacations with meaning and/or life-changing promise.

VACATION QUICK FACTS

Findthedivine.com, a Web site devoted to listing spiritual retreat centers in the United States and Canada, currently gets 143,000 hits a month. That's up from 10,000 hits a month in 2002.[10]

At Outward Bound's Colorado school, the number of adults enrolling in Life/Career Renewal programs has risen by 95 percent in the past five years and 18 percent in the past year alone.[11]

Some favorite vacation ideas include volunteering trips (sponsored by organizations such as Globe Aware and the Sierra Club) like a week spent teaching English in Peru, or restoring an archeological site in New Mexico. Spiritual retreats also top the list, as do Outward Bound–type adventure trips in which travelers face physical challenges as a spur toward self-knowledge and learning trips (for example, a trip to Italy for intense cooking lessons). The goal, as with everything else in an Innerpreneur's life, is to return a changed and better person.

There is an enormous trend of people who have the need to get out and do something different. They're looking for any kind of escape, and if that means "beat me up a little bit," so be it. The point is to work your system to the point where you feel purified.

Gary Mansour, Mansour Travel, Beverly Hills, *The New York Times*, 1/16/04

My family stays in a yurt [on vacation]. They've had them in Oregon State Parks for years. It was like we could learn about the way people across the world from us live, and that makes us appreciate our lives more.

Zach, on Treehugger.com

... staying in Canopy Tower on my Panama vacation, in the rainforest ... over the course of that trip I became acquainted with the notion of fair trade, naturally grown coffee and how it's harvested.

Sharon, on 2020hindsight.org

AGENTS OF CHANGE

Throughout this chapter, we have discussed how an increasing number of Americans are displaying characteristics of the Innerpreneur. Now it's time to devote some time to the most influential among this type: those Innerpreneurs who have inspired the rise of this type in the first place. Better not call them pioneers; we'll consider them rather *agents of change.* The handful of people we explore have used their Innerpreneurial spirits to change attitudes and long-held beliefs, spawn movements, create new pastimes and activities, and otherwise alter behavior on a wide scale. Driven by a very specific (though not always immediately apparent) operating principle, they have introduced their own personal views to the world and have thereby changed it—invariably for the better.

Alice Waters

Followed her vision to create a "delicious revolution" and redefined American cooking.

We had this little fantasy . . . Oh, let's have a little café we said. I wasn't worried about paying for it. I just knew if I did the right thing, people would come.

Alice Waters, The New York Times, 1996

When chef and (now) culinary expert Alice Waters was just starting out in Berkeley, California, in the early 70s, French cuisine was the definition of gourmet. Waters, a perfectionist, was having a hard time finding the right fresh ingredients needed to make the French dishes she loved so much. Rather than change the recipes to align with American farming habits, she instead decided to find farmers who would align with her own (decidedly non-mainstream at the time) philosophy. Along with a group of small local farmers, Waters created a pipeline of fresh ingredients herself. These were harvested and served to customers the very same day. She hadn't set out to change the food industry or start a trend. Waters was just applying her own vision and cooking style to her own restaurants—first the celebrated Chez Panisse in Berkeley, and then its sister restaurant, Café Fanny in West Berkeley.

The Alice Waters philosophy of cooking—allowing fresh, locally grown ingredients to become the star of the plate, and not spoiling their purity with fussy techniques—ended up spreading far beyond Berkeley. Her way of cooking started an entire food movement that some would later call a "delicious revolution." Have you heard about California cooking? New American cooking? Sustainability and biodiversity? The push to use of fresh, locally grown, and organic ingredients? You can trace all of these ideas and trends back to Alice Waters.

Alice Waters changed America's relationship with food. Taste buds were transformed. Diners wanted to know where their food was coming from. It may sound pedestrian today, but in the 80s, Waters was swimming against the tide. Through her restaurants, and later her cookbooks, she proved that food could be a vehicle for social change. The most influential and widespread evidence of this can be found in the success of the organic movement, which Alice Waters helped to propagate.

Though Alice Waters no longer cooks in her restaurants, she still remains a presence on the food scene. One of her recent missions, possibly the most noble, was to bring her simple, nutritious food philosophy to children. Seeking to promote ecological and gastronomic literacy and sell kids on fresh foods instead of junk foods, she created the Edible Schoolyard, a parking-lot-turned-organic-garden at the Martin Luther King, Jr. Middle School in Berkeley, where she not only requires that students tend to their own gardens, but has also created a cooking classroom in which they turn their fresh ingredients into her delicious signature dishes. Food writer R. W. Apple may have summed it up best when he had this to say of our favorite Innerpreneurial chef, "There is no one more influential in American food than Alice Waters."[12]

Jake Burton Carpenter

Do what you love and the money will follow. . . .

When you see some guy in a crazy contraption, you'd better not laugh. They laughed at me. They're not laughing anymore.

FSB (Forbes Small Business), 10/04

Our next Innerpreneurial agent of change is the owner of Burton Snowboards and the father of snowboarding himself, Jake Burton Carpenter. He earned his place in the Innerpreneur Hall of Fame by changing the face of playing in the snow and creating an entirely new popular sport in the process. Snowboarding didn't even exist a few decades ago, and today it has breathed a new, edgier air into ski resorts and even the Olympics. Jake Burton Carpenter made that happen almost single-handedly, all as a result of being driven by desire.

Carpenter turned his passion into a business back in 1977 when, burned out on skiing, he started sliding down small hills in his backyard on a homemade slat of wood. Unsatisfied, he sawed and bent his board into a new shape, that of the current snowboard. Carpenter had a tough time selling both his snowboards and the concept of snowboarding. Customers thought his boards were too expensive, and resort owners were worried about having "these people" on the slopes. Even his own friends told him snowboarding wouldn't be more than a flash in the pan. But believing in this new pastime and satisfied with merely making a living on his sales, Carpenter plugged forward. "I never dreamed it would get as big as it did," he is quoted as saying in a *Playboy* article in 2004. "I just thought I could make a living doing something cool."

The success of Burton snowboards can be attributed to Carpenter's pluck and belief in his product. Eschewing typical market research and focus groups, Carpenter instead followed his gut. Although he made some mistakes along the way—like failing to recognize teenagers as his true target demographic—Carpenter continued to make inroads with the ski community, finally breaking into resorts by the mid-1980s. From there, the sport's popularity grew exponentially and spawned the irreverent and alternative youth culture of "boarding."

With snowboarding one of the fastest-growing sports, Burton Snowboards enjoys about one-third of the lucrative boarding market. And Carpenter, now in his fifties, still has the laid-back attitude of a snowboarder and claims to get 100 days of slope time a year. "If I got buried in an avalanche tomorrow, I would have no regrets," he said.[13]

That's precisely what every Innerpreneur lives to be able to say.

Oprah Winfrey

Do that which will give your life meaning.

For me, the whole celebrity trip doesn't mean a thing unless you have something meaningful to say. What does it mean to be celebrated and have nothing that is worthy of celebration? What does it mean to be put in a position where everyone knows your name and is going gaga over what you have to say if you have nothing meaningful to say?

"Oprah on the Record," *Television Week*, 4/19/04

Oprah has been a TV legend for over 20 years now. But she wasn't always Oprah the Innerpreneur, Oprah the Agent of Change. Sometime in the mid-1990s, she decided that she would either bring meaning to her show (and thereby her life) or stop doing it altogether. She abandoned the salacious topics of other popular talk shows and, running through the audience with a microphone, turned instead to New Agey segments like "Remembering Your Spirit." She encouraged viewers to keep a "gratitude journal" and write down the things they were grateful for. Professionally, she expanded her production company, Harpo Productions, and used it to produce the types of projects she found meaningful. She began *O* magazine, a publication filled with advice on how to live your best life. And she formed the Angel Network, a charity that began as a plea to her viewers to contribute money to The Boys & Girls Club of America for scholarships. The Angel Network has since raised millions of dollars for causes such as Hurricane Katrina relief and educational programs worldwide. And Oprah herself has become a sort of queen of benevolence. Her other charitable works and pet causes are almost too numerous to list. Suffice it to say that her very name is synonymous with phrases such as "giving back" and "following your heart." As her Web site states, "You get from the world what you give to the world." And every day, she continues to use her television show as a forum to urge her millions of viewers to live their best lives and make a difference.

Jimmy Carter

The most important legacy is to have made a positive difference in the world.

Of all the Innerpreneurial agents of change, no other embodies this C-Type's metamorphic tendencies as much as Jimmy Carter. As if it weren't enough to go from peanut farmer to president of the United States, Carter has continued to reinvent himself since he left the Oval Office.

Considered a weak president and even ridiculed while in the White House, Jimmy Carter could have settled into the type of quiet, prosperous life many ex-presidents enjoy: creating a namesake library and collecting enormous speaking fees. Instead, Carter followed a route that would classify him as the quintessential Innerpreneur. He's had many job titles over the years, including author (he's written everything from a memoir to a children's book to works of fiction), professor (he's taught at Emory University), and even mountain climber–adventurer (he's scaled Mount Kilimanjaro and parts of Everest). But Jimmy Carter's greatest legacy lies in his humanitarian efforts.

Carter has worked extensively with Habitat for Humanity, the non-profit housing ministry that builds homes for those in need. And most significant is the worldwide impact he's been able to make through the Carter Center, an organization he formed to advance human rights and alleviate human suffering. Through the Carter Center, the 39th president has helped the global economy and fought disease in third-world countries. Carter Center efforts have even helped to nearly eradicate an entire disease—the deadly guinea worm disease in Africa.

By following his heart, Carter has achieved not only financial success and public approval but also the Nobel Peace Prize. One of only three U.S. presidents to receive the prize, Carter was honored for his decades of human rights work, as well as his attempts to help negotiate peaceful solutions to international conflicts.

MARKETING TO INNERPRENEURS: A CHECKLIST

☑ Innerprenuers shop with their heads and buy with their hearts.

☑ Celebrate the journey, not just the destination.

☑ Brands that challenge convention and carve out new territory are interesting.

☑ Be bold, but not extreme. Change the world, but don't lose perspective.

☑ Be transparent; no gimmicks, tricks, or marketing smoke and mirrors.

☑ Innerpreneurs are inner-directed; market to their creative spirits.

☑ Layer your advertising messages. Sophisticated Innerpreneurs seek to discover things that are less obvious to most.

☑ Rachet up cause marketing: Innerpreneurs want to see your brand visibly involved in causes, not just donating a percentage of the profits.

☑ Innerpreneurs want to learn about the story behind the brand, the reasons for its invention, and the history of its founders.

☑ Innerpreneurs recognize the power of their influence and enjoy leading less adventurous consumers to new things.

DIG A LITTLE DEEPER

FURTHER RESOURCES ON INNERPRENEURS

Innerpreneurs in Print

Raising the Bar: Integrity and Passion in Life and Business: The Story of Clif Bar & Co., by Gary Erickson and Lois Lorentzen
Gary Erickson, the founder of Clif Bar, shares how he turned his idea for a better-tasting sports bar into a successful business, without having to compromise his passion or principles.

The Way of the Traveler: Making Every Trip a Journey of Self-Discovery by Joseph Dispenza
Dispenza, who is clearly an Innerpreneur himself, preaches that all travel is a sacred journey to self-discovery. He encourages fellow Innerpreneurs to "keep a journal of feelings, sketch what you see, and transform yourself in ways that enrich your lives on every trip you take, whether overseas or just across town." Who knew a trip to the store could be a journey of self-discovery?

Transformative Getaways: For Spiritual Growth, Self-Discovery, and Holistic Healing by John Benson

Fodor's Healthy Escapes: 284 Resorts and Retreats Where You Can Get Fit, Feel Good, Find Yourself, and Get Away from It All by Mark Sullivan
When venerable travel guide stalwart Fodor's starts catering to the Innerpreneur crowd, it's clear that this is a trend gaining a strong foothold in the mainstream. Both books above list ideas for vacations that can improve physical, mental, and spiritual well-being, with destinations like spas, family camps, meditation retreats, and wilderness adventures.

Mountains Beyond Mountains: Healing the World: The Quest of Dr. Paul Farmer by Tracy Kidder
Infectious disease specialist and MacArthur Award recipient Farmer is on a tireless quest to bring better medical care to Haiti's poorest. This biography follows him from an unusual childhood, which included living on a school bus and an old boat, to his current work as a modern-day medical Robin Hood.

Second Acts: Creating the Life You Really Want, Building the Career You Truly Desire by Stephen M. Pollan and Mark Levine

Do What You Love for the Rest of Your Life: A Practical Guide to Career Change and Personal Renewal by Bob Griffiths

I Don't Know What I Want, but I Know It's Not This: A Step-by-Step Guide to Finding Gratifying Work by Julie Jansen
These three books seek to help confused Innerpreneurs find their way to ultimately fulfilling work (on their own terms, of course).

Above All Else: The Everest Dream by Jamie Clarke and Alan Hobson
This book suggests that "everyday Everests" can be tougher to climb than any mountain. As you follow the story of how Hobson and Clarke overcame the obstacles when they climbed the actual mountain, they hope it will inspire you to reach your own goals.

Quarterlife Crisis: The Unique Challenges of Life in Your Twenties by Alexandra Robbins and Abby Wilner
When young adults graduate, after almost two decades of regimented schooling, into a world of overwhelming choices—about career, about finances, about where to live and who—to love—they often freak out. They feel helpless, panicked, and indecisive—in the midst of a quarterlife crisis. Of course some people glide carelessly through their twenties, but they don't turn into Innerpreneurs.

Innerpreneurs Online
StevePavlina.com
Steve Pavlina, "perhaps the most intensely growth-oriented individual you will ever meet" according to his Web site, has dedicated the site to helping visitors make conscious decisions about their own personal development. Topics covered include time management, motivation, goal setting, and fulfillment.

BalancedLiving.com
The Center for Balanced Living offers holistic career planning programs to help Innerpreneurs tap into their inherent passions, develop their confidence and communication skills, and finally achieve personally and professionally rewarding lives.

FindYourCoach.com

The Coach Connection (TCC) is the one-stop source for Innerpreneurs looking to connect with the ideal life coach.

FindtheDivine.org

Innerpreneurs wondering where to get in touch with the divine can browse through this site's comprehensive listings (and descriptions) of over 1,100 retreat centers in the United States and about 150 in Canada.

LearningVacations.com

For those looking to bring back more from a vacation than a tan and a T-shirt, this site is a great jumping-off point to find "educational" vacations from guided safaris to golf or cooking classes to language schools.

Outwardbound.com

As the "premier adventure-based education program in the world," this is often an Innerpreneur's first stop when planning a vacation. The organization tries to use the wilderness as a classroom, leading "students" on a mountain-peak ascent, or helping them navigate a boat through zigzagging rapids, all in order to help them develop confidence and self-knowledge in the process.

NOTES

1. Bankrate.com, 3/20/00

2. *The New York Times,* 2/27/06

3. *The New York Times,* 10/2/05

4. *Psychotherapy Newsletter,* 6/05

5. *Detroit Free Press,* 4/11/06

6. *Indianapolis Business Journal,* 2/27/06

7. *The New York Times,* 12/19/04

8. *Running USA*—RRIC Annual Marathon Reports

9. *The New York Times,* 3/16/06

10. *Budget Travel Magazine,* 5/03

11. outwardbound.com, 6/05

12. *San Francisco Chronicle,* 3/19/03

13. *FSB,* October 2002

Middlemen

"

The conveyor belt that transported adolescents into adulthood has broken down.

Dr. Frank Furstenberg, studying the MiddleMan phenomenon for the MacArthur Foundation

A gap between the end of adolescence and the onset of adulthood has appeared in a man's early- to mid-20s, a period in which no traditional markers of manhood apply and income is almost entirely disposable.

Advertising Age, 6/13/05

This group of 18- to 26-year-olds is betwixt and between youthful frivolity and fully committed adulthood. They job-hop, put off marriage and extend education. These people are stimulus junkies.

Dallas Morning News, 8/2/05

"Т he child is father of the man." So wrote William Wordsworth in 1802. Let's give him the benefit of the doubt; maybe when he wrote it the sentiment rang true. Two centuries on, the situation is less clear. Lately it seems that for some males the child is just the father of a bigger child, or (at best) the father of the "guy." Today's young men (and we're speaking here of the generation that has come of age since the early 1990s) appear to be creating a new definition of manhood. This new male type owes more to the jokey carelessness of adolescence than it does to the traditional burdens of adult responsibility.

Bearing in mind that there are exceptions, the average MiddleMan is an unmarried college graduate who most definitely doesn't cook. They don't all live with their parents, although that is true of many. Primarily a highly visible and influential segment of the 21- to 35-year-old male demographic, MiddleMen are defined more by mindset and behavior than life stage. So it's possible to find some examples even among older men. And while there are women who share the same habits and sense of humor as the guys, the wellspring of this C-Type is the preoccupations of the adolescent male.

To be clear, the notion that youngish American adults are in a perpetual state of adolescence is not new. From a 2002 article in *Newsweek* magazine (which referred to them as "adultolescents") to pieces in lad magazines like *FHM* and *Maxim*, the idea that American kids are refusing to grow up has been widely disseminated. It has been in the subject of books (for example, *Rejuvenile: Kickball, Cartoons, Cupcakes, and the Reinvention of the American Grown-up* by Christopher Noxon) and a topic of conversation at dinner parties. Why we think this type is still worth reporting on is the overlooked effect that MiddleMen have had on the culture as a whole, especially the wider culture's construction of masculinity. The MiddleMan type has helped make fantasy sports leagues and video gaming the nation's top pastimes, turned sneakers into collectibles and, most especially, shifted the notion of what we think is funny. The MiddleMan sense of humor has had a profound effect on what the rest of us watch on TV, as well as the kind of films that reap big profits. This type seems well entrenched in the consumer zeitgeist and shows no signs of going away.

One of the most visible MiddleMan markers is their tendency to reside in a parental home even after graduating college. The number of college graduates who move back home has been increasing in recent years for many reasons, but most young men and women remain only a brief time. (For many, male as well as female, the impetus is purely financial. Today's college graduates owe 85 percent more in student loans than the graduates of a decade ago.[1]) Some 54.8 percent of men between ages 21 and 24 now live with their parents but by 25 this number drops significantly.[2] It is this group, the 13.5 percent of men 25 to 30 who still live in their childhood homes, which forms the nucleus of the MiddleMan C-Type. It's not a small group. According to the 2000 census, nearly 4 million people between the ages of 25 and 34 live with their parents.

> I think it's perfectly legitimate . . . conditions in the real world of today almost demand a parent's support—for a while.
>
> **Robert, on the alumni.unc.edu message board**

> We don't want to kick [our 25-year-old] out but we wonder when he'll go . . . there are no indicators to assess his status on the scale of "progress" and "moving ahead."
>
> **Lindsey, on the AARP message board**

FLYING BACK TO THE NEST

Adult children living in their parents' homes isn't just an American phenomenon. Here's the way it's referred to around the world:

ENGLAND: Kippers
An acronym for "kids in parents' pockets eroding retirement savings."

FRANCE: Tanguy Syndrome
This syndrome gets its name from a 2001 comedy about a frustrated set of parents who try to get their 28-year-old to finally leave home.

GERMANY: Nesthocker
This German compound noun literally means "nest squatter."

ITALY: Mammone
The percentage of adult Italians living at home is probably the highest in Europe. The word *mammone*, used to describe them, means "those who won't give up Mamma's cooking."

JAPAN: Freeter
Oddly, this word is half English and half German (a combination of *free* and the German word for worker, *arbeiter*) and connotes an unmarried young adult who lives at home while changing jobs often.

Source: *Time* magazine, 1/24/05

It's worth noting that there are MiddleMan-related marketing implications for which MiddleMen themselves are not the target. Consider the mother of a MiddleMan. She's still the primary shopper and chef for the household and, in a strange way, the old stereotype "mom as gatekeeper" still has relevance in her home. Whether you address her with an empathetic or a humorous tone, you'll still likely gain her loyalty. Taco Bell, a brand that has shown itself wise to the MiddleMan C-Type (see eating habits, below) took the humorous path, with its 2006 "good to go" campaign. In these ads, restless parents use Taco Bell food's portability (". . . it's good to go") to lure their twentysomething son off the couch, out of the house, and into a waiting car loaded with his belongings. This type of advertising strategy could just as profitably be applied to many categories: household cleaners, cough-cold products, T-shirts, etc. Yesterday's mom expected that packing junior off to college marked the end of her housekeeping role, but more and more this is not strictly the case, and that may be interesting to acknowledge in your marketing.

For this C-Type, college is now seen as a life stage, with its own set of rituals and behaviors never intended to be a model for life in the "real world." So when MiddleMen graduate, they are not ready to be truly adult. College may have prepared these MiddleMen to hold down lucrative jobs, but that doesn't mean they're ready to cook, clean, or do laundry for themselves. There are studies to confirm the theory. Social scientists like Frank Furstenberg at the University of Pennsylvania see the emergence of a new phase of life called "early adulthood."[3] And some view this as a positive life trend. Jeffrey Arnett, author of *Emerging Adulthood: The Winding Road from the Late Teens through the Twenties*, suggests, "This is the one time of their lives when they're not responsible for anyone else or to anyone else. So they have this wonderful freedom to really focus on their own lives and work on becoming the kind of person they want to be."

> This time for me is about taking risks. What my parents have done is given me the opportunity not to settle, and I'm taking advantage of that.
>
> **Evan, age 29**

> ... it's just easier to concentrate on finding the right job without having to worry about other stuff. And there is a lot to worry about when you leave home.
>
> **Biggt, on the gamemakergames.com forum**

For many MiddleMen the period after college becomes a period of job-hopping. Those not living with parents are usually found cohabiting with roommates in communal living environments where expenses are shared and therefore reduced. These unmarried men live a life that often resembles life in a frat house, replete with beer in the fridge and a ring around the tub. Surprisingly enough, according to Roommates.com, it's people ages 25 to 34 who form the biggest segment of their users, people whom previous generations would have expected to live independently (if not with a spouse).[4] In addition to the social elements of living with roommates, the sharing of expenses lessens the pressure to stay at jobs that are considered displeasing. Among MiddleMen there is often the attitude that work ought to be, somehow, fun.

These attitudes and behaviors generally last until marriage. Given that the median age for first marriage for men is now nearly 27, this can be quite a few years.[5] A survey for the Integrated Public Use Microdata Series looked at men and women in 1960 and 2000, comparing their level of transition through the "traditional benchmarks" of leaving home, finishing school, getting married, having a child, and becoming financially independent. In 1960, 65 percent of men had passed those benchmarks by age 30. That figure had fallen to 31 percent by 2000.[6]

> Men and women are marrying later, launching their careers or simply sowing oats instead of settling down to start a family with a spouse and kids in their teens or early 20s.
>
> **"Kids flock back to parents' nest,"** *The San Francisco Chronicle,* **3/11/06**

> [This] generation is finicky at best, and full of loners. They don't really date in college—they "hook up," as if sex is just another mechanical accomplishment, to be tallied and put on a resume.
>
> **"The Long Goodbye,"** *Newsweek,* **5/22/06**

Many of the factors that created the MiddleMan phenomenon reach back a quarter of a century to a time when most of this bunch were still tykes. The generation that came of age in the 70s and early 80s grew up at a time when the American family was breaking down, when divorce was becoming commonplace, and when the mood of the country was cynical. There was an absence of positive father figures for many of these boys, both on a personal level (for children of divorced households) and on a macro level. The presidents during the 70s were Nixon, Ford, and Carter—none of them, at the time, was considered a positive, strong male role model—and the overriding message of the culture, at least as it related to personal behavior and interpersonal relationships, was an "if-it-feels-good-do-it" hedonism. In addition, this was a generation where most young men made it into adulthood without a draft or a war to serve as a moral testing ground. It was a time of general prosperity, a time when a segment of pampered boys was uniquely prepared to mature into a cohort of eternal boy-men.

MiddleMen: At Home

Putting aside the issue of where and/or with whom MiddleMen reside, let's look at what fills their homes and what they do when they're there. Foremost among a MiddleMan's possessions is his gaming system. This can be composed of an Xbox, Playstation, Nintendo Wii, or PC (or all four!), and this system is the mainstay of the MiddleMan's recreation time. A recent national online survey regarding relaxation activities of men 18 to 34 found that video gaming outranked even television (39 to 31 percent) as the clear favorite among time wasters.[7] MiddleMen have been in the vanguard in making interactive gaming a cultural phenomenon. It's now the fastest-growing form of entertainment in the country, and not just for kids or teens. (The fastest-growing segment, to be fair, is female gamers, but that's outside the scope of this C-Type.[8]) The average gamer is a 29-year-old adult. In fact, 33 percent of regular Xbox gamers are adults who make over $80,000 a year.[9]

> When I was a kid I could not afford these console toys. Now that I'm an adult, I buy all the games I can. TIME is the problem now.
>
> **Mike, a gamer on Google Groups**

> Unlike my compatriots, I have never really weaned myself off videogames, I still read videogame history, news for oh … uhh substantial amounts of time and I download and play all of the newest games as you can probably tell from my blog.
>
> **Matt M., online blogger**

One good indication of how MiddleMen influence the wider culture is gaming's arrival in the halls of academia. A large number of colleges now offer courses in interactive game theory or specialized game design, and the number offering a major in interactive game design/ entertainment technology has swelled from fewer than a dozen in 2000 to over 100 in 2005.[10] Which means that future generations of graduates will be able to carry a degree in their favorite pastime.

WHAT MIDDLEMEN ARE PLAYING NOW

There are a lot of interactive games for MiddleMen to choose from—but as of October 2006 it seems most are choosing World of Warcraft, made by Blizzard Entertainment. After just two years on the market, the game has almost 7 million paying subscribers and is set to top $1 billion in revenue.[11] That makes it one of the most lucrative entertainment properties in any medium, ever. World of Warcraft has also become a truly global phenomenon (you'd have to go back to Pac-Man to come close). The game has more than 3 million players in China and is hugely popular in South Korea and Europe as well. As with most video games, a clear majority (though not all, by any means) of players worldwide are males between ages 20 and 40.[12]

Gaming's arrival as a mainstream entertainment medium has not gone unnoticed. Savvy marketers like Coke and Wendy's have recognized the power of interactive games as a vehicle for advertising. Straightforward ads appended to popular game titles are a good way of talking directly to MiddleMen, but product placement (à la Hollywood) might be an even more effective way of imprinting your brand on this C-Type's consciousness. According to research firm Parks Associates, marketers spent about $80 million in 2005 on game advertising—from product placement in games to sponsoring gaming events—and this number will only swell as the ranks of gamers continue to grow.[13]

Another recreational activity currently sweeping the cyber world (and spearheaded by MiddleMen) is fantasy sports leagues. Players in these online sports forums create a fantasy team made up of professional athletes, whose success or failure is determined by the performance of real-life players in actual games. Fantasy sports are now estimated to be generating more than $600 million per year in advertising and subscription fee revenues.[14] The men in these leagues stress over the ups and downs of their fantasy teams, and for many it becomes an obsession surpassing even sex. (One e-mail survey of men age 22 and over, asking their number one thought during the day, revealed that for 40 percent of respondents it was fantasy football, compared to only 30 percent for sex!)[15] Much like pickup games serve as bonding activity for youths, these fantasy sports leagues provide a sense of connection for MiddleMen stuck in offices, a link to their childhood days of playing with friends in the backyard.

> Fantasy leagues offer a chance for community and for bonding.
>
> **Psychiatrist Ronald Kamm, president,**
> **International Society for Sport Psychiatry**

There are some real-life games targeted to these guys as well. By combining GenX nostalgia with high-tech toys and an adult environment, Big Games PacManhattan is a perfect example of a MiddleMan activity. This real-world version of the old arcade favorite uses global positioning devices to turn New York City's street grid into a giant version of the video game's onscreen maze, allowing players themselves to enter the world of the game. (Check it out at pacmanhattan.com.) Sports in general are a good way to sell to this C-Type, and that goes way beyond buying advertising time during big events like the Superbowl or NCAA playoffs. Why not sponsor a local ball club or tournament? Or endorse one of the growing number of adult sports fantasy camps, where, for a grown-up fee, MiddleMen can live out a childhood dream by playing a round or inning or period with a (usually retired) professional sports hero?

Moving beyond the game room, what fills the MiddleMan closet? His style, if indeed that isn't a contradiction in terms, unsurprisingly leans heavily toward the uniform of younger males: T-shirt, jeans, and sneakers. No less an authority than the *New York Times* Style Section has noted this fact, asserting that many younger men, "still enjoy dressing the way they did before they started to shave, spending, for instance, more than $13 billion on T-shirts annually."[16] *New York Magazine* did a cover story on this new breed of men who dress and act like youngsters, terming them "grups" (a contraction of "grown ups," from an old episode of *Star Trek*).

> If being a Grup means being 35, using a messenger bag instead of a briefcase, and staying out too late too often, and owning

more pairs of sneakers (eleven) than suits (one)... in short, if it means living your life in fundamentally the same way that you did when you were, say, 22? then I'm a Grup.

Adam Sternbergh, *New York Magazine*, 4/3/06

The "work casual" movement in the 90s was a boon to MiddleMen seeking to avoid the rigor of the suit and tie uniform. While many companies are now shifting back to formal dress codes, in certain industries casual has become the rule (and more casual even than corporate "casual Fridays" ever were: we're talking T-shirts, shorts, and flip-flops). Unsurprisingly, these are the industries, like computer animation, where MiddleMen make up a majority of the workforce. Meanwhile, outside of work, the MiddleMan aesthetic now reigns triumphant in the culture at large. The at-home wardrobes of most men, whether MiddleMen or not, appear to be moving steadily back toward the playground.

The main difference comes in the amount of disposable income they bring to their wardrobes (especially MiddleMen who still live with their parents). These men often have no expenses when it comes to room and board. Every cent they have goes to personal spending. Marketers are taking notice. American Eagle Outfitters, a mainstay of high school guys, is now going after the post-collegiate crowd. (This makes perfect demographic sense, by the way. The number of Americans 25 to 34 will rise by 5.2 percent by 2010, according to the Census Bureau, while those 12 to 18 will fall by 3.3 percent.[17]) The brand is not altering its style much (since this C-Type doesn't want to give up the jeans and T-shirt look), but it's making the clothes slightly more upscale (using finer fabrics, tighter tailoring, and sleeker silhouettes, etc.). This new American Eagle Outfitters chain, called Martin & Osa, started with four stores in fall 2006, but is hoping to eventually outfit an entire generation of MiddleMen.

The casual side of the business shows the greatest growth... jeans, T-shirts and sweaters continue to drive the bottom line.

Kal Ruttenstein, fashion director of Bloomingdale's quoted in *The New York Times*, 1/13/04

When it comes to food, MiddleMen are strangers to the kitchen. If they live alone, or with roommates who are members of their cohort, it's likely the pantry is bare of everything except packaged snacks. Meal preparation, at best, constitutes microwaving a frozen dinner or heating up a prepared meal from the supermarket. At its simplest, meal prep consists of ordering in. MiddleMen are a boon to drive-thru windows, fast food restaurants, and takeout pizza joints. Guys 18 to 34 are the backbone of the fast food industry, buying the majority of fast food sold. One McDonald's exec estimated that this 20 percent of the company's customers is responsible for 70 percent of overall sales.[18] Many fast food trends, like the upsizing of portions, owe a great deal to this C-Type's influence.

Taco Bell aimed squarely at this C-Type with its 2006 "Fourth Meal" campaign. ("Fourth Meal" is another name for late-night eating.) In order to better serve the nearly 50 percent of males aged 18 to 29 (and 30 percent of males 30 to 39) who eat after 7 p.m., most Taco Bells have extended their hours to 1 a.m.[19] According to a company press release, Taco Bell understands that ". . . in addition to functioning as a meal, eating later serves as a way to socialize with friends and extend the night." Further proof, if needed, that Taco Bell has got this C-Type in its sights: the restaurant's Web site features a "Fourth Meal" section consisting of silly, kidlike interactive games, but the players' alter egos look decidedly like adults.

The fast-growing chain In-N-Out Burger (sales at each of the chain's stores are $1.6 million a year[20]) has also captured the hearts and minds of MiddleMen with its "secret menu." Actually, it's not really the menu items that are secret, it's the lingo used to order them. By sidling up to the counter and ordering a burger "protein style" (which means sans bun, wrapped in lettuce leaves) or a 4×4 (which means 4 patties and 4 slices of cheese), grown men get to recapture the fun of being an actual adolescent, when having a private slang was a hedge against parental authority. This is a great way to target this C-Type. If you can create a quirky insider language or catchphrase (remember "Wasssup?") for your brand or business, MiddleMen are likely to be among the first to pick it up and pass it around.

When it comes to drinks, there are certain beverage categories in which MiddleMen can be termed leading-edge. Energy drinks and sports drinks were embraced early by this type, and this once niche category has now become mainstream, clocking nearly $3 billion in 2004.[21] MiddleMan tastes can be clearly seen in the success of Red Bull, whose U.S. sales volume was up by 38 percent in the first eight months of 2005, nearing $300 million.[22] Combining an under-21 attitude with their over-21 privileges, MiddleMen's favorite way to enjoy Red Bull seems to be as a late-night party booster, spiked with their alcohol of choice (usually vodka).

MARKETPLACE EVIDENCE

Domino's Pizza
Delivery giant Domino's Pizza has made a special effort to target this C-Type. The company teamed up with ESPN and ABC Sports in 2004 to sponsor Monday Night Football, an endorsement they continued in 2005. As part of this campaign millions of copies of the Monday Night Football schedule were printed on pizza box tops, and an exclusive Domino's Fantasy Football League was initiated, managed by ESPN. Another noteworthy gesture came in fall 2005 when Domino's raffled off a "Steak Fanatic Pizza Couch" to inaugurate its new steak pizza offering. This MiddleMan couch potato's high-tech dream came complete with remote control caddy bottle opener, a built-in Xbox with three controllers, an MP3 player, an XM Radio, NASCAR headset, DVD player, and not one but two flat screen televisions.

MiddleMen: At Work

When it comes to work, there are two major camps of MiddleMen. The first is made up of those who move from job to job, refusing or unable to settle on and pursue a career. The second, more happily, has found satisfaction in the growing number of fields that allow them to show up at the office in flip-flops and shorts and make use of their specialized aptitudes and attitudes.

In the case of many postcollegiates, an inclination toward remaining an adolescent may be fanned by the flames of a less-than-robust economy. At this point, the average adult under 34 holds a job for only 20 months.[23] Difficulty finding a job only confirms feelings of dependence and immaturity, and the psychological defense against these feelings can often be a retreat into childish humor and the reemergence of the sullen "screw the world" attitude common among dependent teenagers.

> The social shift to a longer transition to adulthood began in the past 10 years. One primary reason for the change is that it takes longer to find a job that pays a living wage.
>
> **Tom W. Smith, University of Chicago**

> It's nearly impossible to support oneself immediately after college, particularly when so many students graduate with thousands of dollars in debt.
>
> **Aaron, commenting on Mahablog.com**

These kinds of MiddleMen tend to switch employers often, though the positions in question are almost always jobs and not careers. The GenX buzzword "McJob" neatly sums up this kind of employment. Data entry, or other sorts of office temp work, also fits here, representing the low-interest, no-chance-for-advancement nature of jobs taken just to make ends meet. (For those living at home, income need only provide spending money, since rent and food are free.) Because they are disinterested and uninvolved in the work they do, it's no wonder that these kinds of MiddleMen take refuge in the world of games and cartoon superheroes.

It's not that there are no ambitious MiddleMen. Some hold down "real" jobs, or even excel in fields that demand a free spirit and a flexible mind. But all MiddleMen share one characteristic: they are unwilling to forgo a laid-back attitude, and a certain amount of irreverence, in pursuit of success. The lucky MiddleMen are the ones who manage to find (or have successfully found) companies where they can behave and dress casually, and combine fun and play with the work they do. Certain fields, needless to say, lend themselves to this kind of workplace more than others. The dot-com boom of the 90s was a godsend for MiddleMen, ushering in, as it did, a proliferation of casual work environments, places where a youthful attitude was seen not only as a sign of creativity but as a key to success in the new, swiftly shifting world of Internet commerce.

Though the dot-com boom is most certainly over, there are still career paths available to MiddleMen that make good use of their particular skills. Video gaming, for one (see above) is a big business. It is a sector that continues to grow and grow, with more work in the decades ahead for future members of this C-Type. Since gaming now pulls in about $7 billion every year,[24] supply has yet to exceed demand in the field of game designers.

All the time spent in front of their gaming consoles may be giving MiddleMen advantages even in industries that might surprise you. One example is in the field of laparoscopic surgery. According to experts, the controls used to maneuver microscopic cameras inside a patient's body are remarkably similar to a computer game's joystick. "The complex manual dexterity required to be a stellar video gamer and minimally invasive surgeon are strikingly similar," says Dr. James Rosser, Jr., chief of minimally invasive surgery and director of Beth Israel's Advanced Medical Technology Institute. Dr. Rosser was a coauthor of a 2004 study that concluded that surgeons who played video games for at least three hours a week were 27 percent faster and made 37 percent fewer mistakes than surgeons who did not play video games.[25] This example is but one among many. So many fields are now dependent upon computers that quick and accurate hand-eye coordination is becoming a valuable skill comparable to a fast typing speed 20 years ago. Given that it's a common accomplishment for MiddleMen, maybe mom should stop worrying about whether a son who'd rather play with his Xbox than do homework will ever be able to hold down a job.

MARKETPLACE EVIDENCE

CollegeHumor.com

The simplest way for MiddleMen to be sure of a happy work experience is to found a company themselves. CollegeHumor.com, founded by four young guys hanging around in front of their computers in their boxers and bare feet, is now one of the most popular humor sites on the Internet. Though they claim the for-profit Web site was originally launched merely to score "beer money," they now hope to use it to launch a multimedia brand (like *Mad Magazine* or *National Lampoon*) with spin-off movies and books. Their first book, *"The CollegeHumor Guide to College,"* was released by Penguin Group USA in spring 2006 with more to come. But lest you think they have become more mogul than MiddleMan, the founders insist: "We have fun at what we do. We'd be doing this if we were making less money. The point is, we're doing something we enjoy."[26] When it comes to business, that could be the MiddleMan credo.

MiddleMen: Culture and Society

A perfect MiddleMan night out combines both adult and childlike pleasures. Venues and activities that allow them to play games or act immature while also drinking (or smoking cigarettes—or smoking something else) or socializing with friends (or flirting with the opposite sex—or, well you get the idea) are the ones that attract and keep the MiddleMan clientele.

> On any given night, places like Dave and Buster's are packed with patrons shooting at aliens with a plastic gun in one hand and a beer in the other.
>
> *Chicago Daily Herald,* 4/28/05

> I've met a few people around my age who live with their parents, and they all tend to live way out in the suburbs. That

really imposes a cost in terms of limiting one's ability to
socialize.

Dlamming on his blog, Saccharomyces.blogspot.com

Because of the defining circumstances of their lives, MiddleMen
have the time and the discretionary incomes to allow the bars, clubs, and
restaurants they frequent to become "homes away from home." This is
even truer for MiddleMen still living with their parents. For them, the
need is great for a place where they can hang out with compatriots in an
unstructured way, where they can feel autonomous and independent.
Online communities meet some of this need, but the nature of Web interactions cannot equal having laid-back drinks with the guys.

The combination of drinking with game playing is perfect for MiddleMen, and they are at the center of this moment in bar culture. The
past few years have seen drinking games move from frat houses to more
mainstream venues, and to an older, postcollegiate crowd. The most successful of this new breed of drinking games is Beer Pong, and its success
is indicative of a pervasive, nationwide MiddleMan influence. Bing
Bong, a company created in summer 2004 specifically to sell portable
Beer Pong tables, sold more than 2,000 tables in the first year alone.[27]
While the game originated on college campuses, many bars in big cities
now hold matches every week. Players toss or hit table tennis balls into
cups of beer; when one team sinks a ball into a cup, the other team is
required to drink the beer. Beer Pong tournaments are sponsored by large
beer distributors who help advertise the events and supply the prizes.
Miller Brewing Company awarded the prizes for a four-day Beer Pong
tournament in Atlanta which drew hundreds of people, while Anheuser-
Busch had a promotion in 2004 called "Bud Pong."[28] And in January
2006 the first World Series of Beer Pong was held on the outskirts of Las
Vegas. With its combination of gambling, gaming, strippers, and, of
course, plentiful alcohol, the American city most representative of MiddleMan fantasies writ large.

God bless beer pong. Why in the hell it's not an Olympic sport
is beyond me.

Billy, age 30, on GreekChat.com

When it comes to less alcohol-suffused entertainments, the MiddleMan influence is also pervasive. The Sporting Goods Manufacturers Association says 2.6 million Americans now regularly ride skateboards, just as many as play the (old) national pastime baseball.[29] New to periodical racks (as of September 2006) is a revamped version of the classic juvenile humor magazine *Cracked*, targeted to an older (if not an appreciably more mature) group of readers. The premier issue featured sarcastic "articles" on face transplant surgeries, speculative plot points for the new season of *Lost*, and a found document purporting to be a sex contract for Paris Hilton. It's too soon to say if the revised magazine will succeed, but *Cracked*'s new publisher and editor-in-chief feels he's onto a MiddleMan winner, because, "*Cracked* is a comedy brand that all men, growing up, have picked up and read."[30] Nostalgia often works wonders with this C-Type. Imagery and messaging that can transport him back even just a few years, to his high school or college days, resonate, and translate to brand loyalty.

In Hollywood, MiddleMen rule—at least, when it comes to comedy. Major stars like Jim Carrey (*Ace Ventura: Pet Detective* and *Dumb and Dumber*) and Adam Sandler (*The Water Boy* and *Big Daddy*) have made names for themselves playing man-children, characters with whom it is a point of pride that they are childlike. The 2006 movie *Failure to Launch* about a thirtysomething guy who still lives with his parents took direct aim at the MiddleMan target and made him fodder for a comedy that was funny precisely because it rang true. The core of this type in Hollywood is the so-called Frat Pack. Spearheaded by performers such as Will Ferrell, Owen Wilson, and Ben Stiller, the pack hangs together in real life, appears in each other's movies, shares a goofy, spoofy sense of humor, and seems to be making movies as much to amuse each other as the audience.

> The Frat Pack [is a] hedonistic, ain't-it-cool-to-be-smart-but-act-dumb boy's club.... What you're seeing is a definition of what American comedy looks like, sounds like, and jokes about in the early 21st century. And that's not hyperbole.
>
> *Toledo Blade* (Ohio), 7/24/05

As someone in the same age group as the main characters, perhaps I related too much, but the idea is great: Three 30-something guys decide to recapture their college glory days ... these men serve no purpose in society, but that's the significance of the frat house ... say what you want about the random nudity and cussing, this film is life affirming for all men hitting their 30s.

oldman29 on imdb.com chatboard for the film *Old School*

Much current television programming also owes a debt to this C-Type's particular melding of the childish and the adult. The doctors on *Scrubs* (NBC) seem to have made it through medical school without growing up, and for much of the run of *Everybody Loves Raymond* (CBS), Ray's brother Robert (played by nearly 6'9" Brad Garrett) lived at home and allowed his mom to do all the cooking and cleaning. Now that's one tall MiddleMan! Trey Parker and Matt Stone, the thirtysome-things behind the animated show *South Park*, belong to the subset that has managed to make a full-time career out of being MiddleMen. Animation in general is big with this C-Type. A full 26 percent of the regular audience for Nickelodeon's *SpongeBob SquarePants* is over 18.[31]

"When we got ratings in, we were shocked to discover that a third of the viewers were adults," says Mike Lazzo, the creator of and senior VP in charge of Adult Swim [the new network spun off from the Cartoon Network]. "I think that people that grew up with cartoons—a certain type of person, let's put it that way—continue to watch cartoons."

Mediaweek, 9/5/05

I'm 22 and my favorite show on TV is SpongeBob, and I watch Jimmy Neutron all the time.

Smashley, on Answers.Yahoo.com

Even more sophisticated, intellectual programming like *The Daily Show* (Comedy Central) often can evince a subversive MiddleMan quality. A punchline on *The Daily Show* is just as likely to consist of calling the president a "doody head" as it is to be a reference to world affairs or history. The joke of Stephen Colbert's *Colbert Report*, a spin-off of *The Daily Show*, is the spectacle of helpless interviewees (real people) being faced with an irascible child's mind trapped in a faux-right-wing, grown man's body.

Much reality TV programming, too, seems to be aimed at (and created by) MiddleMen. On *Punk'd* (MTV), prankster Ashton Kutcher took practical jokes to the next level by targeting celebrities, while NBC's *Fear Factor* featured goofy gross-out games for adults—with a very grown-up $100,000 prize. MTV's *Wild Boyz* was a spin-off of the same network's *Jackass*, starring two MiddleMen who travel all over the globe being mischievous. *Jackass* itself made the leap to the big screen with *Jackass the Movie* (2002). This R-rated version allowed Johnny Knoxville and his band of maniacs to perform the same sort of MiddleMan stunts and pranks they pulled on the small screen without having to worry about the network censors. The movie's gross-out gags translated into a gross of almost $65 million in its initial release (plus spurred first week DVD/VHS sales in the region of 3.5 million units[32]) proving that its appeal has moved way beyond just the MTV generation.

It seems that our society currently derives humor and fascination from any image of a grown man behaving like an immature kid. Why? Impossible to say. But it's a pervasive truth, and the joke obviously resonates with almost all audiences. And it has moved beyond programming into advertising: one good example is the Six Flags ad campaign (summer 2004–2005) which was simply a little, bald, elderly man gettin' jiggy (i.e., dancing) to youthful pop music.

MARKETPLACE EVIDENCE

Best Buy Escape

Mega-retailer Best Buy's new offspring, Escape, is a boutique shop specifically aimed at those tech-savvy men between 26 and 35 who have to have the latest and greatest before anybody else. The store's most innovative features are "luxury rooms" which customers can rent to try out products or to host gatherings like bachelor parties and the like. They hold up to 10 people, contain the latest in home audio systems, flat screen televisions, projection screens, video game consoles, plus couches and comfy chairs. If they had beds, they'd probably never get MiddleMen to leave.

MARKETING TO MIDDLEMEN: A CHECKLIST

☑ You can never be too irreverent.

☑ Cheap thrills = big bucks.

☑ Bells and whistles count; little extras can generate big sales.

☑ Sex sells; "relationships" don't.

☑ Responsibility is a downer.

☑ MiddleMen love literally wearing their brands on T-shirts, caps, keychains, and so on.

☑ MiddleMen travel in herds (and often defer to a "leader of the pack").

☑ Life's a game. (To the victor go the spoils.)

☑ Life is now. (Don't appeal to future needs.)

☑ MiddleMen are often nostalgic for childhood—leverage iconic characters from movies, cartoons, games.

☑ Interactive gaming is a critical medium for messaging and building brand awareness.

DIG A LITTLE DEEPER
FURTHER RESOURCES ON MIDDLEMEN

MiddleMen in Print

Mom, Can I Move Back in with You? A Survival Guide for Parents of Twentysomethings by Linda Perlman Gordon and Susan Morris Shaffer
This book is geared toward the often frustrated parents of Middle-Men—and, really, can you blame them for being frustrated?

Triple Platinum: Fever Pitch/High Fidelity/About a Boy by Nick Hornby
There can't be many authors who've given their name to a distinct sociological "type." But so it is with the Nick Hornby man. The British writer has become known for chronicling the foibles of a certain kind of feckless modern male: confused, childlike, self-centered, and crippled by a fear of commitment. Yup, sounds like a MiddleMan by a different name.

Xbox Nation
Electronic Gaming Monthly
Game Pro Magazine
There's a wealth of gaming magazines out there (these are just a few), and even a cursory glance at the advertisements inside will tell you that their target reader isn't 12 years old!

The Peter Pan Syndrome: Men Who Have Never Grown Up by Dan Kiley
A classic from way back in the 80s, but one that still has relevance today. Some of those original 80s Peter Pans still haven't grown up.

Arrested Adulthood: The Changing Nature of Maturity and Identity by James Côté
Côté, a sociologist at the University of Western Ontario and the author of several books, takes on the conundrum of the MiddleMan from a psychological perspective.

Emerging Adulthood: The Winding Road from the Late Teens through the Twenties by Jeffrey Jensen Arnett
A book which posits that today's adults are more like adolescents and seeks to answer the questions: Why do so many adults seem to drift and avoid responsibilities such as work and family? As the traditional family breaks down and marriage and child rearing are delayed, what

makes a person an adult? As these half-adolescents/half-adults pursue personal fulfillment, they merely morph from a prolonged youth into a vague and insecure adulthood.

MiddleMen Online

RockstarGames.com
Wonder what the next big game will be? Check out this Web site to see what's new from the company responsible for video games like "Grand Theft Auto: Vice City" which have become icons in the pantheon of popular culture.

GameNation.com
This site boasts enough free games to keep the most fickle Middle-Man busy.

CollegeHumor.com
See "MiddleMen: At Work" above.

MIDDLEMEN: ASPIRATIONAL ICONS

Spike Jonze
This former skateboard magazine photographer turned movie director (*Being John Malkovich, Adaptation*) was voted one of "The Creativity 50: The most influential creative people of the last two decades" by *Creativity* magazine. The idiosyncratic and fantastical worlds he creates on film combine the uninhibited imagination of a child with the incisive intellect of a grown man.

Wes Anderson
Another film director, the case for Anderson as MiddleMan was made perfectly in a *New York Times* profile back in 2001: "The appeal of movies like *Bottle Rocket* and *Rushmore* . . . comes from the fact that Anderson has retained a boy's way of conceptualizing the world . . . he recreates the fun and cruelty of youth in a lexicon that real adults have forgotten and real children have yet to acquire."[33]

Tony Hawk
Just because he retired at 31 doesn't mean Hawk no longer skates—it's just that now he does it because it's fun. The former king of the competitive skating world, and idol of millions of boys (and men), was

voted the best vert skater 2006 by readers of *Transworld Skateboarding* magazine. According to *Forbes*, Hawk was personally responsible for generating $300 million in retail sales of clothing, skateboards, tour income, and video games in 2003, and now headlines his own 30-city tour of professional skateboarders.

Daniel Peres

The editor-in-chief of the men's magazine *Details*, Mr. Peres is living proof that casual Friday will never totally disappear. He wears Converse All Stars with a suit and prefers a tousled bed-head to a neatly combed "do." And, according to a *New York Times* interview, he almost never tucks in his shirt. "Day, night, all situations, it's out," he said. "O.K., maybe for a funeral I would tuck."

NOTES

1. *Time*, 1/24/05

2. *San Francisco Chronicle*, 3/11/06

3. *San Francisco Chronicle*, 3/11/06

4. *The Denver Post*, 9/4/05

5. U.S. Census Bureau, American Community Survey 2002–2003, Census Supplementary Survey 2000–2001

6. *San Francisco Chronicle*, 3/11/06.

7. Jupiter Research and Nintendo, 3/04

8. *USA Today*, 7/11/06

9. BuzzSponge, 2004

10. International Game Developers Association, sourced in *The New York Times*, 11/22/05

11. *The New York Times*, 9/5/06

12. *The New York Times*, 9/5/06

13. *USA Today*, 7/11/06

14. *Forbes Magazine*, 9/03

15. *Business Wire*, 6/21/04

16. *The New York Times*, 1/13/04

17. *The New York Times*, 9/5/06

18. *Chicago Tribune*, 2/17/05

19. *University Wire*, 5/17/06

20. *The San Diego Union-Tribune*, 7/27/03

21. Mintel International Group Ltd., 2/1/05

22. *Financial Times*, FT.com, 11/10/05

23. *Newsweek*, 5/22/06

24. Entertainment Software Association's 2005 Annual Report

25. *The New York Times*, 2/24/05

26. *Richmond Times Dispatch*, 4/4/05

27. *The New York Times*, 10/16/05

28. *The New York Times*, 10/16/05

29. *The New York Times*, 8/3/05

30. *The New York Times*, 9/12/06

31. Nickelodeon, 4/04

32. BPI Entertainment News Wire, 4/3/03

33. *The New York Times*, 12/2/01

CULTURE CROSSERS

Look at Forest Whitaker playing a samurai swordsman in Ghost Dog: The Way of the Samurai. *Look at the imagery by [Wu-Tang's] the RZA. [Pop culture] is an upside-down pyramid, and it's just getting exponentially bigger and bigger.*

"Cool Characters; Ancient Asian Symbols Have Become a Hot New Street Fashion" by Kevin L. Carter, *Pittsburgh Post-Gazette,* **5/31/00**

I have worn dreadlocks for the past six years. I am an Irish American blonde-haired, blue-eyed white man . . . I'm a Rasta. I did not choose my faith, nor did I choose my appearance. THEY CHOSE ME.

Ron, 25

Members of our next C-Type are defined as much by what they aren't as by what they are. Which is to say, they define themselves by whom they choose to be, not by the culture, class, or ethnicity they're born into. They choose freely from all the world has to offer and leap over differences and social boundaries as if they aren't there—hence the name Culture Crossers. Visit any high school, open any youth magazine, or turn on MTV, and you'll be struck by the fact that what you find not only celebrates diversity but embraces and builds on it to an extent unimaginable in the past.

Culture Crossers primarily exist within the 15- to 30-year-old consumer demographic, making them the youngest of our C-Types. They may or may not belong to an ethnic minority; they may or may not be multiracial. Whatever their background, they're engaged in cultural ideas from outside the United States. They define themselves in totally new—foreign if you will—ways, bulldozing through boundaries to find what's cool and different.

It's important to note that we're not referring here to suburban kids who mimic their favorite hip-hop stars by wearing their jeans slung low and adopting "thug" attitudes. Culture Crossers are not just white kids bored with vanilla pop culture; they can be of any race and class. What unifies Culture Crossers is an interest in appropriating styles and customs from cultures other than their own. They're part of the new frontier in coolness, picking and choosing from a world of global trends to create a new and idiosyncratically personal image. Culture Crossers are the young people to watch if you want to know where tomorrow's trends will originate.

It's easy to see why Culture Crossers have emerged now. As members of the most diverse and open-minded generation in American society, they've grown up hearing buzzwords like "multicultural" and "inclusive" incessantly. Their social and educational circles likely have included peers of varied ethnic backgrounds. Maybe they've even attended classes in racial harmony at school. Some were (or have friends who were) born overseas and brought to this country to be adopted by American parents. Others may be recent immigrants or the children of immigrants whose families have made it a point to maintain their cultural identities.

This generation is accustomed to seeing mixed race couples treated with nonchalance, whether on television or in real life. The television hit *Grey's Anatomy* features an Asian-American medical resident dating an African-American surgeon, but it is not a factor in the couple's plotline—it's just the way the roles were cast. Interracial celebrity pairings, like model Heidi Klum and musician Seal, exist in the spotlight without controversy. And this generation's role models come in all shapes and colors. Some—like super-golfer Tiger Woods, who has referred to himself as *Cablinasian* (a word that combines "Caucasian," "black," "Indian," and "Asian")—are themselves an amalgam of ethnicities.

> I have Sikh, Hindu, Pagan, Neopagan, and Christian friends, and most are fine with my choice of religion [Wicca] and with each other's. I do not tolerate those out to bash other religions—or race, or sexuality, come to that.
>
> **Fey Scissorhands at greatestjournal.com**

Culture Crossers grew up exposed to the world, not just through television but through the Web. They barely, if at all, recall life without the Internet—the one technological breakthrough that has turned all of us into global citizens. Ideas, trends, products, and music from all over the world can be accessed by the touch of a keyboard button.

In short, a changing cultural landscape, amazing technological advances, and a new climate of open-mindedness have slowly merged. Yesterday's "melting pot" has been replaced by today's "salad bowl." Individualism, the preservation of customs and habits, and celebration of personal differences are in.

CULTURE CROSSERS: A SHRINKING WORLD

The idea of Culture Crossing is not new. The habits and practices of this C-Type have been bubbling up in society, especially among the most avant-garde, for the past decade or so. For instance, the 2004 book *Transculturalism: How the World Is Coming Together* is a collection of essays and observances by and about young adults living multiethnic, multicultural, boundaryless lives. The book's editor, Claude Grunitzky, also edits *Trace*, a favorite Culture Crosser periodical.

> Transculturalists lead lives some may consider unusual. They often . . . date or marry outside of their race, religion or nationality. They travel on a whim to faraway lands and codify their own styles. . . . They are comfortable listening to, creating and criticizing music outside of their original cultures and often display high levels of creativity in various progressive disciplines. Some people call transculturalists heretics; many call them the future.
>
> **From the Web site www.transculturalism.com**

Absorbing influences from other parts of the world is a defining characteristic for this C-Type. As noted earlier, nothing has contributed to the accessibility of ideas and influences from all over the world as has the Internet. Who can forget a few years back when a clip of a few Chinese teens lip-synching and dancing to the Backstreet Boys' sappy ballad *I Want It That Way* made its way around the globe via e-mail and Internet sites? A portion of that video even made it to *The Today Show* on NBC. Similar videos find a worldwide audience each day by way of the explosively popular site youtube.com, which allows visitors to view and/or upload homemade videos. As with the Japanese video, many of the most-viewed clips provide a window into life in some other part of the world.

Youtube.com is not the only site providing a window, only the most visible. (At least, as of this moment. As we neared completion of this book, new sites like dailymotion, liveleak, and stickam were gaining traction. The last of these three especially, with its emphasis on live Web cam feeds, appears poised to bring a new immediacy to cultural exchanges.) Google Earth, for instance, allows users to zero in on satellite images of any locale, landmark, or even house anywhere on earth with just a few clicks of a mouse. Similarly, Amazon's A.9 BlockView offers street-level color photographs (complete with natives milling by) of addresses in cities all over the United States and soon, presumably, the world. Even Yahoo!'s worldwide maps let you "find and see every city, town, and major land feature in the world," according to the company.

With technology like this, the world doesn't seem very large, and it has helped more and more American youths to think of themselves as members of a global community. You can see this on sites like Myspace.com, the social networking site that boasts more than 90 million users around the world. As a group, Culture Crossers take an active stand on many of the injustices and atrocities requiring attention around the globe. The Washington, D.C.-based Save Darfur Coalition has publicly credited college students with being at the forefront of addressing the crisis in Sudan. STAND, or "Students Taking Action Now: Darfur," was formed by students at Georgetown University, and now has affiliated groups at more than 100 colleges. TakingItGlobal.org, an online community that lists information and opportunities for young people who want to make a difference, claims hundreds of thousands of visitors a month.

> You can see the beginnings of the American educational system taking international and cultural education more seriously.
>
> **Christine Vogel, vice president of AFS Intercultural Programs/USA**

> I have a different point of view on everything now. . . . The world seems smaller; it doesn't seem so big. Kids all over the world can be the same.
>
> **Emmalee, who lived in India for four weeks,**
> *The Cincinnati Enquirer*, 3/29/05

One interesting example of the increasing Culture Crosser influence is the greater choice students now have when deciding which foreign languages they'd like to study. Not too many years ago, the choice was between Spanish, French, and maybe German or Italian. Today, students can (and do!) choose to study Chinese, Japanese, and Arabic. The number of Chinese language programs around the country has tripled in the past decade, and some estimates are that more than 50,000 American students are now studying Chinese.[1] Also helping to expand Culture Crossers' horizons is the U.S. Department of Education's National Security Language Initiative, which encourages schools to offer nontraditional "critical languages," such as Arabic, Chinese, Korean, Farsi, and Hindi. The initiative provides resources and incentives to schools, as well as scholarships and summer-abroad opportunities for students and teachers.

Study-abroad programs are enjoying increased popularity, and are spreading to children younger and younger. Thousands of high school (and even grade school) students now spend summers, spring breaks, or semesters abroad. The concept of a "gap year" (a year between high school and college, generally focused on travel and real-world education) has also begun to catch on, even if thus far the numbers are minuscule compared with Europe, where gap years are a regular feature of many students' lives. America's Council on International Education Exchange (AIEE), which previously offered only high school study abroad programs, has recently expanded to offer gap year programs in China, Japan, and the Dominican Republic. And Harvard University's Web site now devotes a page to explaining, and encouraging, applicants to take a year between secondary and higher education to explore the world and other cultures. The traffic runs the other way as well. The numbers of foreign students traveling and studying on these shores has remained high despite the visa restrictions imposed after 9/11. In fact, were it not for 9/11, it is believed the number of foreign exchange students in the United States would have risen by quite a bit.

> You can learn a lot about cultures from a classroom in the US but meeting people and experiencing their culture in person gives you a new understanding and appreciation for the world and its diversity.
>
> **Vanessa, on blogabroad.com**

Noneducation-based foreign travel has also increased, for both young and old. Eager to experience the world they've been exposed to through peers, language classes, or the Internet, Generation Y is embracing global travel even before they're old enough to fly alone. And on the other end of the spectrum, Baby Boomers, (parents of this C-Type,) travel more often (and to more places) than their parents did. Many Boomers value one-of-a-kind experiences for their offspring and are thus more likely to have kids in tow on their worldwide adventures. A 2006 Yahoo Travel and Harris Interactive poll found that travel outside the country had not only reached pre-9/11 days but it was far exceeding it— for instance, a reported double-digit increase in travelers visiting Europe.

CULTURE CROSSERS: FASHION AND STYLE

Perhaps the easiest way to identify a Culture Crosser is through the clothes he or she wears. Fashion is an area in which this C-Type can easily reference other cultures: an Indian batik print here, African beads there, or even a keffiyeh (a patterned scarf common in the Arab world) around the head to pull off a controversial look that some derogatorily refer to as "terrorist chic."

> Want to make your parents angry and want to be provocative? Wear a keffiyeh.
>
> **David Abitbol, cofounder of the blog**
> **jewlicious.com, _L.A. Times_, 4/9/06**

> i wont confine myself to just asian fashion, it will be mostly about My-kinda-fashion. :) or in other words, whatever i like.
>
> **fashionista.blogspot.com**

Culture Crossers and the fashion industry alike look for sartorial inspiration outside of the United States. In 2005, South Asian colors, beading, and embroidery were all over the runways. And it isn't just high design that's being influenced. The references have trickled down all the way to mass market retailers such as Target. That year, Target introduced a new concept called the "Global Bazaar," in which furniture and other housewares from India and Asia, Latin America, Africa, and Europe were for sale. Affordable pieces from all over the world? Perfect for cash-strapped Culture Crossers just beginning to set up households of their own.

When it comes to street fashion, Culture Crossers probably idealize Japanese design more than any other. The most notable brand is the monstrously successful A Bathing Ape (affectionately referred to as BAPE by brand loyalists), which attracted a cult following in Japan before doing the same in the United States (see Marketplace Evidence below). By some reports, the loud colors and cartoonish prints of Tokyo pop (which includes lines like BAPE) have bounced back to the young, urban market in the United States, from which it took its earliest cues. A checked fedora worn with custom Nike Air Jordans and a bright blue, cloud-covered hoodie might be an example (at least at this writing) of a Tokyo pop-style combination you might see on the street.

> My friend's going to Japan, and I asked him to bring me back a BAPE hoodie. I don't even care what kind, as long as it's not available here.
>
> **Kernohan, on the SoleCollector.com message board**

> Temporary guerrilla stores, traveling boutiques and hybrid emporiums, selling everything from Belgian fashion experimentalia to limited-edition Japanese toys, are just some of the novelties setting the stage for a serious denouement at the cash register.
>
> **Horacio Silva, in the *New York Times Magazine*, 5/29/05**

Of course, sneakers and T-shirts reign as the favored uniform of all youth. Microproduced, limited-edition tees, with obscure or foreign images and text are de rigueur for Culture Crossers. Online retailers like San Francisco-based Trainwreck Industries sell tees that mix American and international references (one shirt features Che Guevara made up like a member of Kiss—another, Chairman Mao as a DJ). The messages on the T-shirts may not always make sense to the average viewer, but that's just the way Culture Crossers like it.

Like T-shirts, sneakers are (in most cases) affordable enough for anyone to maintain a collection. In fact, some of the most popular Culture Crossing blogs include rambling musings on sneakers. The transition from word-of-mouth to word-of-blog has expanded the circle of influencers and opened up a whole new world of information exchange. Now they can find what they're looking for (or even what they didn't know they were looking for) by going online. In stores like New York's Flight Club and Alife, sneakers are even displayed on walls like they're art works in a gallery. Channeled in hip hop (Run DMC's 1986 classic "My Adidas" being one of the earliest, most noted examples; The Pack's 2006 hit "Vans" being one of the more recent), this global sneaker culture might have initially been controlled by brands like Adidas and Nike, but today's informed Culture Crosser demands a greater selection of colors and styles than even megabrands can provide.

> When you walk into a room, people look at your feet first.
>
> **Miamian Gregory Fago, "Freaking for Sneakers,"**
> *Time Magazine,* 4/06

For Culture Crossers, this need to have apparel that is unique and hard to find creates extreme pressure for manufacturers. While ordinary consumers may complain about styles that are "last year," Culture Crossers will decry anything that's "too seen," even if they were all over it last month. One solution (that every marketer, no matter which category, should consider) is to invite the most cutting-edge, taste-making Culture Crossers to be part of the design and marketing team. Two notable, and noteworthy, examples come from Nike and Diesel, each of which plucked an artist from the underground art scene to join their efforts. Nike hired Stash, one of the best known and most notorious New York graffiti artists of the 80s, to design both T-shirts and sneakers. Diesel, meanwhile, commissioned the design work of Paul Pope, the only American comics writer and artist to have worked for Japan's largest *manga* (Japanese word for comics and print cartoons) publisher, and the man behind DC Comics' *Batman: Year 100*, a look into what the superhero might be like in the year 2039. As Culture Crossers find their inspiration in leading-edge figures like Stash and Pope, smart marketers can't go wrong by enlisting their assistance.

MARKETPLACE EVIDENCE

BAPE

The Tokyo-born clothing line, A Bathing Ape, took Japan by storm in the mid-1990s. The store followed the rules of "cool marketing" nearly to the letter. It didn't market itself, had no advertising campaign, and let the products (everyday streetwear like jeans and sweatshirts) speak for themselves. The store quickly became a cult brand (wearers claimed they felt part of a secret society), and soon the most leading-edge Culture Crossers stateside caught on. Fast forward about a decade later and BAPE has a record label, hair salon, café, and toy line! BAPE scores extra kudos for producing only limited-edition designs and allowing Culture Crossers to feel that they set the trends, and not the other way around.

CULTURE CROSSERS: SHOPPING

Culture Crossers like to pick goods from a global market—whether the old-fashioned way (in person) or online. In fact, foreign retailers, in many cases, have an easier time prying dollars away from this C-Type than established domestic brands. In some cases this happens because the items this C-Type is seeking are themselves part of a foreign trend or category. For example, manga, a comics style born in Japan, has reenergized the comic book purchasing for Culture Crossers. Representing one of the fastest-growing segments of the publishing industry, manga is known for its large-eyed heroes and heroines, sometimes mystical settings, and occasionally ultraviolent storylines as well as soap opera–like tales of high school outcasts, young love, and more. Sales of manga have skyrocketed since the turn of the millennium, and today sales have reached about $300 million in the United States.[2] American comic book companies have certainly taken notice by publishing OEL (original English language) manga (sometimes called *Amerimanga* in the States), by non-Japanese artists heavily influenced by traditional manga style. Fans of manga and anime (manga in its animated form) can chat about storylines, trade images, and otherwise share through the site www.anime.com.

> Manga isn't going to save the American comic industry—it's going to replace it.
>
> **William, commenting on the**
> **mildmanneredreporter.blogspot.com blog**

> Manga is cool because in between panels, as the reader's eyes crosses the gutters, their minds can go wild adding more to the book.
>
> **Ed, on comicworldnews.com**

> If the American comics industry doesn't want manga to close the book on American comics, they would be well advised not to close the book on manga.
>
> **Sean, on Blogcritics.org**

Hello Kitty may be a bit too mainstream for Culture Crossers, but they're not too grown up to collect other (cool) toys from around the globe. The collectible vinyl and plush toy industry may have gotten its start with graphic designers in Hong Kong and Japan, but it's now a truly global business. Described as "more lowbrow art than play thing" by the *Los Angeles Times* in 2002, collectible vinyl/plush toys vary in size from just a few inches to over a foot tall and can range from smoking bunnies to Martians on skateboards. One popular brand, Uglydolls, sells plush monsters that look nothing like the stuffed animals most of us cuddled as children—extra eyes and limbs are a regular feature. Shawnimals, another purveyor of stuffed oddballs, has a line that includes creatures like a moustache with big eyes and an angry garlic clove. These toys aren't meant to appeal to kids, but to Culture Crossers looking to celebrate nostalgia and global pop culture. And thanks to the early success of stores like KidRobot, with out-posts in San Francisco, New York, and Los Angeles, these toys are now available online and in shops all over the country.

Concept stores appeal to Culture Crossers, as long as it's not last year's concept. One store popular among this C-Type as this book is be-ing written is Surface to Air in Paris. A combination studio-gallery-store dedicated to showcasing and fostering creativity (surface2air.com), its pa-trons are a mix of European, Asian, and American tourists, mainly teens. Designers and artists from all over the world consider it a must-visit shop when in Paris. Its shelves are stocked with books, limited-edition Surface to Air–designed sneakers and T-shirts, sought-after jewelry from small de-signers, and other hard-to-find, much coveted wares.

MARKETPLACE EVIDENCE

superfuture.com
Want to travel around the world—eating and shopping as though you're a real live Culture Crosser? Don't even think about leaving home without first consulting Superfuture. Created by a Tokyo-based Australian designer as a resource for jet-setters as interested in cutting-edge design, fashion, and street culture as he is, the site includes shopping guides and tour maps for cities all over the globe, including New York, Sydney, Tokyo, Amsterdam, Shanghai, and Paris as well as user-generated reviews on places to visit in over 150 cities.

CULTURE CROSSERS: NEW MEDIA

Culture Crossers inherently have a strong desire to both express them-selves and share ideas with others. In this way, Culture Crossing has grown from mere behavior to lifestyle. Though not necessarily turned off by traditional media, Culture Crossers are deeply immersed in the alternatives.

Blogging

The amount of influence that blogs have had on the Culture Crosser movement is almost impossible to overestimate. Blogs are the easiest, most timely way to keep up on new ideas. Photo-heavy sites like Thecobrasnake.com and Lastnightsparty.com are staffed by party-hopping photographers whose pics of reveling hipsters are now influencing both fashion industry insiders and regular kids all over the globe. Lastnight's party, alone, is said to receive more than 20,000 unique visitors a day, many of them from thousands and thousands of miles away from wherever the featured party was held.[3] The people, places, and even hairstyles shown in the pictures spark industry trends, and some promoters don't consider a party a success unless it's covered by one of these morning-after, self-appointed arbiters of cool. Culture Crossers seek out sites like these for ideas; if you're a marketer interested in the latest trends, you should too.

Magazines

Culture Crossers are, without a doubt, magazine junkies. The number of international magazines available on newsstands and online is astounding, and new ones are popping up every day. They offer a relatively inexpensive way for Culture Crossers to view the world at their fingertips (although they're not opposed to shelling out twice the cost of a standard magazine for a German fashion title or Dutch shelter glossy, complete with amazing photography and ads for interesting international products). Whether their focus is on travel, design, lifestyle, or sports, their views are never narrow. When it comes to content, anything goes for these publications—the more far-flung and unusual, the better.

> "It's like this whole culture," said Chris Young at the Westcan Printing Group in Winnipeg, which prints many of the alternative publications: *The Believer, Lemon, Clamor, Swindle, Anthem, Beautiful/Decay, Bidoun, Re:Up, Archetype, The Drama.* "There's so many!"
>
> **From "Remember Zines? Look at Them Now,"**
> ***The New York Times*, 5/7/06**

The alternative press idea is not new. Today's alt press owes a debt to category pioneers like *The Village Voice, Rolling Stone, Paper*, and more. The irreverence and opinionated journalism in those periodicals was liberating (*Rolling Stone* once offered a free roach clip with a subscription, with a slogan that read, "Act now, before the offer is made illegal"), but it took technological advances and falling printing costs to allow the army of would-be publishers to indulge in their own brands of free-thinking journalism. Thanks to this new ease of production, today's Culture Crossers can enjoy a plethora of idiosyncratic magazines that make it easy to keep track of what's cutting edge all over the world. See the sidebar for just a few of the most leading edge.

FOCUS ON: LEADING-EDGE ZINES AND MAGAZINES

Giant Robot
It started as a black-and-white, photocopied zine about Asian pop culture trends, but it's now a regular glossy that has spawned a store and more. Credited with featuring Chow Yun Fat and Jackie Chan long before they were mainstream, *Giant Robot* now appeals to a much larger audience than just Asian-Americans.

Lemon
Lemon publishes twice a year and is known for merging 60s and 70s pop culture with today's. Its production values exceed some of its fellow underground magazines by a mile: Issue 1 even carried a light lemon scent.

The Fader
The Fader offers the voice and look of the street, covering music, style, and lifestyle topics.

Trace
Launched by *Transculturalism* (see above) author Claude Grunitzky, this culture and style magazine documents the interconnected worlds of music, fashion, film, art, politics, and today's multicultural world youth. Annual features like the "Black Girls Rule" issue and an issue

entirely devoted to one nation (Japan, South Africa, and Mexico have all received treatment) are popular draws.

Anthem
Anthem magazine's content focuses on film, music, style, and art design—but with a global perspective.

Tokion
Its title basically translates into a made-up word for "the sound of now" in Japanese, and its coverage of the latest in pop culture and the arts certainly follows suit. In addition to print editions, the New York- and Tokyo-based magazine hosts the annual Creativity Now conference in New York City: a huge draw for creative types from all over the globe.

Beautiful/Decay
This magazine features the illustrations, design, and other works of emerging artists, some most definitely Culture Crossers themselves.

Flaunt
Flaunt magazine is groundbreaking for its outsider culture highlights—a mix of art, music, fashion, entertainment, and literature.

CULTURE CROSSERS: MUSIC TRENDS

Few things can unite an international group of young people in quite the same way as music. Today nearly anyone from anywhere can hit big as long as the music sounds good (or new or unique) to this generation. Culture Crossers will not only embrace it, they will likely create a community—again, a global one—around it.

Remember back to the 80s and early 90s when most music that came from outside North America or England was given the overly simplistic label of "world music." Now that mislabeled genre has not only exploded, it has splintered into dozens of recognized hybrids and subgenres. Gypsy-punk, baile funk, Afro Cubano—those are just some of the many musical styles that Culture Crossers are listening to on their iPods.

The American "discovery" of world music is ongoing, and the work of many.

DJ Earball, on Soundroots.org

The important thing people need to understand is: Just because YOU are not familiar with the Singer/musicians DOES NOT mean that the music is weird. Not Everyone in the World listens to american top 40 music. . . . You would be surprised at how many people have never heard of Britney Spears, Snoop Dogg, Ice Cube, Shania Twain, Journey, etc.

RickiiRock, on eBay.com reviews

[Japanese rappers] Rip Slyme absolutely rock. I don't understand half of what they say, but they certainly know how to say it.

Gavin, on TVinJapan.blogspot.com

Musician celebrities are taking advantage of the Culture Crosser moment to broaden their musical horizons and explore new (to them) musical traditions. Madonna and her sister in pop Gwen Stefani are two good examples. In the mid-1990s, Madonna gave vent to many Culture Crossing impulses: she covered herself with Indian henna tattoos, sang a song ("Shanti/Ashtangi") entirely in Sanskrit on her CD *Ray of Light*, and began to practice the ancient Jewish mysticism of Kabbalah. In the same vein, Gwen Stefani brought Harajuku girls (fashion-forward young Japanese women who reside in the Tokyo district of the same name) to wide attention, referencing them in a number of songs on the CD *Love. Music. Angel. Baby.* and has even devoted an entire song's lyrics to them.

THE INTERNATIONAL MIXTAPE PROJECT

Mixtapes have been around for as long as, well, as long as cassette tapes. The International Mixtape Project, which includes people from more than 30 countries, has evolved with the help of Myspace.com. It's like a modern-day, pen pal project for Culture Crossers. After joining, it's your responsibility to create a song compilation and send it to other music-minded pals in your international group. Talk about worldwide music exposure! For more information, visit www.my-space.com/mixtapeproject.

Here again, the Internet has helped the Culture Crosser agenda, fueling the spread of musical styles from all over the world. Some estimates say that 40 million Americans a month listen to Internet radio. Internet stations can be as niche or as inclusive or as musically diverse and far-reaching as they want to be—which gives listeners thousands of stations to choose from at any given time. They're no longer bound by where they live or the bandwidth of their local stations. We're quite sure a number of the deejays on Internet stations are members of this C-Type, playing music that has not been heard on traditional radio stations. Creamyradio.com (based in Tempe, Arizona, but broadcast online) says its global reach stretches as far away as Australia and Bahrain. And Pandora.com is a free Web-based service that can "create" stations for users based on their preferences. When, for example, a user types in one of his or her favorite songs, Pandora searches its database to find other tunes and tracks that might similarly appeal to the user. Pandora's founders say their intent is to "broaden people's horizons," which, come to think of it, sounds a lot like the philosophy of Culture Crossers themselves.

MUSIC MASH-UPS

Nothing has done more to unite diverse musical styles and sounds than the mash-up. Mash-ups are made by fusing two or more songs into one. The trend started underground, as a new, albeit illegal, variation on remixes and covers. Musical artist and producer Danger Mouse is credited with creating the first mash-up to really receive widespread attention. The bootleg mix of Jay-Z's *Black Album* and the Beatles' *White Album*—sold as *The Grey Album*—sparked a sensation, and Danger Mouse faced legal action brought by the songs' original artists. Other artists have been similarly perturbed. Nirvana's Dave Grohl is said to have hated the mash-up of his band's "Smells

Like Teen Spirit" and Destiny Child's "Bootylicious." Christina Aguilera sought legal action after a London radio station mashed her "Genie in a Bottle" with the Strokes' "Hard to Explain." Yet some artists have decided to join rather than fight the trend. Kylie Minogue was said to be thrilled with the combination of her hit "Can't Get You Out of My Head" and New Order's "Blue Monday." And David Bowie actually invited fans to his Web site to mash up songs from his CD *Reality*. Even Warner Brothers Records joined the mash-up party when it released an entire Jay-Z/Linkin Park mash-up CD *Collision Course*. The CD debuted at the top of the Billboard charts, and MTV (at the time this book was written) had plans to devote an entire series to mash-ups. Is all this attention the kiss of death for the mash-up? Or will Culture Crossers simply begin combining music in a whole new way?

It really astonishes me that two disparate songs can be welded together so neatly—listening to some of these mashups, you can't imagine them being done any other way.

Rob, on typepad.com

THE NEW "WORLD MUSIC": A GLOBAL SAMPLING

Here is a sampling of a few influential Culture Crosser artists and Culture Crossing styles in the world of music. The number of artists and musical styles from around the world who have made an impact on this C-Type is astounding. It's interesting to note that without the Internet and other technological advances that allow music to be shared so easily, the list couldn't possibly be as extensive.

CULTURE CROSSER ARTISTS

Wu Tang Clan
Undoubtedly one of hip hop's most distinctive groups, and also one of the genre's most influential. Hailing from Staten Island, they were among the first to make Asian influences central to their sound, something so widely copied it's nearly become a hip-hop cliché. Band-

member RZA found inspiration in Hong Kong action cinema and Samurai films, and has composed the score for the Japanimation series *Afro Samurai*, as well as the *Kill Bill* movies.

Bjork
Although best known by the average American for showing up at the Academy Awards draped in a swan, the Icelandic siren's seven solo albums have featured collaborations with musicians from Turkey, the United States, India, Iran, Brazil, and Denmark, just to name a few.

Gogol Bordello
Gogol Bordello's unique brand of gypsy punk and notoriously explosive live shows have made them a huge draw worldwide. Fronted by Ukranian-born Eugene Hütz, the band of Ukrainians, Israelis, and Russians bangs out a mix of ska, flamenco, and rock.

Kronos Quartet
This San Francisco string quartet has been creating music for more than 30 years and has long been known for collaborating with a wide and diverse range of other artists. Most recently the quartet has opened their arms to musicians like Rahman Asadollahi, an Azerbaijani accordion player from Iran, and Zhang Hai Yue, an instrumentalist from southern China. They represent the classical edge of Culture Crosser music.

Lyrics Born
Hailing from California, Lyrics Born's Japanese and Italian roots make him fairly unique in the world of hip hop. Music critics credit his "hard to place" voice and virtuoso rhymes for gaining him the kudos he's received from fans all over the globe.

Matisyahu
Though his name may sound Japanese, Matisyahu is the world's most notable Hasidic reggae star (it's hard to believe, but there's more than one). His reggae-rhythms-mixed-with-ancient-Hebrew formula makes for a surprisingly uplifting mix.

Hip-Hop Hoodios
Hoodios is Spanish for "Jewish people," and this band's works are one part klezmer (traditional Jewish music), one part cumbia (Colombian folk), and one part hip hop.

M.I.A.
Sri Lankan-born, UK-based M.I.A.'s music is a schizophrenic mix that includes hip hop, electro, reggae, garage rock, and Brazilian baile funk, served up with a side of politics.

Lady Sovereign
She's been called an English Eminem for her musical style, which is—you guessed it—decidedly un-"Ladylike" English hip hop.

CULTURE CROSSER MUSICAL STYLES

Bhangra
This traditional Indian music originated as a harvest celebration dance for farmers. True to its beginnings, it still has a down-to-earth feel, but in the 70s and 80s it entered the club scene mixed with house and hip hop. Today, bhangra remix artists like Panjabi MC, have helped popularize this style in the United States.

Reggaeton
Reggaeton is a sexy blend of reggae, hip hop, salsa, cumbia, and meringue. The reggaeton craze began in Panama and Puerto Rico, before moving to the U.S. club scene. It's especially popular in heavily Latino cities, namely New York and Miami.

Baile/Baile funk
Born when Miami bass arrived on Brazilian shores, early baile or baile funk deejays took this American sound and blended it with samba drums and screechy lyrics to create something entirely new. No matter what you call it, it's a strange and funky combination of traditional Brazilian sounds, hip hop, and 80s electronic dance.

Bongo Flavas
Take hip-hop sounds from the Bronx and mix them with native African sounds and flavors, and you've got bongo flavas, a style of music that started in East Africa (where it still remains popular).

CULTURE CROSSERS:
ART AND CREATIVITY

The coolest C-Type is also one of the most creative. Despite their relative youth, they shine in an art world that knows no geographical boundaries.

As art and technology collide, art from all over the globe is more accessible, making this generation's taste and creative influences more international. Today's most interesting artists can be found anywhere, not just in New York, London, or Paris, and an art movement can, in record time, spread from backyards and backstreets to the main stage in the virtual world. The very same media sources that Culture Crossers look to for other advice and information regarding music and fashion devote coverage to the arts as well, almost without exception. Much of the coverage is editorial (that is, capable of exerting strong influence over more middle-of-the-road Culture Crossers), with recommendations about exhibits to see and individual artists to pay attention to. When weekly newsletter *Flavorpill* innocently promoted an event held by the Lower Manhattan Cultural Council, the show's small space was flooded with attendees. *Flavorpill* had no idea of its drawing power, but make no mistake—the Culture Crossers out there were paying attention.

DANCE OR SPORT?

Participation in the global, not-quite-a-sport DDR (for dance dance revolution, the dance/exercise craze that swept through Japan before hitting the United States), is growing by the day. DDR first appeared in Japanese video arcades in 1998 as a game played on a dance pad with four panels. Players move their feet following the signals on a computer screen facing the game. Within the past five years, the game has spread to the United States where at-home versions are now available.

Capoeira is another, more exotic example of a Culture Crossing activity. This Brazilian-born martial art is often mistaken for dance but includes punches, spinning kicks, and head butts intermingled with elegant back handsprings and cartwheels. Sometimes used in fight scenes in American movies (*Catwoman* and *AeonFlux*, for example), it has also gained popularity among some diet-crazed Americans who recognize its calorie-burning effects. An estimated 20,000 Americans currently practice capoeira, but that number seems sure to grow.[4]

Long before he was hired by Nike (see above), Stash made his name in graffiti, one of the few art forms to so clearly manifest the melding of and overlapping of cultures. With an audience once limited to city dwellers or tourists or the very few readers of graffiti magazines, Culture Crossers halfway around the world can now view freshly painted graffiti on walls anywhere from Berlin to the Bronx thanks to digital cameras and the help of the Internet.

VANDAL TO VIRTUOSO: GRAFFITI GETS THE FINE ART TREATMENT

You're all over the place, but no one knows who you are.
Graffiti artist "Twist"

Graffiti has grown so big that it's spawned worldwide competitions. Events like Write4gold, or France's annual Kosmopolite, bring together artists from all over the world to do things like work their wonders on temporary walls, and they're attracting thousands of aspiring and accomplished graffiti artists and fans each year. For those who want to see the best work from the comfort of their own home, they can visit the Streets Are Saying Things: The Original Online Graffiti Museum. Begun in 2002, it's the largest online compendium of graffiti art anywhere. The interactive Internet museum also allows visitors the opportunity to "meet" and chat on message boards with other graffiti fans about featured works and artists. But one of the most well-organized and popular online forums has got to be 12ozProphet.com. Visitors to the site are encouraged to post work they like (preferably not their own) and solicit feedback from others in the graffiti community.

GRAFFITI ARTISTS TO WATCH
Barry McGee (aka "Twist")
A traditionally trained artist, McGee was introduced to graffiti more

than two decades ago by a friend and quickly began spreading his work all over San Francisco, where he earned his nickname. His work now shows in galleries and museums all over the country.

Fafi
One of the few women popular in the world of graffiti today, Toulouse-based Fafi is known for her pouty, sexkittenish Fafinettes and strong color sense. Her murals have shown up in cities all over Asia, the United States, and Europe. She also has a clothing line and has collaborated with the handbag brand LeSportsac.

Art fairs that attract Culture Crossers include Art Basel Miami Beach, the younger, cooler sister of the Swiss event of the same name. Art Basel is a showcase for the contemporary international art world, and with each year the crowds grow bigger and satellite exhibitions more numerous. A showcase of both established and more cutting-edge artists, the event is always worth checking out. Similarly, RESFEST, an annual traveling film and multimedia festival, is another event that attracts global art and design insiders. Attendees can enjoy installations, screenings, and live performances (and parties!). On the opposite end of the media technology spectrum is lomography, an international photography movement, based around the intentionally low-tech Lomo (a small manual camera with no fancy accessories or even a flash), which users are encouraged to tote everywhere. Culture Crossing lomographers can then post these off-the-cuff snapshots in the WorldArchive on the Web, where the Lomographic Society International hopes to produce the most comprehensive photographic documentation of humanity around the globe.

CULTURE CROSSERS: YOU ARE WHAT YOU DRINK

As has been made clear, Culture Crossers are on the leading edge of trends in many categories. The beverage arena is no exception. Unlike some of their more provincial peers, Culture Crossers are notable for their openness to adventure. Add to that the element of cool imparted by, say, sipping an obscure sake poured from a well-designed bottle, and as marketers, you've got a whole new set of inclinations to explore.

For Culture Crossers over 21, global influences can easily be seen in what they order at the bar. Cocktails like mojitos, a Cuban creation, and caipirinhas, from Brazil, have been incredibly popular for the last few years. Hipster bar owners are pushing this trend even further. Audrey Saunders, the owner of the trendy Pegu Club in New York's Soho, makes it a point to offer some of the more obscure alcoholic drinks from around the world: rhum agricole (from the French Caribbean), chartreuse (a European herbal liqueur), Madeira (a fortified Portuguese wine), and pisco (a Peruvian brandy). This last, being a solid 90 proof (45 percent alcohol) is becoming a particular favorite among younger, bar-hopping Culture Crossers.

> Also on the radar screen is the Pisco Sour, a tangy libation getting a public relations boost from the growing appreciation of Peruvian cuisine.
>
> **Cheers**, 10/1/06

> In putting together the bar and wine list at Uovo, a restaurant in the East Village, the beverage manager and sommelier Richard Ervin has made it a policy to carry only small-scale liquors and wines that come from mom-and-pop vineyards. . . . his shelves are lined with High Wine rum from Guyana, made from Demerara sugar; jenever from the Netherlands; and Zubrowka vodka, made with bison grass culled from the last primeval forest in Poland and Belarus. "People get excited because they haven't seen these labels in liquor stores," Mr. Ervin said. "It makes it more fun."
>
> **The New York Times**, 1/4/06

The foreign import that may have seen the most interesting kind of growth is sake. Sake (sometimes called Japanese rice wine, though it's brewed like beer) has been around for more than 1,000 years, but its appeal in the States has really been noticeable only since the mid-1990s (and primarily in cosmopolitan areas). Interestingly enough, sake's really become "hot" as Americans have begun drinking it cold—in accordance with Japanese tradition—rather than warmed up as it's served en masse in a lot of American sushi restaurants. It's difficult to quantify just how popular sake has become, because sales are not always recorded under the same class of alcohol. Sake is sometimes grouped with wine, other times with spirits. But the numbers that do exist are impressive. The Pennsylvania Liquor Control Board, for example, reported a 10 percent increase in sake sales from 2004 to 2005.[5] And anecdotal evidence shows that sake is now being drunk with everything from sushi to Italian food, and even barbecue.

> I never tried sake until I went to Japan and learned that there are like over 100 different kinds. Now I try to find my faves to order near me, but I have to order online.
>
> **Geishfan, on travelpunk.com**

Another alcoholic beverage from Asia that's become a bit of a sensation on American shores is shochu, a vodkalike, grain-based spirit (it's even listed as Korean or Japanese vodka on some menus). Much was made in Japan of shochu's (unsubstantiated) health claims that suggest it helps the body produce enzymes that can prevent heart attacks and strokes. The growth of shochu's popularity overseas inevitably spread to southern California (where, incidentally, many if not most U.S. cocktail trends start). The Sushi Roku, with branches in the LA area and Las Vegas, claims the drink is rivaling sake in terms of sales, especially among their younger clientele.

Culture Crossers are also expanding their horizons and becoming more adventurous with beer. Rather than bellying up to the bar for a Bud, or even standard imports like Stella Artois or Heineken, Culture Crossers are sipping harder-to-find Belgian ales or lambics (naturally fermented beers brewed with a combination of malted barley and unmalted wheat that produce complex flavors). Lambics are also making their way into cocktails, mixed with spirits like flavored vodkas, or with champagne.

On the nonalcoholic front, specialty teas seem to have captured the interest of Culture Crossers. Tea connoisseurs speak of their favorite

MARKETPLACE EVIDENCE

The Boba Invasion
Boba tea, also called bubble tea, is a fruit-flavored concoction that has bubblelike, edible pearls of tapioca suspended inside it. Created in Taiwan decades ago as a way to get kids to drink tea, it made its way to this country through immigrant Asian communities. When cool-hunting Culture Crossers discovered boba, they couldn't get enough of it, and the drink spread like wildfire all over the country. It suddenly became hip to carry a big boba drink (with an extrawide straw to suck up the pearls). You can now find Culture Crossers hanging out after school in boba cafés in nearly any city in the country.

brews in much the same way wine lovers speak of favorite grapes or vintages. For evidence of the increasing popularity of tea and the growing sophistication of tea drinkers, just look at the wide variety of flavors and types available through Starbuck's Tazo brand. With varieties like "Zen" and "Chinese Green Tips," Tazo has shown American consumers that tea doesn't necessarily mean black tea. Even Lipton has taken notice, introducing Lipton Chai, a packaged version of the cardamom- and cinnamon-spiced East Asian blend. In 2005, American consumers spent $5 billion on tea. That's still less than what they spent on coffee, but five times what they were spending five years ago, with rooibos as the fastest-growing variety.[6] Along with rooibos (a red tea), white tea has also exploded onto the market, thanks to the cold tea purveyor Teas' Tea, which produces a deliciously unsweetened bottled version.

Another hot, steeped beverage currently entering American culture is the South American mainstay yerba mate. *USA Today* called it, "the hottest U.S. beverage since green tea and chai," noting that it's been taken up by celebrities like "Matt Dillon, Madonna, Alicia Silverstone and rocker Flea, among others. Musician Moby even sells it at Teany, his New York City cafe."[7] It may seem, at first glance, similar to tea, but yerba mate is brewed from the holly shrub of the South American rain forest. This gives it a unique taste all its own, plus health benefits that range from the lungs, liver, and kidneys to the stomach. It also carries with it a series of preparation and consumption rituals (it's traditionally drunk through a straw) that make it even more enticing to Culture Crossers looking for a full-bodied beverage experience.

Culture Crossers: Follow the Leading Edge

It bears repeating that Culture Crossers may be among the hardest of all the consumer types to reach and effectively influence. The very things that make them who they are—fickle, hip, anticonformist, interested in discovering things on their own—present formidable obstacles for the marketer. Forward-thinking marketers are instead relying on the influential, leading-edge Culture Crossers themselves—tapping into the people who live the trends and lifestyles rather than hiring someone who's merely found a way to report on them.

Some such taste-makers have already caught on to the power they harbor and are capitalizing on it. Blogger Josh Rubin, formerly of Razorfish, and his team of Culture Crossing editors and contributors wax poetic daily about the art exhibits, gadgets, design objects, fashions, and music they find interesting. Major companies, like Audi, Nike, and American Apparel, clamor to advertise on his site. Josh Spear offers his favorite art, books, design, gadgets, fashion, and food on his blog joshspear.com. And charlesandmarie.com, a site geared toward global shoppers, considers itself the arbiter of cool and one-of-a-kind products from all over the globe. Some, in fact, are sold through their site, but each item only for one day. After its 24-hour posting period, the lamp or bag or whatever it may be is no longer available.

If you plan to try to market to Gen Y (or even Gen X), invite Culture Crossers into your fold. Not only do they live and breathe the trends you're looking to uncover, they're creating them. Make this leading-edge C-Type a part of your team, commission them to create designs for you, or consult with them on packaging. At the very least, run your marketing campaigns by them. When it comes to this cool-obsessed, globally minded, marketing-savvy C-Type, it's really the only way to ensure that your efforts stand a chance of being youth-relevant.

MARKETING TO CULTURE CROSSERS: A CHECKLIST

☑ You can never be too underground or too avant-garde.

☑ Celebrate diversity.

☑ "The City" rules. "International" rules.

☑ The thrill is in the discovery, being first to know.

☑ Let them find you. Be understated and laid back.

☑ Don't market to them; market with them.

☑ Cultural identity is a choice.

☑ Art and Music = Life

☑ Culture Crossers live by the indie rule: independent magazines, movies, and restaurants.

☑ This type moves from coffeehouse to club. Make sure your brand can stay up all night.

☑ Use local media and local heroes to get the word out.

☑ While generally not flush, Culture Crossers will spend significant dollars to buy a few style-defining products.

DIG A LITTLE DEEPER

FURTHER RESOURCES ON CULTURE CROSSERS

Culture Crossers in Print

Postethnic America: Beyond Multiculturalism by David A. Hollinger
Noting the shift to voluntary affiliations as opposed to ascribed and fixed identities, Hollinger argues that modern ethnicity has increasingly become a construct of choice (as evidenced to some degree by Culture Crossing youth).

Hip: The History (P.S.) by John Leland
The word *hip* comes from the Wolof word *hipi* meaning "to open one's eyes" and, of course, open eyes and minds have always been the cultural core of cool. This expansive rundown flips through hip's many forms; an analysis of cool from the Bowery Boys in the nineteenth century all the way to Sparks swilling hipsters in the twenty-first.

Graffiti World: Street Art from Five Continents by Nicholas Ganz
An auteur-based approach to the wild world of global street art featuring beautiful photographs of the works of some of the best practitioners, past and present. Artist profiles are organized by region and include everything from stickers to expansive murals.

Cool Shops, Restaurants, Hotels Series by teNeues House
Covering Hamburg, London, Milan, New York, Barcelona, Berlin, Hong Kong, Munich, Paris, Tokyo, and more, this series is ideal for aesthetically minded Culture Crossers as they crisscross the globe.

The Life and Death of Bling Bling: A Story of Innovation, Proliferation, Regurgitation, Commercialization and Bastardization by Matthew Vescovo
Follow the life (and death) of the word *bling*, from coining to co-opting to the end of its cool career, in this clever picture book, written in verse. A short and witty lesson on a common theme in contemporary culture and the thing of any leading-edge Culture Crosser's nightmares.

Transculturalism: How the World Is Coming Together by Claude Grunitzky
The basic premise of this book is that some individuals transcend their initial culture in order to explore, examine, and infiltrate alien cul-

tures. These people and their experiences seem to him to prefigure a time when it will be difficult to identify and separate people according to ethnic and racial delineations.

Culture Crossers Online

Flavorpill.com

Flavorpill began as a weekly e-mail newsletter on the best events in New York City (gallery openings, experimental hip-hop shows, and everything in between) but has since spawned Artkrush (global art news), BoldType (book reviews for the smart set), Earplug (for the latest in music), JC Report (global fashion trends and news) as well as Flavorpill guides for LA, San Francisco, Chicago, and London.

Gridskipper.com

This snarky and irreverent travel blog from Gawker Media is for the young and adventurous by the young and adventurous. Covering everything from budget travel to luxury hotels, it's as much a resource for those looking for the next vacation hot spot as those looking for quirkier excursions.

Generationmix.org

Seattle's Generation Mix seeks to bring to the fore issues facing multiracial youth and families. It's sponsored by the Mavin Foundation, which was founded in 2006 by Matt Kelley, the son of a white father and Korean mother.

Karmaloop.com

Karmaloop takes the work out of global shopping by offering only the brands a taste maker would approve of. Its method for success is simple: a team of people as young and savvy as their audience to spread the word.

NOTES

1. *The New York Times*, 10/15/05
2. Universal Press Syndicate
3. *The New York Times*, 10/30/05
4. *The Columbus Dispatch*, 4/25/05
5. "Sipping Sake: The once-searing Japanese drink has mellowed," Joseph A. Slobozian, *Philadelphia Inquirer*, April 2006
6. *The Providence Journal*, 10/6/04
7. *USA Today*, 3/3/06

GEEK GODS

They pore over 130-page computer manuals to glean details about wares soft and hard. Never intimidated, they view computers as intellectual puzzles and talk to each other for hours in a lingo non-nerds can't comprehend.

Pittsburgh Post-Gazette, 12/11/05

In pre-Industrial times, the real catch was a man of muscle. Who better to bring home the bison or protect the hearth from threats of invading clans? But [now] there's a new order of alpha male: the techie.

Hillary Hull, from the *Los Angeles Times*, 4/28/05

Geeks are taking over the world. They make the most popular movies and games, pioneer new ways to communicate using technology, and create new ideas that will change the future.

Leena on IP-SJ.org

I t's safe to say that most consumers have a love/hate relationship with technology.

Not Geek Gods.

Geek Gods are the guys (and we're not being sexist; this C-Type is definitely male) who live for the latest gadget, systems upgrade, or other technological advance. Call them hooked-up, wired, or teched-out; just don't call them ambivalent. The Geek God's relationship with technology is a real love affair.

While the Geek God moniker may seem like an oxymoron, it really isn't. Today we live in an age when almost everyone under 40 totes an iPod, is wirelessly connected to the world around them, and does an increasing amount of shopping online. (Online holiday spending totaled $19.6 billion in 2005, a 25 percent surge from the same period in 2004, according to comScore Networks.) In this tech-driven world, Geek Gods play revered roles: those of teacher, motivator, trendsetter, and sage. The former computer nerd or AV club geek from your high school now possesses both the power and status of a god . . . or, well, at least a demigod.

As mentioned earlier, we've sculpted this C-Type as male. It's not that there are no tech-savvy females—far from it—but the contours of the type, as you will see, go beyond a facility with computers and gadgets. When it comes to social matters and the like, the smaller number of tech-head women exhibits a different set of characteristics and behaviors.

The majority of Geek Gods fall into the 20 to 35 demographic, are single, and have a fair amount of both money and free time (being a Geek God takes a good deal of time). A typical Geek God might spend hours a day perusing his favorite Web sites and posting messages on the latest software, the best deals, or some crafty way to outsmart "the system." Another might spend hours rewiring his toaster to send a text message to his cell phone when his toast is ready. One Geek God we met recently told us he runs computer searches on the same 20 high-tech products every day until he finds the price he's looking for. Once he snags his deal, he's on to the next one. This type will do anything short of breaking the law to ensure that they maintain their position atop the technological power pyramid.

> When I bought my first Mac I wasn't thrilled . . . so I upgraded the RAM myself.
>
> **Adam on Lifehacker.com**

> I have the most sophisticated home entertainment system of anyone I know . . . and you won't believe how little I paid for it. You just have to know how to work the system. . . .
>
> **Brian, on about.com home electronics message board**

The rest of us, rather than begrudge Geek Gods their superior knowledge, love them for the fact that they are so inclined to share it with us. A Geek God's interest in sharing his discoveries, and being generous with his time and technical know-how, cannot be overstated. This type finds satisfaction in getting the information before anyone else and then in spreading it to others. If you're lucky enough to be the friend, family member, or colleague of a Geek God, you know what we're talking about. There's no need to do the research yourself. Tell your friendly Geek God your budget, and he'll find the perfect digital camera for you. He helped you set up your iPod three years ago. And he can always retrieve your lost data.

> My friend is a computer geek. He put together his own PC, and he helps me figure things out.
>
> **MrMike on the-junkyard.net**

> My friends often call or email and ask computer questions. I use a program that lets me see their computer screen from my own.
>
> **Bob on www.askbobrankin.com**

Almost everyone will agree that knowledge is power. And Geek Gods not only possess knowledge but they also possess the type of knowledge that's of-the-moment. In his bestselling *The World Is Flat: A Brief History of the Twenty-first Century*, the *New York Times* Op-Ed columnist Thomas Friedman argues that globalization is driven by the technical advances of the digital revolution. It's a belief shared by many. Good news for Geek Gods, as this theory puts them in demand. It also secures them a seat at the proverbial table, whether that table is social or professional.

I have done more tech work for my coworkers off the job than I have on the job most months.

GenericTech commenting on AssociatedContent.com

I've got a family gathering coming up, which means that I'll be cornered by aunts, uncles, and cousins asking me about Registry keys and device drivers. I've been functioning as the unofficial Bass family help desk for years.

Steve Bass from "Helpfulness Is Next to Geekliness"
on About.com, 4/30/03

MARKETPLACE EVIDENCE

Geeks on Call

In 1999, before the Internet bubble had burst, Geeks on Call first opened its doors (so to speak). The company, which now has hundreds of franchises across the country and was ranked number one on *Entrepreneur* magazine's list of top-20 franchise companies in the United States for 2006, offers services such as hardware and wireless network installations, computer repairs, consulting, and upgrades. No problem (including figuring out how to use that gadget you got for Christmas) is too small for the company's hired "Geeks," who drive around in blue Chrysler PT Cruisers. Turning a C-Type into a business, they do what comes naturally to Geek Gods, but charge a premium for it. For more information, visit www.geeksoncall.com.

Geek Gods and Sex

Despite the lingering stereotype of the socially awkward, dateless computer nerd, Geek Gods usually have a wide circle of friends and even (gasp!) romantic lives. This is not so surprising when you consider the qualities this C-Type, as a group, embodies: intelligence, diligence, curiosity, and financial stability. While they may not have the qualities typically associated with sex appeal (e.g., physical attractiveness, athletic prowess), their technological savvy often becomes their passport to relationships.

Intimacy, however, does not come easily for Geek Gods. Since they're defined by gadgets and computer bytes, it makes sense that they might find more comfort in hardware than in the murky waters of emotions. Thankfully, the Geek God doesn't have to navigate these waters without help from technology. Their preferred method is not much different from the way in which most modern-day teens interact: abbreviated text messages, emoticons to express very real physical reactions, e-mail flirting.

> [Text messages are] little electronic waves and nods that, just like real waves and nods, aren't meant to do much more than establish a connection—or disconnection, as the case may be—without getting into specifics.
>
> *The New York Times Magazine*, 1/22/06

Technology affords connection without intimacy, a tempting barrier that preserves the power of the Geek God. It's also important to note that technology is often the topic of conversation, as well as the method, for this type. Remember, it's what Geek Gods know best and what they use to connect with others, from family members to colleagues to romantic interests.

Although the typical Geek God is unlikely to have six-pack abs (or to waste much time worrying about not having them), there is, as with everybody, the desire to be seen as sexy and desirable. This creates an opportunity for marketers. You can use this tension in your advertising to create humor or empathy by playing against what is typically considered sexy, and positing intellectual and nerdy as "sexy" instead.

Actually, the idea of the nerd as a sex symbol might not be that far-fetched. Lately there seems to be a newfound passion for Geeks. Fashionable T-shirts have appeared emblazoned with slogans like "I Love My Geek." The TV show *Beauty and the Geek* followed the cohabitation of a group of self-defined geeks and a troupe of buxom beauties. The goal of the program (ostensibly) was to show that the two groups have much they can offer each other: knowledge on the one side, social panache on the other. One woman, interviewed by an Australian newspaper, explained geek appeal very simply, saying, "Geeks are cool, because it's about being able to do things other, less tech-savvy people can't."[1] On its simplest level, knowledge is sexy, and the Geek God's kindness, sensitivity, loyalty, and helpfulness are actually winning him dates these days.

> I want someone who'll take me to concerts AND anime-cons. Someone who can reformat my hard drive for me and keep me up to date on which programs are best to pirate software and mp3s with. Someone who can help me with website layouts and . . . and . . . and . . . I want a geek, dammit!
>
> **Mandysrad on the GeekCulture.com message board**

> The true test of a sexy geek is Making Stuff. Robots, art, what have you—we go for guys who can design and build some cool and unexpected thing. That is HOT! Watching someone do what he's good at is a turn on that beats a Calvin Klein underwear model body.
>
> **Jane on gamegirladvance.com**

MARKETPLACE EVIDENCE

Apple Genius Bar
What do you call a bunch of Geek Gods gathered behind a bar help-ing tech-weary customers? Why, Geniuses! Several years ago, Apple created the Genius Bar, a special section in its flagship Manhattan store, where folks could bring their iPod- and computer-related problems. The technicians—known as "Geniuses"—have proved beyond a shadow of a doubt that computer geeks can be sexy! Ac-cording to many reports, the bar is more like, well, a bar, and there's anecdotal evidence that many a love match has been made between a Genius and a damsel in tech distress!

GEEK GODS AND THEIR GADGETS

Collectors, but not pack rats, Geek Gods collect toys and gadgets with an unspoken understanding that their joy will be fleeting. This C-Type recognizes that today's hot item will inevitably be followed and replaced by tomorrow's. Manufacturers are aware of the short shelf life of today's hot tech toy, and, in fact, a planned obsolescence is standard. Smart marketers create a new gadget or piece of software fully aware that they will replace it with a newer, even better version of the product the following season. The Geek God quest, therefore, is to find the hottest, most current products and then spread the word about them before they become obsolete. Their strategy might be termed, "scout, embrace, and reboot." For the Geek God the search for the next cool thing ("scout") is constant; to find it ("embrace") is a real, if momentary, high; and then he starts the search process all over again ("reboot").

One reason Geek Gods are so important to marketers is what they do during the "embrace" part of the equation. As soon as they are infatuated with a new gadget, Geek Gods are relentless about promoting it to their entire circle, both real and virtual. Given their standing among friends and family, a recommendation from a Geek God is usually taken to heart and often results in a purchase.

The scouting process is never-ending, fueled by a constant stream of gear magazines as well as online message boards at sites like slashdot.org. (We thought about trying to assemble a list of the hippest and coolest gadgets of the moment, but without a doubt it would look humorously retro by the time this book is published. The cycle of must-have to who-cares spins mighty fast.) There is a definite competitive element to this search for the "newest of the new." Much like the stereotypical Los An-gelino's obsession with what car he drives or a fashionista's determina-tion to wear something no one else in the room is wearing, Geek Gods feel defined by the gadgets they carry with them. Within a Geek God group (and many Geek Gods have circles of friends within the C-Type), hierarchy is determined as much by who has the coolest tech toys and most cutting-edge devices as it is by who is the best at debugging a piece of Linux programming or building a computer from spare parts.

> ... everyone whips out their cell phone and puts it on the table. If some guy has the latest phone, it's the first five minutes of conversation. It's as much a part of their identity as the suit or tie they are wearing.
>
> **The New York Times, 4/15/04**

It should be noted that although Geek Gods are always looking for the next best thing, there's a warm place in their heart reserved for a number of products from the past. At the moment, there's a resurrection of interest in analog—similar to the slow food movement among food-ies. Analog recording is seen as a means of recapturing the aura of hu-manity, of real-world input, that digitization erases.

Out-of-date products may hold special meaning for Geek Gods for any number of reasons. It could be a nostalgia for the gadgets that first sparked a love affair with objects and technology. Or nostalgia for a cer-tain item that was introduced during a meaningful period in the Geek God's life (like a kid's first Walkman or camera). Or perhaps, even, be-cause the product was *so* revolutionary for its time that a thrill still lingers (like the first PCs). Enabled by eBay, where any obsolete, romanticized gadget can be found and purchased, many Geek Gods give in to their nostalgia, amassing collections of outmoded technologies that can rival their collections of the latest ones.

GEEK GOD PRODUCT HALL OF FAME

Here are just a few of the antiquated objects of desire that set nostalgic Geek God hearts aflutter.

Apple Newton
Introduced in the early 90s, the Apple Newton was part of the genesis of the personal digital assistant (PDA) category. The handheld device was mocked for its shortcomings and even though it's been discontinued, it nevertheless enjoys a cult following.

Atari
Today's insanely lifelike video game systems owe a nod of gratitude to Atari, the classic gaming system popular in the 80s. Geek God fans of Atari were thankful for the introduction of Atari Flashback Classic Game Console several years back. The unit allowed users to play approximately 20 classic games, such as Asteroids and Breakout.

8-Track
Today's young people wouldn't even be able to identify an 8-track cartridge, but full-grown Geek Gods appreciate this blast-from-the past product. According to Malcolm Riviera, Webmaster of www.8track-heaven.com, "people always focus on the flaws, but they have to realize that between 1965 and 1970, the 8-track was the best portable tape system there was."

Reel-to-Reel
Digital threatens to make reel-to-reel recordings obsolete, but purists say analog has a better, warmer sound. And some old-school recording artists are responding by sticking with reel-to-reel for their new CDs.

Putting oneself in the Geek God mindset, the ideal future would be one in which gadgets become ever more complex. Once a technology becomes so commonplace (like the old land-line telephone, let's say) that the average consumer feels not only comfortable with it but also fully understands it, the Geek God's raison d'être disappears. As far as Geek Gods go, technological products cannot be overengineered. You can hardly swamp them with too much information. Don't be afraid to include graphs and flowcharts in your marketing materials; this C-Type wants specific terminology. Within their own circles, Geek Gods speak in a sort of insider slang, a techno-babble that non-Geek Gods can barely comprehend. If you can generate a new term or phrase associated with your brand or product that Geek Gods will incorporate into their slang, that's a very good thing.

GEEK GODS AND "OPEN SOURCING"

As mentioned above, whatever information Geek Gods acquire is meant to be communicated to others, a trait that makes them uniquely suited for the concept of *open sourcing*. Open sourcing was started by software programmers who shared the source code they developed with other programmers. (The source code is the actual lines of words, numbers, and incomprehensible clusters of characters that tell a computer what to do and how to do it.) They gave it away for free, because tech folks in general believe information *wants* to be free.

As the code moved from programmer to programmer, it was read, changed, and redistributed. Performance upgrades were made; bugs were discovered and fixed. Through the open source process, software has evolved and advanced to new levels, at record speed. Open source has been so successful that it's precipitated a fundamental shift in how code is now being written. Many pieces of code are now being "open sourced." An army of Geek Gods took command of the operating software for Google maps and reprogrammed it to create Google map mash-ups. These mash-ups allow users to overlay fun, sometimes meaningless, data, such as the locations of potholes, taco stands, and UFO sightings, over the map of a given locale. It's just one way Geek Gods have left their imprint on highly utilized pieces of technology. In an odd twist of the capitalist marketplace, some companies that market technological products have taken the code that's been reworked by open sourcers and incorporated the changes into the new products they sell. The clock and calendar functions on Apple's iPod were originally written into the iPod software by Geek God hackers. When the company saw how popular these functions were, they added them to the official iPod package.

> I really thought the idea of putting my subway map onto my iPod was cool. Why should I keep it all to myself? If it's helpful to me, then why not to the rest of you?
>
> **William Bright, design director for Nerve.com whose site www.ipodsubwaymaps.com was one of the first to create an MTA map of NYC downloadable onto an iPod.**

> Early users of the Roomba, a robot vacuum cleaner, are rewiring it to serve as a "mobile security robot."
>
> *The Washington Post,* **7/12/05**

Through open sourcing, leading-edge Geek Gods have created a community of sharers and collaborators, a virtual "team" that works together toward synergistic, if not common, goals. One must possess creativity, intelligence, and cutting-edge insight to become a part of this community. Herein lies Geek Gods' power. There's an inherent desire to continually move forward, to work together, and to create the next best thing. Thankfully, technology (via the Internet) makes it easy for Geek Gods to both find and share with each other.

Bulletin boards are popular among Geek Gods because they easily facilitate communication and allow this C-Type to share ideas and information. Geek Gods can speak to each other and seek advice, expert to expert. Non-Geek Gods, beware. If you're not a member of the type, you may not understand the language spoken here! Companies marketing to Geek Gods need to be wary too. Geek Gods are outspoken with their opinions, and the Internet gives them an easy podium from which to spread the word—good or bad. And don't assume that they chat only about the high-tech stuff, either. This type can make or break products from a variety of categories, simply because the Web gives them extraordinary reach, and their technical facility means that they know the fastest and most effective ways of delivering their messages.

> In the consumer technology industry, for example, Gizmodo (www.gizmodo.com) is widely read. If the writers on the Gizmodo site are unhappy or disgruntled with a product, a lot of people will read about that.
>
> *Chicago Tribune*, 7/17/04

In addition to community boards, Geek Gods also populate technology blogs. Although specific blogs come in and out of favor (like everything else in the Geek God kingdom), as this book is written, many Geek Gods were turning to Gizmodo, a blog about gadgets; Boing Boing, a virtual scrapbook for tech ideas; and Lifehacker, a site that offers up "the downloads, web site, and short cuts that actually save time."

> It's not like tech geeks have all the answers in their heads, but they know how to get the answers. It looks a lot simpler to people than it actually is.
>
> *The Journal News*, 10/10/05

For marketers, the open sourcing practice has wide application across categories other than tech gadgets and computers (imagine, for example, open source baby food products that allowed consumers to play with the list of ingredients). Open sourcing also provides us with increased insight into the Geek God community and the Geek God mindset. This C-Type wants things transparent. They will figure out if you are not being straight with them. This is a community that also has a "first to market" mentality. Within the open source community, new ideas bubble up organically, and it's considered disrespectful to take credit for ideas that are not your own. (Use the idea, sure, but don't lie about developing it.) Geek Gods respect true innovators versus fast followers.

MARKETPLACE EVIDENCE

Linux

There's arguably not a better open sourcing (and Geek God) success story than Linux. The operating system was started in 1991 by a 21-year-old Finnish software engineer named Linus Torvalds. When Torvalds posted a note on a computer message board asking for input on his new system, Linux, the system quickly became a group effort for software developers worldwide. Fueled by an unrestricted pool of contributors and freed from the restrictions of corporate-backed efforts, Linux grew into a powerhouse of a system that is, today, supported by corporations such as IBM and Intel. And only 2 percent of the program was written by Torvalds himself!

GEEK GODS IN TRAINING

Tyler Marshad owns a cell phone, iPod and a PlayStation Portable. But what sets him apart is his age. Tyler is 12. "The fact that he's technologically savvy is very important," said the seventh-grader's father. "It's part of growing up in the year 2005."

New York Daily News, 11/27/05

It's amusing to answer our front door and have a neighbor asking if [my son] is home. . . . I must admit I was at times tempted to say, "No, Ryan can't play right now." But these adults, twice or more his age, were coming to ask Ryan computer questions and began paying him to work on their PC's!

Susan Fischer Benigno, in an article on www.folksonline.com

Gadgethead mania has taken hold of children, and the toy industry knows it. Manufacturers are filling the aisles with gadgets like two-way radios, mobile phones, portable digital video players, cameras, camcorders and hand-held games—for children as young as 6 years old.

The New York Times, 11/2/05

Today's Geek Gods better watch their backs. A new generation is right at their heels, ready to take over the kingdom. This generation, sometimes referred to as Generation IM (in honor of Instant Messaging, their preferred mode of communication), is chock-full of a whole new breed of Geek Gods. These Geek Gods in Training have the advantage of never having known life without their beloved technologies. Forget dolls and toy trains. This bunch is growing up with the most technologically sophisticated gadgets in human history. According to one international toy and game industry study, sales of electronic and video games doubled over the first five years of the decade, increasing from 20 percent in 1998–1999 to 40 percent in 2004–2005, while sales of nontech toys remained stagnant.[2]

This early fascination with technology quickly becomes mastery, and in many households it is the children who become the teachers. Parents are placed in the awkward position of going to their kids when they need help. In fact, one survey showed that over 80 percent of youths (ages 12 to 17) said they had been asked to help an adult do something online that the adult wasn't able to do.[3] Being placed in this role of authority in the household (at least in some matters) can have a strong effect on the psyches of these burgeoning Geek Gods, affecting "their confidence levels, the kind of employees they will be, companies' marketing tactics and even family dynamics."[4] Kids learn early that tech skills are a prized commodity and pay off big time.

Far from being passive users of these new technologies and gadgets, tomorrow's Geek Gods are becoming active participants in the process of evolving and shaping the tech world around them. They have created a shortcut language for text-messaging and IMing that is nearly impenetrable to their parents, and over 57 percent of the teenagers active online (that's about 12 million) are busy creating their own digital content, from Web pages to original artwork, stories, and blogs.[5] The upshot of all this is a generation poised to surpass even today's Geek Gods and to beat them at their own game.

The more kids are involved with digital content creation, the more thinkers will emerge that will eventually produce tomorrow's innovative products.

Brendan, a 15-year-old student at Seabreeze High School in Daytona Beach, quoted in *The New York Times News Service*, 11/12/05

Within a year of our household acquiring a computer I'd outpaced the adults who paid for it and claimed it almost wholly for my own.

Posting by AnonymousHeroin on GeekPress.com chatboard

Geek Gods and Brand Loyalty

Geek Gods can be among the most brand loyal of consumers—or among the least loyal, if they feel slighted or if they feel that a brand or company has put out a shoddy product. This C-Type reveres companies like Apple, Sony, Leica, BMW, and so on, all of whom have a longstanding tradition of quality and innovation. But Geek Gods are also the first to call them out for inefficiencies or missteps.

I've used blackberry products since their inception for my business. I've personalized them for the way I use them, and I'll never switch.

BigD commenting on bbhub.com

I don't care how many features the other sites have, I'm not sure if I could ever give up my Google. I switched to it about 5 years ago and have never looked back. Plus, there's something about that logo that makes me feel all warm and fuzzy inside.

Nick, commenting on Lifehacker.com

Smart companies hoping to go after the Geek God target need to recognize that, in this information age, forward-thinking consumers hold the keys to tomorrow's technology. Geek Gods want to be acknowledged as the market force they are. There can be, and should be, a symbiotic relationship between this C-Type and marketers. Geek Gods want to be "the first to know" and you should want the same, because Geek Gods will help refine and build your idea. Beta testing with this type (again, think about categories that reach beyond software) is critical if you want your Geek God consumers to feel involved and if you want to gain the benefit of their informed opinions.

Don't get hung up on old brand equities as a driving force when it comes to these consumers. In the technology arena, new brand awareness is something that can be created overnight, if it is linked with a new product or service that meets an emerging or unmet need. Look at Gizmodo or YouTube. These brands have universal recognition within this target, and yet, just a few years ago, they didn't exist.

SIZE MATTERS

For Geek Gods, size definitely counts—but bigger isn't always better. In fact for most technologies the rule of thumb is, "The smaller the cooler." Mobile phones emerged from the suitcase-size shells they had to be carried around in the late 70s to become the brick-size analog phones of the late 80s which gave way to the ever slimmer and smaller pocket cellular models we lust after now. Portable MP3 players are another perfect example. A quick look at the history of the genre's bestseller, the Apple iPod, reveals that, since its introduction in 2001, the iPod has gotten smaller and thinner while increasing its memory capacity from 5 GB to 80 GB (plus it now has a color display screen). In the same vein, the iPod's original little sibling, 2004's iPod mini, was replaced only a little over 18 months later with the iPod Nano, which was 62 percent smaller by volume (while maintaining the same 4 GB of memory). The smallest of the small, 2006's clip-on iPod Shuffle (a screenless player) was approximately the size of a matchbox, yet could hold 240 songs. The only real competition for Apple, when it came to small, was 2005's MobiBLU's DAH-1500. This dazzlingly small, sugar-cube-sized player (just one cubic inch) offered an FM radio, while playing both MP3 and WMA files and weighing in at less than one ounce.

One technology that is going in the opposite direction is television. In this category, big still sells. In television's infancy in the 50s, a 16-inch TV set was the biggest available. In the 70s, the biggest TV screens were 25 inches. Today, sales of TVs with screens 27 inches or larger are rising, while TVs smaller than 20 inches show falling sales. Projection TV screens can grow even bigger (thanks to new technologies that make the projection box much smaller and more den-friendly) with some brands offering 60-inch plus models. How big home television screens will get no one knows, but it seems unlikely that, for them, small will ever be "in."

No matter what product you sell or category you are in, this type is addicted to information. Technical specs, product development histories, compatibility, and the like, are important to Geek Gods, and they'll patiently pore over whatever data you allow them. Create ways for them to understand your backstory via the Internet. Don't be afraid to create layered campaigns that unfold over time or require a little legwork on the part of consumers to fully uncover. Digging beneath the surface is a game to a Geek God, and uncovering "secrets" is half the fun. The key to successfully reaching this C-Type is to touch their intellectual *and* creative nerves, and to be witty and/or humorous in your execution without dumbing down your message.

There is one exception to the notion of transparency when it comes to designing and/or developing products for Geek Gods. It has nothing to do with the actual working of products, and is secondary to all we've said about what drives Geek Gods in their everyday lives and social interactions. That's why we've saved it for last. It does, however, cast a light upon the Geek Gods' sense of humor and their capacity for innocent delight, something that we haven't really touched on yet. The exception is called *Easter Eggs*.

These Easter Eggs have nothing to do with the holiday—or with chickens. In tech terms, Easter Eggs are hidden features or novelties that programmers have put in for their own (as well as the finder's) amusement. It can be anything from a hidden Web page with a tribute to the designer, or an off-color animation that appears after a certain series of keystrokes. Easter Eggs can also be found on DVDs (extra bonus features) or CDs (usually a "hidden" final track) where they are revealed through a lucky, or accidental, combination of button pushes.

Knowing that many designers purposely include them, Geek Gods love to stumble upon these hidden delights, and some spend many hours looking for them. To find a new one that none of your friends has found is a cause for crowing (as soon as an Easter Egg surfaces, it's quickly posted on the Web for the delectation of others). Easter Eggs are a great way to make this C-Type feel smart and in the know—and can cause Geek Gods to have a positive association with your brand or product.

THE EASTER EGG: A GEEK'S DELIGHT

According to www.eeggs.com, a Web site that as of January 2006 had cataloged over 9,000 Easter Eggs (from software, DVDs, interactive games, and more), a true Easter Egg must satisfy the following criteria:

1. It's undocumented, hidden, and nonobvious. An Easter Egg can't be a legitimate feature of a product. It stands out precisely because it doesn't fit in or serve any real purpose.

2. It's reproducible. Any user of the product must be able to produce the same result given the instructions.

3. It's put there by the creators. Easter Eggs originate during product development and are usually a homage to their creators' personalities.

4. It's there for fun, not to do damage. We're talking fun finds here, not viruses.

5. It's *entertaining!* This is the most important element; if it's not there for entertainment, it's not an Easter Egg.

Source: www.eeggs.com

Examples of Easter Eggs You Can Try *(Thanks to eeggs.com*
contributors)
Grand Theft Auto: Vice City—The Obscene Egg
1. Go into the parking lot behind the Malibu club.
2. Look at the skyscraper across the street; this is the building
   where you'll find the egg.
3. At 23:00, some of the windows in the building will light up
   and create a certain image. Also, at 15-minute intervals
   (23:15, 23:30, . . .) a jet of "water" will be sprayed from the
   top of the building.

Quark XPress, v. 4.0—New Bigger Alien to Delete Old Alien
1. Draw a box in the center of the screen. Leave plenty of room
   on both sides for action.
2. Press Shift-Option-Command-K to get original alien. Repeat
   keystrokes at least 5 times.
3. The new alien appears randomly, usually after 5 to 12 tries.

MARKETING TO GEEK GODS: A CHECKLIST

☑ This C-Type yearns for real innovation. Lead your category; don't follow.

☑ Geek Gods are loyal to brands they believe in.

☑ Geek Gods are benevolent; they love to share and give others tech advice and counsel.

☑ Geek Gods embrace ideas with exuberance. Keep your message upbeat.

☑ Information is the key to their hearts.

☑ This type loves to use technology to snag deals and save money. Contests, rebate programs, and consolidation sites are right up their alley.

☑ Create a symbiotic innovation relationship with Geek Gods; use them as beta testers, and they'll reward you with idea refinements. Make them feel included, and they'll become brand evangelists.

☑ Knowledge is sexy.

☑ Easter Eggs!

DIG A LITTLE DEEPER

FURTHER RESOURCES ON GEEK GODS

Geek Gods in Print

Kick Me: Adventures in Adolescence by Paul Feig

Superstud: Or How I Became a 24-Year-Old Virgin by Paul Feig
The author, creator of the cult classic TV show *Freaks and Geeks*, offers personal experiences in these two nonfiction titles about the trials and tribulations of growing up geek.

Just a Geek by Wil Wheaton
This collection of stories from the actor who played Lt. Wesley Crusher on *Star Trek: The Next Generation* includes nostalgic tales of his discovery of the joys of HTML, blogging, and Web design.

Geek Chic: The Ultimate Guide to Geek Culture by Neil Feineman
The author agrees that we're in the midst of a sort of heyday for geeks.

Gonzo Gizmos: Projects & Devices to Channel Your Inner Geek by Simon Field
The ultimate how-to for nerds, Field explains how to make something (e.g., a simple radio) out of something else (iron, circuits, and a few pennies).

Geek Gods Online

Gizmodo.com
Super Geeks and regular folks alike check in daily with this granddaddy of gadget-centric Web logs for up-to-the-minute news on everything from hybrid smart cars to quirky flash drives made of wood.

Thinkgeek.com
This one-stop shop for the "smart masses" carries all of the essentials for the geek in your life: gadgets, toys, and "funny" T-shirts. (Although Geek God humor is sometimes oblique, e.g., a T-shirt slogan like "There are 10 types of people in the world: Those who understand binary, and those who don't.")

iPodlounge.com
Whether you're a newbie looking for advice on purchasing your first MP3 player or a Mac guru on the hunt for advanced hacks to personalize your iPod, this lounge is the center of the iPod universe.

Engadget.com
If you're looking for a place to find news on Japanese rescue robots or maybe just some useful gadgets with great design, point your browser to this tech-loving Web log for great geek coverage.

We-Make-Money-Not-Art.com
Wanna know all about Tokyo's Dorkbot performers? Or find out how to test your mushrooms for "magic" hallucinogens? While the name of this Web log may be misleading (it does cover plenty of art), you'll find geek-focused content here that you won't find anywhere else.

I4U.com
Full of news, reviews, and tips, this online geek emporium is a great place for tech-heads to research, price, and even buy all their geeky gear, all without leaving the comfort of their desktop.

Makezine.com
For geeks who want to go the DIY route, this online magazine offers all the tips and tricks to build or modify their own techy toys.

Pandora.com
Just like you turn to your local geek for advice on the newest software, geeks-in-the-know look to Pandora for a leg-up on the newest music. This service analyzes your favorite songs and recommends new artists based on similar patterns within the music, all in a streaming radio format that's like listening to your own personal DJ.

Slashdot.org
If geekdom were a religion, this message board and clearinghouse for geek stories would be the temple.

GEEK GOD ROLE MODELS

Famous Geek Gods throughout the ages . . .

Archimedes (287 BC–212 BC)

Proving Geek Gods coexisted with the Greek gods, Archimedes was the ancient world's foremost mathematician and inventor. He discovered pi. He created the Archimedes screw (the first device for raising water from a lower to a higher elevation). He invented the catapult, the lever, and the compound pulley. The legend says he was killed while drawing an equation in the sand during the battle of Syracuse. Probably apocryphal, but who are we to argue with a legend?

Ben Franklin (1706–1790)

Preeminent scientist/inventor/renaissance man of the American colonies. He famously investigated the properties of electricity with his kite and key and invented across many fields, creating the first bifocals, a metal home furnace (the "Franklin stove,") an early type of odometer, watertight bulkheads for ships, and (as a result of all that kite flying) a protective lightning rod for rooftops.

Thomas Edison (1847–1931)

Dubbed "The Wizard of Menlo Park," this inveterate tinkerer was the inventor of the phonograph, the incandescent light bulb, and motion pictures, to name just the most impressive. He was one of the first inventors to apply the principles of mass production to the process of invention, making him truly a forerunner of modern Geek Gods, and was eventually the holder of 1,093 U.S. patents (the most ever issued to one individual).

Howard Aiken (1900–1973)

Harvard Ph.D. and physics instructor who created the Mark I, the world's first computer (the IBM Automatic Sequence Controlled Calculator), and also started the world's first computer science academic program.

Nicholas Negroponte (1943–)

Founding chairman of MIT's Media Laboratory and founder of MIT's Architecture Machine Group, a combination lab and think tank which studies different approaches to human-computer interface. Chairman of One Laptop per Child (OLPC), a nonprofit organization created to distribute inexpensive laptops to provide every child in the world with access to knowledge and modern forms of education.

Steve Jobs (1955–)
CEO of Apple, which he cofounded in 1976, and Pixar, the Academy Award–winning animation studio, which he cofounded in 1986. Fired once from Apple, he is now back at the helm and helping to keep that company in the forefront of the tech race (and the Geek God consciousness).

Larry Page (1973–) and Sergey Brin (1974–)
More commonly known as the Google Guys, this pair founded the world's most popular Internet search engine.

NOTES

1. *The Courier Mail*, 5/7/06

2. Ibisworld Australia report, quoted in *Sydney Sun-Herald*, 10/23/05

3. Parents & Teens 2004 Survey, Princeton Survey Research Associates International, for the Pew Internet & American Life Project

4. *The Columbus Dispatch*, 12/30/05

5. Pew Internet & American Life Project survey "Teen Content Creators and Consumers," 11/2/05

E-LITISTS

"

This group is practicing altruism of convenience . . . they want to do good, but will not go too out of their way to be green.

Devin Gordon, *Newsweek*

So imagine that you're in charge of [a car] company. . . . To the environmentally conscious, you sell the prospect of saving the earth even as you appeal to the class vanity of affluent customers who might otherwise never dream of buying an American car. Ford just might get it . . . the Sierra Club joined Ford to promote a new hybrid version of the Mercury Mariner sport utility vehicle.

***The New York Times*, 7/24/05**

What's wrong with a little flair with your environmental do-goodedness?

Lisa, on Workerbees.Typepad.com/HipAndZen

ince the beginning of the environmental movement in the early 60s, environmentalists have been called many things, none of them very positive. Tree huggers, Greenies, Enviros, and EcoFreaks are just a few examples. Though varied in their missions, these individuals had one thing in common: heavy-handedness. They were strident in their causes, often anarchistic and always against what they saw as our culture's rampant consumerism. Definitely not the darlings of marketers.

But just as the environmental movement has evolved over the years, so too has the environmentalist. Enter the E-litist, the first environmentally associated consumer group that is made up of just that: consumers. And somewhat mainstream consumers at that. E-litists are green, but they're a new green. The *New York Times* Style section dubbed them "light green."[1] They're not replacing the old diehard environmentalists but are a refinement of the type, a new wing on the (pardon the bad pun) greenhouse. Here's a simple comparison to encapsulate the difference: a hand-crocheted sweater made with undyed, homespun yarn? That's Old Green. Designer duds made with organic cotton, or better yet hemp? That's E-litist—and good news for marketers.

E-litist consumers are easier, and more profitable, to target than their green forebears because they want it all: style, comfort, and quality as well as "greenness." They're willing to pay for a product that has all four of these virtues, which, for them, represent the new super-premium.

Consider the Toyota Prius—a stylish, spacious, fully loaded hybrid car that gets better mileage with fewer emissions. The E-litist shopping for a Prius doesn't need to compromise. He or she is able to enjoy the car-buying excitement, is given a large selection of cutting-edge features and accessories to choose from, and still ends up with an economical car that's better for the planet.

E-litists are most often found in the 25 to 55 age range, and among the well-to-do. As members of the privileged classes, they juggle their green values with an appreciation of luxury. E-litists are able to make luxury and social consciousness jibe through a willingness to use their money to effect positive change. They view green-tinged purchases as badge items, and very definitely want their purchases to make a statement; they are proud of their choices and want others to know it and emulate them. This is the greatest achievement of E-litists—that their money has helped create a market for environmentally friendly products, thereby allowing those products to migrate into the realm of the less financially advantaged consumer.

Some might wish to deride E-litists as moneyed dilettantes. Environmental purists may scoff at the fact that most E-litists don't have a very deep knowledge of issues and may be focused only on the most publicized threats (lately that would be global warming, the dangers of pesticides, diminishing natural resources, overprocessing, etc.) And, yes, it's true: E-litists are not known for delving deeply into issues, preferring instead to receive information and advice from the media. But in the very short time they have existed (less than a decade), E-litists have done more for the image of the environmentalists than any other green faction ever. E-litists not only spread the word, but they make environmentalism both fashionable and aspirational. Because of E-litists, an ever-growing proportion of the population is finding that, finally, it's easy being green!

ARE BOOMER E-LITISTS LATENT HIPPIES?

Many members of the Baby Boomer generation are former hippies who grew up, got a job, and never looked back. Or did they? We have our theories, and one of them is that ex-hippie Boomers with money, who were practically weaned on environmentalist ideals, are now coming back to the cause. The group is reconnecting with the ideals of the 60s, but doing so in a less angry, less "Abbie Hoffman" way, bringing a millennial, guilt-free flair to it.

HOME, E-LITE HOME

Home is an arena where E-litists are in the vanguard of society. They have the income and the interest to make their homes concrete symbols

of their commitment to civic and societal responsibility, as well as repos-
itories for all of today's latest conveniences and luxuries.

> For so many people in wealthy worlds, simplifying has also
> become an industry which, ironically, turns out an array of
> alluring products: toxin-free paint so wholesome it's known as
> "milk"; clothing woven from hemp fibers; even the fat, glossy
> magazine *Real Simple*.
>
> **Elizabeth, on Grist.org**

The most obvious manifestation of the E-litist homeowner's commitment to the environment is that line of recycling bins by the curb.
Many consumers recycle–it's the law in most places– but E-litists often
go to extremes to do their part. One study showed that residents in areas
with high recycling levels tend to be mostly white, affluent, and well-
educated. In other words, the prime E-litist demographic. In fact, the
study went on to show that most people who recycle regularly earn at
least $60,000 a year.[2] Some E-litists' homes have whole rooms designated
as "recycling centers" to make sorting waste simpler. They can spruce
the recycling room up with such fancy accoutrements as Design Within
Reach's elegant set of color-coded refuse containers, or Stacks and Stacks
recycling cart with wheels (to make the journey from house to curb
easier).

> Builders are going green because it's finally starting to make
> sense economically. And if we can save the planet at the same
> time, so much the better.
>
> **Architect Eric Schamp, *Los Angeles Times*, 9/25/05**

> I have a long-standing love affair with chic, modern modular
> homes, particularly those built with eco-friendly materials and
> techniques (which is most of them, these days).
>
> **David, on Gristmill.grist.org**

People are willing to pay up to live in a healthier environment.

James F. Gill, the chairman of the Battery Park City Authority,
The New York Times, 5/17/06

There is a demand among E-litist consumers for luxury housing built with a green conscience, and developers who satisfy those demands can turn tidy profits. According to research by the National Association of Home Builders, as of 2004 about 15,000 new homes a year currently meet either local or regional green building standards. Southern California developers are considered to be at the leading edge of ecologically sound home design. The county of Santa Monica, for one, offers building grants for LEED-certified buildings (see LEED sidebar). Some of New York's newest residential developments are going green as well. Battery Park City, a relatively new area of Manhattan (created from landfill) near the island's southern end, drafted its own green building guidelines in 1999, requiring that every residence in the area meet strict sustainability criteria. The Battery Park City Authority requires buildings to contain photovoltaics, which capture heat from the sun and turn it into electricity. Also, 75 percent of a building's nonmechanical roof area must be a Green Roof (meaning a roof with a covering of plant life which serves not only to insulate the building but also helps clean the air). All the parkland in the development is run organically, using horticultural soap instead of pesticides, and the ball fields' restrooms feature waterless urinals and composting toilets.

I think it's great that green buildings are getting the recognition they deserve. So what if these are luxury buildings—it means they have more money to spend on innovation and green initiatives.

Aqua Fille, on Gristmill.grist.org

One of the luxury condominiums built in Battery Park City, the Solaire, provides a good example of the way E-litist building practices slowly but surely trickle down to the mainstream. A number of the products that were custom-made for the Solaire during its construction—adhesives, kitchen appliances, paint enamels—are now sold at Home Depot. Even though 15 to 17 percent of the $120 million Solaire, completed in 2003, went toward its green features, the same developer's next building had an added green cost of only 8 percent, according to his calculations, thanks to the increased availability of these green-friendly building supplies.

LEED CERTIFICATION— WHAT DOES IT MEAN?

The U.S. Green Building Council, a coalition of corporations, builders, universities, government agencies, and nonprofits, pioneered the green housing movement in 1993, when it created the commercial standards by which housing could be rated for environmental impact. Similar to an EnergyStar Rating, LEED certification, for Leadership in Energy and Environmental Design, designates a building or housing project as environmentally friendly.

Although LEED is used for commercial housing only, a number of ratings programs for residential homes are currently in the works. Recognition of this nature, by independent organizations, is especially important for this C-Type. E-litists desire assurance that they are making truly environmentally friendly purchase decisions, but they don't want to have to wade through data on the subject themselves. If your brand can gain certification of some sort or an award (like the U.S. EPA Climate Protection Award or The Global Environment Leadership Award, etc.) which attests to your commitment to the environment, it will help give your brand the cache E-litists are looking for.

One sure sign that building green doesn't have to mean giving up luxury, style, or modern-day amenities is that some of the country's current leading-edge architects are E-litist. Noted architect William Mc-Donough built a new plant for the Ford Motor Company that features the world's largest green roof. (It doubles as a habitat for animals.) Mc-Donough, considered a prophet for sustainability, also designed a building at Oberlin College in Ohio designed to make more energy than it needs to operate. In 1999, *Time* magazine named him a "Hero for the Planet."

Another example is the firm Cook + Fox Architects, headed up by Robert Fox and Richard Cook. Their philosophy is simple: unite high design with sustainable technology and a connection to the environment. Their buildings, which include One Bryant Park in New York City, have special green features, such as a new wall technology that dissipates heat from the sun, carbon dioxide monitors, and a system to collect and reuse rain and waste waters.

The attitude and ethics of these architects, who've made their names in green design, are trickling down (or perhaps trickling "up") to some even more famous architects, who were not previously known for paying attention to environmental concerns. Architectural icon Richard Meier is one example. He recently joined the fold with his latest project (at least, as of this writing)—a Beverly Hills condominium looking to get a LEED rating and planning to not only meet but surpass California's strict environmental building codes.

Moving on to the interior of E-litists' houses, it probably comes as no surprise that these C-Types fill their homes with products that combine green with grand. Peek inside the laundry room, and you might see the Duet washing machine from Whirlpool. It has an elegant, vaguely art deco look and a large load capacity, but uses reduced energy and water to operate. It fulfills both the functional and emotional needs of the E-litists, plus it provides an opportunity for them to reaffirm their benevolence while (thanks to cost and design) boosting their status. In the basement, there's likely to be a tankless water heater that heats water only when it's needed, thereby saving energy. Throughout the house, light fixtures probably contain compact fluorescent light bulbs (CFLs), which are more expensive than regular bulbs, but use less electricity and last longer. And on the walls, you can expect low VOC paints. (VOCs are volatile organic compounds emitted by standard wall paints, which can cause respiratory distress.) The VOCs, however, are the only thing low about these paints—prices for this premium wall cover run high.

I have been using a [renewable]-bamboo spatula for cooking for ages and it's the best thing available.

Luc, on Treehugger.com

Ecover laundry whitener is a fabulous addition to my armory against grass stain and indeed other marks on my son's cricket whites.

Susan, on DigitalDivide.net

I'd been looking for some stylish wine glasses for a while and finally ordered some 100% recycled ones from Metro Wine Glasses.

Marky, on Treehugger.com

When ABC Carpet & Home, one of Manhattan's higher-end home stores, starts concerning itself with eco-friendliness and social responsibility, you *know* the green mindset has made it to the upper crust. The store, known for its eclectic and expensive offerings—everything from faux imperial china to hippie-chic jewelry to bedding and carpeting—has turned E-litist. Over the past few years, owner Paulette Cole has made it her mission to offer merchandise that, whenever possible, is environmentally and socially responsible. The quality and high style remain, but much of the furniture is now made in ways that don't destroy the world's rainforest. Even the store's packing materials are now biodegradable. The store has also started the ABC Home and Planet Foundation, which assists more than a dozen do-good organizations.

My goal is for the store to be 100 percent responsible design.

Paulette Cole, owner of NY's ABC Carpet & Home,
***The New York Times*, 5/25/06**

On the West Coast, look for E-litist goods at LivinGreen in Culver City. All of the store's home furnishings and accents (handmade natural-fiber baskets and pillows, organic bed systems, and repurposed fabrics and textiles) are made from natural, nontoxic, or recycled materials. In addition, the store also has some practical green-living items such as energy-efficient bulbs, green cleaners, and nontoxic paint. What lifts LivinGreen even more is the look and feel of the store, which rivals the hippest furniture and design stores, and includes an attached art gallery featuring handicrafts from around the world.

CLEAN GREEN: AN E-LITIST CLEANING PRODUCTS BRAND SORT

E-litists find selecting environmentally preferable and/or natural cleaners a no-brainer. But many of the brands out there currently are just *too* green for E-litists, or rather a shade of green that clashes with their décor. So, when it comes to the current crop of green cleaners on the market, who's doing it better in E-litists' minds?

Seventh Generation
Although a favorite brand of old-guard environmentalists, some complain that Seventh Generation tissues and paper towels are not as soft as mainstream brands. It's not enough to be green—E-litists demand top-notch service.

Simple Green
Simple Green's products are natural and nontoxic, and they work well, but the packaging is decidedly plain. E-litists want a product that looks good as well as works well.

Ecover
This brand of "ecological cleansing and detergent agents" gets high marks on efficacy and E-litist kudos for a more modern, clean look.

Method
They get it just right when it comes to satisfying and appealing to E-litists. Method barely pays attention to its greenness, letting the chic, artsy package design, great colors, and appealing modern scents speak for themselves. Still, the products are all nontoxic and come in

recyclable packaging, and the company highlights a catchy "People Against Dirty" campaign for green living on its Web site. Now that's the way to be green and hip at the same time!

Repurposing is a very of-the-moment concept gaining ground with E-litists when it comes to home furnishings. *Repurposing* can refer to products that are made from recycled goods or items that enjoyed another existence and have now been incorporated into something else. Either way, the purchase of a repurposed product helps consumers feel better about their "footprint," or the impact they're having on the environment. Another key E-litist byword is *sustainability* (also discussed below with regard to farming and food production), which here refers to the process by which the item was made, not its ability to last. The Q Collection is a good example of sustainable furniture. There's nothing crunchy or overtly natural about the line's classically inspired, sleek, and sexy pieces, which have been featured in *Elle Decor, Town & Country*, and *Gentry* magazines. They are certainly more suited to a mansion or luxury condominium than a log cabin, but the company remains committed to creating (in its words) "furnishings that are 'health aware' and 'eco-friendly.' The company strives to be at the forefront of sustainable design by acting today in a manner to protect and preserve our planet for tomorrow."

MARKETPLACE EVIDENCE

Terramor Village
Located in Orange County, California, more than 1,200 homes and townhouses are being built in 12 neighborhoods collectively known as Terramor. Terramor is being called the largest green-oriented village of its kind. And believe us, it's no hippie commune. Prices for Terramor's upscale homes begin at $500,000 and rise well past $1 million. The neighborhood's greenness comes by way of solar-paneled roofs, recycled insulation, kitchen recycling areas, drip landscape watering systems, and electrical vehicle recharging outlets in the garage.

These are just a few examples of the high-end retailers and designers who cater to E-litists. For more examples check out some of the Web sites listed in the Dig a Little Deeper section at the end of this chapter, or just browse your local furniture store. You may be surprised at how synonymous eco-friendly has become with premium when it comes to home goods.

E-LITISTS: FOOD AND DRINK

At the core of the original green movement lurked a distrust of anything activists hadn't grown or made themselves. Happily for marketers, that isn't remotely true of E-litists. On a very basic level, E-litists believe labels and rely on claims like "organic" or "local" to lead them to healthy choices rather than investigating what these nutritional claims represent. Saddled with busy lives, E-litists appreciate the convenience of mass-manufactured goods as long as they are made with at least some attention to environmental concerns. "Good for the Environment" is not an all or nothing proposition with them. Even if you can't fully reformulate a product to meet strict green demands, something as simple as changing your packaging to a more earth-friendly plastic (and highlighting it, so E-litists are aware you've done it) can be enough to help your brand gain points with this C-Type.

So what bywords and catchphrases are E-litists currently excited or intrigued by, when it comes to potables and comestibles (to be fancy about it)? Here's a rundown of some of the most popular.

Organic
Organic food sales have been rising by about 20 percent a year in the United States since 1990, according to the Organic Trade Association. The OTA's 2006 Manufacturer Survey reported that organic food sales totaled nearly $14 billion in 2005, representing 2.5 percent of all retail food sales. To E-litists, organic might as well be synonymous with "better quality." A simple rule of thumb is that, for E-litists, the higher up in the food chain the product (for example, meat, dairy), the more likely

an E-litist is to buy the organic version. E-litist parents are especially sus-
ceptible to the organic label when selecting prepared baby food, which
allows them to enjoy convenience without the guilt.

For years, organic represented the leading edge in the pure foods
movement. But, thanks in part to the trickle-down effect of E-litist influence, food giants like Kraft, General Mills, and Safeway now offer an
increasing number of organic products. In some cases they've even created their own fully organic food lines. A huge signal that organic really
has gone mainstream, though, was Wal-Mart's 2006 decision to start
stocking organic foods, and at only a 10 percent price premium over its
nonorganic goods. While traditional "greens" were horrified by the news
(fearing the term "organic" would become debased to the point of mean-
inglessness by the mega-retailer's reliance on factory farming and mass
production techniques), E-litists mostly perceived this as a good thing, a
sign that the world was moving in the right direction.

Sustainability
Although there is no FDA-regulated definition of sustainability, the
World Commission on Environment and Development defines it as,
"Meeting the needs of the present without compromising the ability of
future generations to meet their own needs." In regard to food, sustainability refers to the treatment of animals and conditions on the farms
where crops are raised. Because it appeals to their view of themselves as
guardians of their children's future world, sustainability is a big buzzword among E-litists and lends a huge helping of credibility when it's af-
fixed to a product label.

One good place to see sustainability in action is Blue Hill at Stone
Barns, in Pocantico Hills, New York. Merging restaurant and farm, Stone
Barns is an 80-acre pasture owned by the Rockefellers (can't get much
more old-school elite than that!) with a restaurant run by one of New
York City's top chefs, Daniel Barber. A fan of local foods, Barber creates
high-end dishes using food that is almost exclusively grown or cultivated
on the land at Stone Barns. Another fine example of sustainability in action is Portland, Oregon's New Season Market grocery. Almost all of the
store's meat is locally and sustainably raised, and the fish are graded ac-

cording to a system developed by the Monterey Bay Aquarium's Seafood Watch (a program that monitors fishing practices and their environmental impact). Local produce from the Oregon, Northern California, and Washington area is clearly labeled with a sustainable sticker.

Local Foods
E-litists want to feel close to both the earth and their own community. They seek out foods that come from within a 100-mile radius (the official definition of "local," according to the locavore movement; for more information, see *Locavores* in the "Food Psyche" spectrum in Part 3), because they recognize that it will be fresh and tasty, and because they believe buying locally will have a positive impact on their neighbors. Local as a label, especially on restaurant menus, also adds a certain cachet.

Farmers Markets
In 1970, there were a mere 340 farmers markets across the United States. By 2004, there were 3,706.[3] New York City's Union Square Greenmarket, the city's most popular farmers market, lures more than 60,000 visitors on a typical summer weekend. It's almost impossible to find anyone who doesn't approve of farmers markets. Growers love the markets because they can sell their goods for more than they get from wholesalers, while consumers love the quality, selection, and good-old, close-to-the-earth country feel. E-litist favorites at the greenmarket? Rarer produce varieties (heirloom tomatoes, etc.) and handmade, dinner-party-ready baked goods.

Biodynamic
Is this the next big buzzword? Our first inkling came when we heard about several vineyards that were being farmed biodynamically. What does this mean, exactly? Think of it as organic with a splash of the spiritual. Biodynamic farms seek to be self-sustaining, with an overall goal of attaining perfect balance. Like organic farming, biodynamic farming rejects the use of pesticides and fertilizers, but it goes even further; ideally, everything used on a biodynamic farm comes from the farm itself. Additionally, solar, lunar, and astrological rhythms are considered and

respected. It all sounds very New Agey, but even skeptics might find the proof is in the pudding. Many of the wines produced on biodynamic farms, for example, Quivira Vineyards in the Dry Creek Valley of Sonoma County, are praised for their high quality. Biodynamic farming isn't cheap, of course, but to an E-litist that makes the wine even sweeter.

> For years I've been a fan of Newman's Own. It's one of those companies that does things right, from its focus on quality products to its ethos of giving back to the globe-at-large.
>
> **Tanya, on Epicurious.com**

It's worth noting that many of the top organic brands are now subsidiaries of the world's largest food producers. Organic yogurt maker Stonyfield Farms sold a 40 percent share to food giant Groupe Danone in late 2001. (Eventually Danone increased its stake in the company to 80 percent.) In 2000, Kraft Foods swallowed up Boca Burger Inc., known for its veggie burgers. That same year, Vermont-based ice cream maker Ben & Jerry's sold itself to an Anglo-Dutch consumer products group, Unilever NV, for $326 million.[4] Thus far there seems to be no consumer backlash to corporate intervention.

If there is a single store that delivers everything the E-litist consumer wants, it's Whole Foods Market. The philosophy of this $4.7 billion natural foods store chain aligns perfectly with E-litist ideals: It offers customers the best quality foods and food products, beautifully arranged in a clean, chic setting. Whole Foods has its own organic brand, "365," offering everything from peanut butter to cereal to ground coffee in attractive, cleanly designed packages. Prices can be steep (there's a reason the chain is sometimes called "Whole Paycheck"), but for those who can pay, and E-litists can, no other store offers such a wide range of healthy and eco-friendly products with an unmatched level of service and convenience.

THE E-LITIST SHOPPING CART

What brands do E-litist consumers gravitate toward? Here are just a few:

Amy's Organic
One of the first natural-organic brands, Amy's is still number one in terms of sales and consumer popularity. The brand's stature is well-deserved. With scores of frozen foods and meals to choose from, Amy's has made organic, healthy and convenient for E-litists.

Annie's
The first brand to make macaroni and cheese in a box acceptable to E-litists, Annie's still holds a warm place in the hearts of this type. E-litists especially favor this brand when it comes to feeding their kids.

Newman's Own Organics
Paul Newman's namesake company was one of the earliest all-natural and organic lines to market and package itself in a way that would bring in E-litists. It was also a pioneer in the use of "cause" marketing, where part of the purchase price gets donated to a worthwhile cause. With fun names like Fig Newmans, and a smart and approachable brand personality, Newman's Own merges a "good-for-you and good-for-the-planet" aura with fun and great taste.

Stonyfield Farm
E-litists can't help but buy in to the good that Stonyfield Farm is doing for the planet, such as donating 10 percent of its profits to environmental efforts and going to great lengths to recycle the yogurt cups.

EnviroKidz Organic
E-litist parents can feed their kids this brand of cereal and not worry that they'll reject it. The colorful and cheery, animal-centric packaging and names like Gorilla Munch and Cheetah Chomps keep their attention, as well as boosting global wildlife awareness.

MARKETPLACE EVIDENCE

Maury Rubin's Birdbath

Maury Rubin, of New York's (and now Los Angeles's, too) famed City Bakery, has opened another outpost that's part bakery and part E-litist social statement. Officially unnamed, it goes by the codename "Birdbath." From City Bakery, Rubin has brought his outrageously large signature cookies, made with organic ingredients, of course. As for the décor, everything is made from eco-friendly, sustainable materials, such as wheat and sunflower seed walls and a floor made of cork. Even the staff is outfitted in hemp and linen jackets. At press time, the shop was less than six months old, but Rubin has promised to change the design every six months or so. To check it out, visit his site at www.buildagreenbakery.com.

E-LITIST FASHION AND BEAUTY

Aesthetics matter. You can be cool and hip and still give a f#!_ about the environment.

GreenGrrrl, on About.com's Environmental Issues forum

In February 2005, during the hoopla of Fashion Week in New York, a phalanx of models strolled down a catwalk wearing hemp/silk gowns, organic-wool dresses, and bustiers made from recycled polyester.

Wired Magazine, **"Rise of the Neo-Greens,"** 5/06

As with home furnishings, E-litists are looking for clothes and accessories that combine high design with eco-friendly materials. Though the notion of clothing and personal accessories catering to green consumers is not new, early green brands (like North Face and Birkenstock) were created more for nature lovers and outdoor people than fashionistas. For them, function always prevailed over fashion considerations. While a few green brands like Patagonia have, over the years, attained an aura of cool, they aren't quite high design enough for E-litists, who want status cues as well as environmental ones. E-litists spend money on their wardrobes, and even the most socially conscious among them aren't willing to give up the style and quality to which they're accustomed.

> Like with all paradigm shifts, as the new green design paradigm takes hold, outdated designers will eventually conform to the new principles and embrace them as their own.
>
> **Josh, on LazyEnvironmentalist.com**

> Eco-chic is about wearing things that are cutting edge, and knowing that the choices one makes are geared at protecting the world we live in.
>
> **Goldie, on GoldieBoutique.wordpress.com**

In the past few years, however, new brands and designers have emerged that make it easy for E-litists to have their cake and eat it too. "luxury green" clothing lines like Stewart + Brown combine high-fashion with an environmental conscience. Founding partners (and soul mates) Karen Stewart and Howard Brown aspire to "the highest standards of quality and functional style while extracting the bare minimum from Earth's precious capital." The Stewart + Brown line features cutting-edge styles made of eco-friendly materials like organic cotton, hemp, and Mongolian cashmere.

Another line, Edun (that's "nude" spelled backwards) is the brain-child of U2's Bono, his wife Ali Hewson, and designer Rogan Gregory, known for his Loomstate line of organic cotton jeans. Sold at upscale emporiums like Barneys, Nordstrom, and Saks, Edun is committed to sustainable employment practices and produces fair-trade T-shirts, jeans, and sweatshirts made in factories in Africa, South America, and India where workers earn fair wages. It's worth noting that each of these fashion initiatives comes complete with a backstory. This is always a good thing to have when marketing to E-litists. They usually have their own story about how their eyes were opened to the environmental cause and they want to know yours. If your brand or company has an eco story, don't hide it—highlight it.

> I've read about this denim company called Del Forte that uses 100% organic cotton. I LOVE jeans, and I'm so excited to see the sustainable choices coming out.
>
> **Natalie, on Treehugger.com**

> Levi's organic line of jeans is a bold move for this company that I think deserves our applause, as it appears that Levi has thought through the entire lifecycle of this product.
>
> **Mark, on Treehugger.com**

As with food, an "organic" label attached to a garment is practically enough by itself to convince an E-litist that it's worth a premium price. It's also a highly desirable attribute when it comes to the personal care category. Sales of organic nonfood, nonpersonal care products (a broad swath that includes towels, linens, and clothing, as well as pet food and nutritional supplements) grew by 32.5 percent in 2004–2005 to reach $744 million,[5] while sales of natural personal care products topped $2.6 billion in 2002, a 52 percent jump since 1998.[6]

Mainstream brands are slowly joining the party as well. Sports outfitter Nike has set a goal of using organic fibers for at least 5 percent of its cotton-based garments by 2010. And Wal-Mart's Sam's Club now sells 100 percent organic-cotton active wear by Chaus, with prices as low as $10 per piece. The number of clothing brands that use organic cotton has risen to more than 250 today from fewer than 100 in 2002.[7]

More news that shows the increasing influence of E-litists in the marketplace is the acquisition by major players of most of the bestselling boutique green brands in the personal care category. L'Oreal paid $1.1 billion in 2006 for The Body Shop's chain of 2,085 stores, not to mention its reputation for eco-friendly packaging and high animal-testing standards. In 2006, Colgate announced that it was buying Kennebunk-based Tom's of Maine, the number-one natural oral-care brand with products including mouthwash and dental floss. (Natural dental care products represent a $3 billion market that's growing by 15 percent a year, according to Colgate's own figures.) While purists worry that the corporate mentality might damage these brands' souls, it's undeniable that with this new marketing power behind them these small brands will reach a much wider audience than they did before.

MARKETPLACE EVIDENCE

IIKH

The brand's tag line—Smart. Stylish. Sexy. Green.—says it all. IIKH, a Manhattan-based seller of body, home, baby, pet, and gourmet goods, was formed when a trio of eco-conscious fashion and luxury goods insiders decided to bring a new level of sophistication to the booming market of eco-friendly products. Now isn't that what E-litism is all about?

E-LITIST POWER SOURCES

As the world's oil crisis spirals out of control, many kinds of consumers are trying to do their part to help. It's an arena where E-litist's "luxury-with-a-conscience" has really come to the fore, and where their influence is highly visible. The most obvious example (as noted in this chapter's introduction) is the rise of the hybrid car.

> I own a Civic Hybrid . . . I bought it for the eco-benefits, but to my surprise, I received numerous compliments on "such a stylish car."
>
> **JimBor, on associatedcontent.com**

According to hybridcars.com, which follows this trend closely, U.S. hybrid sales have generally doubled every year since the turn of the century, from fewer than 10,000 in 2000 to over 200,000 in 2005. A sure sign that many of these hybrid drivers are E-litists is a 2003 study by J.D. Power and Associates which found that the average household income of new hybrid car buyers was $15,000 higher than those of nonhybrid car buyers.[8]

It's a truism that consumers use cars as an extension of themselves. E-litists use their hybrid cars as a way to wear their green identities on their sleeves. One study concluded that drivers of these cars bought the vehicles mainly because of what the purchase said about them, noting that when the cost of the car and gas money were factored in, hybrids provide owners with no noteworthy savings.[9] The study's researchers thus hypothesized that the benefit was purely psychological. A 2006 episode of the TV cartoon *South Park*, entitled "Smug Alert," mocked this tendency of hybrid drivers to feel so good about their purchase they want to trumpet it to the world. As one character on the show stated, "Ever since Gerald Broflovsky got a hybrid, he thinks he's so much better than the rest of us."

Some green movement activists move even further to the left and fill their cars with cooking oil. (For the specifics on how this works, check out www.greasecar.com.) Grease Nation, a gathering held in Westchester, New York, in spring 2006 attracted dozens of drivers who favor vegetable oil over diesel, their cars festooned with stickers like "Veggie-Powered" or "Refueled at Rosa's Pizza" on the rear windows. Thus far, this solution has not been embraced by most E-litists, since there is something decidedly downmarket about it. Though some committed members of this C-Type are grease enthusiasts, at the moment this is a good example of an idea E-litists might embrace if some enterprising company packaged and marketed it in a more upscale way.

ON THE DIAL

Whatever the car they drive, there's one radio station that draws more listeners of this C-Type than any other. No, it's not Top 40. It's NPR. Aligning with and/or sponsoring shows on National Public Radio will likely garner your brand positive attention from E-litists, who care as much about the medium (and its perception related to the cause) as the message.

Moving away from automobiles and into home energy sources, one company that really understands the status-marketing angle is Con Edison of New York. It's recently introduced a premium energy option, NY Clean Choice, which allows Big Apple consumers to upgrade to cleaner, renewable, and local electricity sources. Although the number of Con Ed customers who've signed up for the Clean Choice option is relatively small, you can bet that a good many of them are E-litists. And New York is not the only state with a green power option. An article in *Vanity Fair* says that utility companies in 35 states currently offer green-power pricing plans.[10]

> In one of life's little ironies, solar power is gaining a toehold in the most unlikely of places—the world of SUVs, big-screen TVs, and two-fridge families—the 'burbs. And if it can gain acceptance there, some analysts say, the technology is on the cusp of widespread acceptance.
>
> **Christian Science Monitor, 2/12/04**

> Most of our grid-tied customers [those with solar panels plus a link to public fossil fuel plants] today are people with multiple TVs, pools, even luxury homes.
>
> **Sam Nutter, Massachusetts Technology Collaborative**

For a long time, hard-core environmentalists have also been exploring various ways in which they might create their own energy—from installing solar panels on their roofs to spearheading the creation of wind farms. These concepts have now begun to take root among E-litists. Building a new home with solar panels can add $20,000 to its cost, limiting the technology generally to the well-to-do. But many states offer programs to help defer the cost and allow homes with solar panels to remain connected to the grid. Which means that E-litists, with their energy-intensive lifestyles (computers, air conditioners, etc.) no longer need to shy away from solar power for fear that they will not produce enough electricity. The federal government is doing its part to help "wind entrepreneurs."

There are billions of dollars in subsidies and tax credits available to those who install their own wind power stations (for example, a windmill).[11] Though wind power now produces less than 1 percent of U.S. electricity, some of the wealthiest E-litists have begun installing private wind farms on their estates. Public wind power, however, remains something of a political football for E-litists. Several states (including Virginia, New York, New Jersey, Maryland, Massachusetts, and Delaware) are exploring proposals for offshore wind farms, but these projects have drawn strong opposition from the affluent shoreline residents who contend that the wind farms would mar the natural beauty of the coastlines and damage property values, tourism, and recreation.[12] As of this writing, not one offshore wind farm has actually been built in the United States.

Overall, though not necessarily willing to selflessly sacrifice personal comfort for the good of the planet, E-litists clearly are interested in doing what they can to conserve energy. Because they have the incomes to explore options that don't necessarily save them money, but allow them to showcase their green values, E-litists are at the forefront of many green transformations that will one day soon become more cost-effective and thus trickle down to the mainstream.

MARKETPLACE EVIDENCE

OZOcar
Car services are notorious for sending a black Lincoln Town Car to pick up customers, but E-litists in New York City turn to OZOcar. It's New York's first all-hybrid car service. Clients still ride in style, though it's a nongas-guzzling style. The company's fleet of Toyota Priuses comes complete with leather seats, Wi-Fi, and Sirius satellite radio. Even better, the price runs about the same as traditional car services. Check it out at www.ozocar.com

E-LITISTS AND TRAVEL

Ecotourism has become a major trend in travel.

Amy Ziff, Travelocity editor-at-large (from Business Wire, 4/18/05)

For most E-litists, the first introduction to travel-with-a-conscience was probably back in the late 90s, when it became commonplace among trendy hotels like South Beach's The Delano to place little cards in the rooms which allowed guests to request that sheets and towels not be washed every day, thereby conserving water. Today, E-litists are going to greater lengths to bring their green lifestyle attitude on the road with them. Instead of just taking small steps to minimize their environmental impact while traveling, many E-litists are choosing vacations that revolve around helping the planet or at least that celebrate environmental awareness. Of course, the usual E-litist requirements apply: the vacation must first and foremost be relaxing, indulgent, and luxurious.

E-LITIST HOT SPOTS

If you're wondering where E-litists travel to indulge their hedonistic green selves, check out these uber eco-destinations (as featured in a 2006 issue of *Plenty* magazine):

Canadian Mountain Holidays (candianmountainholidays.com)
Located in the western province of Alberta, this collection of remote mountain lodges seeks to minimize traveler's negative impact on the environment. Gas is piped, rather than shipped in, and the group makes ecological demands on all its suppliers.

3 Rivers Eco Lodge in Dominica (3riversdominica.com)
Dominica is the only Caribbean island to be completely eco-certified, and 3 Rivers is one of the best options on the island for enjoying paradise without the guilt.

The Kandalama Hotel in Sri Lanka (aitkenspencehotels.com)
Situated on a mountain lake, The Kandalama is surrounded by a wildlife reserve and is Green Globe 21-certified (see below).

The Zion Lodge in Zion, Utah (zionlodge.com)
This sanctuary in Zion National Park features more than 146,000 acres of cliffs, canyons, diverse plants, and animal life and is run by Xanterra, a company that tries to incorporate sustainability and conservation in its resorts and destinations.

Many services have sprung up to help E-litists travel green without forcing them to undertake a lot of research themselves. Founded in 1998, Green Map System (GMS) is an international organization that sponsors and encourages the creation of city maps that highlight environmental sites of interest. At a glance, these maps tell visitors which regions are doing a better job of sustainable energy consumption and/or production, sites of environmental interest to visit (green markets, museums, etc.), and the location of successful green initiatives they might want to replicate in their own city. There are approximately 250 different city maps currently published, with another 100 in the works, each one the result of a locally driven process, but created under the aegis of GMS. For more information, visit GreenMap.org.

The travel industry also has a certifying body somewhat analogous to the building industry's LEED certification. Green Globe 21 is a worldwide benchmarking and certification program for sustainable travel and tourism, developed at the 1992 Earth Summit in Rio de Janeiro. Hotels and resorts that are Green Globe 21-certified have met a certain number of environmental requirements, and are reassessed yearly to ensure compliance. The Green Globe 21 program not only encourages travelers to be conservers of the environment, but it also supports economically responsible tourism which respects and preserves (and supports financially) the well-being of indigenous peoples.

MARKETPLACE EVIDENCE

Hilton
The Hilton Vancouver Washington is one of the few hotels outside of eco-lodges that considers itself "green." The first hotel to become LEED-certified, it received an award for its environmental features from the Washington State Hotel and Lodging Association and features a heat-reflecting white roof, landscaping with native plants, and an air recycling system. Green visitors with electric cars can even plug them into specially designed outlets in the hotel's state-of-the-art eco-friendly parking garage. Even the construction of the Vancouver Hilton is environmentally friendly: Local material was used in order to cut down on transporting and fuel costs, and all waste materials were recycled.

E-LITIST HALL OF FAME

A number of celebrities and organizations are responsible for helping to drive forward movements that have inspired the E-litist C-Type. As consumers of popular media, E-litists respond favorably to eco-minded brands endorsed by celebrities or notable charities (those with high visibility and prestige). The following are just some of these entities, along with their E-litist claim to fame:

Laurie David
Best known as the wife of Larry David (*Seinfeld*, *Curb Your Enthusiasm*), Laurie David is a talent booker turned environmental crusader. A committed recycler, David is credited for turning the green movement into a celebrity cause. In 2005, she worked to incorporate environmental topics into television shows. And she produced the documentary *An Inconvenient Truth*, starring Al Gore.

Al Gore
Long known for his green activism, Gore made a big eco-splash in 2006 with his feature film documentary *An Inconvenient Truth*. Opening to (mostly) rave reviews, the film was also "impressive in attracting large audiences to theaters—especially the elusive 'sophisticated' adult audience."[13]

The Sierra Club
Less radical and more easily embraced by mainstream consumers than Greenpeace, the Sierra Club has long been able to mobilize individual Americans, E-litists among them. Since massaging its image in recent years, to become less left of center and instead more E-litist, the group's popularity has soared.

The World Wildlife Fund (WWF)
Who can resist the cute panda? That icon, adorning every piece of literature sent out by the World Wildlife Fund (plus being a conservation leader for more than 40 years) puts the WWF on the top of every E-litist's charitable giving list. In addition to protecting endangered species and their habitats, WWF is also addressing global threats such as pollution and overfishing. Recently the WWF has also under-

gone the same image shift as The Sierra Club, shedding an overly strident image for a more populist, we're-in-this-together stance.

Robert F. Kennedy, Jr.
A staunch defender of the environment, Kennedy is chief prosecuting
attorney for Riverkeeper, an environmental neighborhood watch program that protects the nation's waters. Kennedy has also worked on
environmental issues across the United States, Canada, and Latin
America. The New York City watershed agreement, which he negoti-
ated on behalf of environmentalists and watershed consumers, is regarded as an international model in sustainable development.

MARKETING TO E-LITISTS: A CHECKLIST

☑ Cost is not the bottom line. Style, status, and bragging rights are.

☑ Luxury is not a dirty word.

☑ E-litists believe in their ideals—but they won't suffer for them.

☑ Make it "easy to be green." Do not underestimate the value of ease-of-use, convenience, look, design, and emotional appeal.

☑ Every brand can be a bit greener.

☑ Companies and brands that have solid green credentials need to consider the aesthetic factor. (Could your packaging, product feel, product attributes, and/or marketing or advertising campaign use a face-lift?)

☑ E-litists like to be recognized as marketplace leaders.

☑ Traditional green movement authorities and organizations may be too left of center to have clout with an E-litist.

☑ Celebrate the sexy side of "green-friendly" ingredients.

☑ A compelling brand backstory is as important as the product and/or service you deliver.

DIG A LITTLE DEEPER
FURTHER RESOURCES ON E-LITISTS

E-litists in Print

Plenty magazine

This slick media entry hit newsstands in January 2005, promising readers that, "If we, as individuals and as a society, make the right choices, we can still have a world of PLENTY." The ensuing issues have delivered on that promise, outlining exactly how to enjoy fashion, food, and design without disrespecting the planet. "[*Plenty* magazine] unabashedly tries to celebrate both sustainability and abundance," said respected environmental writer Joel Makower, on his blog (see below).

The Healthy Home: Beautiful Interiors That Enhance the Environment and Your Well-Being by Jackie Craven

Conscious Style Home: Eco-Friendly Living for the 21st Century by Danny Seo

Both these books, illustrated with glossy color photographs worthy of a décor magazine, can help guide consumers to the perfect E-litist interior, one that's as elegant as it is natural, and manages to still honor the earth.

Eco Chic: Organic Living by Rebecca Tanqueray

A complete guide to living an environmentally conscious life, covering food and drink, interior design, health and beauty, and fashion. Tanqueray shows readers how they can look after their bodies and the environment without sacrificing style.

Big and Green: Toward Sustainable Architecture in the 21st Century by David Gissen

Eco-Tech: Sustainable Architecture and High Technology by Catherine Slessor

The first of these two books examines the history and engineering technology behind sustainable, earth-friendly skyscrapers, with specific discussions about recent high-profile examples. The second is much lighter on text, but is lavishly illustrated with beautiful photographs of these examples and more by photographer John Linden.

Real Food: What to Eat and Why by Nina Planck

Previously a successful manager of urban green markets, Planck has poured her life experience into this not-quite-cookbook. She outlines her theory that most food products introduced in the modern era can't hold a candle to their old-world all-natural counterparts. "Planck links good nutrition to sensible enjoyment of food in all its variety," said Mark Knoblauch of the American Library Association.

PERIODICAL PICK OF THE DECADE

Green never looked as good as it did in the May 2006 issue of *Vanity Fair*, which was, appropriately, dubbed the magazine's first green issue. Not only was the magazine's text printed in lovely shades of green, the cover models included beautiful people (and celebrity E-litists) George Clooney and Julia Roberts. The issue replaced *Vanity Fair*'s usual blend of pop journalism and celebrity interviews with some grim revelations of what the world will look like if we continue on the environmentally dangerous path most of us are taking.

E-litists on the Air

The Lazy Environmentalist

This nationally broadcast radio show airing weekly on Sirius Satellite Radio and LIME Radio informs listeners about cutting-edge, eco-friendly products and services.

NPR (National Public Radio)

This internationally acclaimed nonprofit radio network offers news, talk, and entertainment programming for an educated, cultured audience of 26 million Americans each week, and regularly features news items and commentaries on issues of environmental interest.

E-litists Online

Treehugger.com

This site's motto is, "The future is green. Find it here." For design-obsessed E-litists this is the first stop on the Web. Treehugger can connect them to everything from an ultra-chic eco-crib to an "ethically made" wedding dress and even an eco-vacation. One indication that the site targets E-litists and not real tree huggers? One of its product categories is titled "cool but ugly." Green absolutists wouldn't care.

Haworth.com

This is the online home of global office furniture and architectural interior expert Haworth. The company has more than 250 patents under its belt, and more than 50 LEED-certified professionals on staff to help E-litist remodelers who log on looking for eco-solutions.

Alonovo.com

This site's tagline is, "Social Values-Guided Shopping," and it promises to help E-litist consumers make a statement with every purchase. Alonovo matches buyers with products and companies that share their values, and every product comes with a "values rating." Each vendor listed also gets a "company report card," outlining how that company fares on social responsibility, healthy environment, fair workplace, business ethics, and customer commitment.

idealbite.com

"We know that you would just love to 'do the right thing' for yourself and the planet" runs the home page copy of idealbite.com, "if it were convenient, fun, inexpensive, and made you feel good." Sounds like a perfect pitch to E-litists. The site offers a free, daily e-mail tip with ideas on what to do and buy (although most of the products it recommends tend to come with a premium price tag). "Ideal Bite has come along at the right time, with the right attitude. Relevant tips and insight on how to live a green life, without giving up style or creature comforts," writes site user Kim Hoffman, of San Francisco.

Gaiam.com
Ecowise.com

These online lifestyle companies offer a little bit of everything. Users can shop for a set of organic cotton bath towels or nontoxic cleaners, or peruse the many articles and links to learn more about environmental issues and how to live an eco-healthy life.

GREEN BLOG: MAKOWER.COM

The Associated Press has called Joel Makower, "The guru of green business practices," and it would be hard to disagree. He is the founder and executive editor of GreenBiz.com, as well as Climate-Biz.com and GreenerBuildings.com, and he is also cofounder and principal of Clean Edge Inc., a research and publishing firm focusing on building markets for clean energy technologies. His blog consists of daily news captures, as well as his informed and generous personal take on the state of the globe.

NOTES

1. *The New York Times*, 5/14/06
2. 2006 study by the Oklahoma Recycling Association, *The Oklahoman*, 7/17/05
3. *Newswire*, 3/13/06
4. Organic Exchange, 2005
5. Organic Trade Association, 2006
6. U.S. Market for Natural Personal Care Products Show
7. *Knight-Ridder Tribune Business News*, 3/25/06
8. *Business West*, 5/2/05
9. University of California, Davis, study on Toyota Prius and Honda Civic and Insight drivers, 2004–2005
10. *Vanity Fair*, May 2006
11. *The Seattle Times*, 4/25/06
12. *Pittsburgh Post-Gazette*, 2/28/05
13. Indiewire.com, 6/13/06

ANALYZING UNIVERSAL ASPECTS OF CONSUMER LIFE

3.1 THE PSYCHE CONSTRUCT

Consumer typing is an invaluable tool when it comes to sorting a mass of undifferentiated consumers into comprehensible and, more importantly, usable cohorts. Starting without preconceptions allows you to make connections and see similarities that sometimes transcend obvious commonalities like age or economic status. But there is a different, narrower kind of consumer typing that can also prove valuable upon occasion. It's a sort of filtered typing, using one universal aspect of life as a screen. Only attitudes and behaviors relating to this universal aspect are considered, and consumers are then grouped and typed according to these.

What do we mean by a "universal aspect"? It's something we all deal with—interact with—and usually every day. An aspect of life like food or sex. (Okay, sex might not be a daily occurrence for everybody, but even a lack thereof affects thoughts and behaviors.) We've also used less primal aspects as screens, things like interactive technologies, health care, or fashion. It's often amazing, and instructive, to see how this sort of typing can make strange bedfellows (so to speak) by joining consumers who would never belong to the same C-Type into a shared category.

We call these shared categories Consumer Psyches, and we've included two collections of them in this chapter, based around food and sex. Obviously Psyches are not multidimensional (in fact, by definition, they are unidimensional), but since they succinctly and handily represent how consumers please their appetites for sex and for food in the context of the world today, we think they will prove useful for marketers across many categories. Remember, we're not talking about sexual persuasion here, or the obesity epidemic, but rather the multitudinous ways consumers can react and behave given the same basic stimuli.

So how do Psyches relate to C-Types? It's simple. Each of us contains multitudes. So while Karma Queens have a clear approach to food (eating organic, etc.), Karma Queen Jane may also be an avid foodie, who can't get enough of watching the Food Network, while Karma Queen Joan may always be on a diet. Similarly, Geek God Harvey may be a Functional Eater who simply wants to get nourishment quickly and efficiently with little concern for the hedonics of the experience, while Geek God Henry is a Young Man in the Kitchen who likes to cook elaborate meals for his girlfriend. C-Types are full-bodied portraits driven by the complexity of consumers; Psyches are behaviors driven by emotional and physical needs.

The basis for what you're about to read, however, is the same as for the C-Types. The Psyches described below are the ones that have risen to the top as we've gone about our consumer research over the past decade. Some had their genesis in an interesting consumer behavior or activity we read about in a leading-edge publication. Others came to our attention through the hundreds of expert interviews we've conducted or emerged during our interactions with consumers themselves.

3.2 Portfolio of Sex Psyches

Everybody knows that "sex sells." Who said it first? It really doesn't matter. It was already implicit in Eden, when the snake picked Eve to be a spokesperson for the apple. From that day forward, humans' sex practices have run the gamut from exuberantly kinky to boring to nonexistent—the Marquis de Sade to Queen Victoria to the Pope. The trouble for marketers was identifying consumers' Psyches from their outward appearance. (Queen Victoria did have nine children with Prince Albert; clearly *some* sort of mojo was working in their bedroom. And as for de Sade, isn't it said that people talk loudest about what they don't do?)

Today, thanks to the Internet, anyone can easily learn about the habits and behaviors of their neighbors, aligning with others who have similar predilections or exploring the dark recesses of their own desire. Confirmed by this sense of community, what once may have seemed odd or extreme sexual behavior now seems less so. And with increased visibility and awareness also comes greater scope for those who would use sex to sell.

While by and large most of our work has skirted product categories directly related to sexuality, we have conducted more than a few projects in which sex and sexual behavior were topics du jour (projects relating to health care, fragrance, and the like). What follows is our peek through the keyhole, highlighting some of the more interesting and surprising Sex Psyches that have emerged in our current, post-sexual-revolution America.

Sexy Seniors

Sex is definitely not just for the well-chiseled guys and curvy women in various states of undress featured in most of today's perfume ads. There's a whole group of older Americans who are sexually active, who approach sex with the same energy and gusto that their younger counterparts do, or perhaps even more. Pop culture has noticed. In the 2004 film *Meet the Fockers*, it's the grown son (Ben Stiller) who's embarrassed by the pro-sex antics of his parents (Barbra Streisand and Dustin Hoffman). The phrase-turned-title *Still Doing It* is so popular recently that it's been snapped up for both a new book (about 60+ sexuality) and a new documentary (about female seniors' sex lives). With the leading edge of the mammoth Baby Boom generation now hitting 60, the number of Sexy Seniors is only going to increase.

Primers

Not quite old enough to be called seniors but definitely not 22 either, these women (often referred to as Cougars) are independent, healthy single women in their middle years who are still very much on the prowl for sex. Primers (in "the prime of their lives") take a page from the hordes of middle-aged men who date women 10 or 20 years their junior and look for partners much younger than themselves. Demi Moore is a poster child for this Psyche, having traded in Bruce Willis (7 years her senior) for Ashton Kutcher (16 years her junior). But she's not alone. A 2003 AARP survey found that 34 percent of women ages 40 to 69 were dating younger men (3 percent date men 15 or more years younger, 5 percent date men 10 to 14 years younger, and 11 percent date men 5 to 9 years younger). An article entitled, "Older Women Seeking Relationships with Younger Men," sums up the Primer ideal neatly. "Older women pairing up with younger men is becoming mainstream, barely raising eyebrows as women in great shape and good health find themselves attracted to men sometimes young enough to be their sons. All those Baby Boomer girls who watched Anne Bancroft seduce Dustin Hoffman in the 1967 film *The Graduate* are middle-aged and trying out May-December relationships for themselves."[1] Whatever the reason, this is one sex psyche that appears to have legs.

Celibatarians

Whether married or single, some consumers have decided to opt out of sex altogether. The National Health and Social Life Survey, although conducted back in 1992 (it hasn't been attempted again, yet), showed that nearly one-third of 18- to 59-year-olds have sex a few times per year or not at all.[2] Some Celibatarians may have lost desire for their mates but decide to remain in the relationships anyway. (There are estimates that up to 20 percent of all marriages are low- or no-sex, and the book *The Sex-Starved Marriage* hit number three on Amazon.com's bestseller list, which has to mean something!)[3] Others choose celibacy for religious or moral reasons. Lauren Winner recently wrote a book *Real Sex: The Naked Truth about Chastity* (Brazos Press, 2006) to convince her devout but sophisticated young Christian brethren that "just saying no" can be hip. The lead singer of Weezer, Rivers Cuomo, proved that even a rock star can forgo sex, having recently made good on his vow of two years of celibacy. For some Celibatarians, celibacy is merely a transitory state, due to a stressful period in their lives or general exhaustion. For others it is a lifelong choice. One thing is certain; thanks to the choice they've made, Celibatarians have more time to devote to the rest of their interests and activities!

Cuddlers

You can find their ads on craigslist requesting partners for cuddling rather than sex or spot them at any of the nationwide Cuddle Parties where groups of adults snuggle and hug under the watchful eye of "lifeguards" who make sure everyone's following the rules in the cuddle pool. (Those rules, according to www.cuddleparty.com, are designed "to create an event for adults to get together and explore affectionate touch and communication without it becoming sexualized.' ") In case you think this behavior is too mild to belong in a roundup of sex Psyches, here's what Helen Fisher, author of *The Anatomy of Love: A Natural History of Mating, Marriage, and Why We Stray* (Ballantine Books, 1994), has to say on the subject: "Human skin is like a field of grass, each blade a nerve ending so sensitive that the slightest graze can etch into the human brain a memory of the moment." Cuddling may not really count as a sexual activity, but on the plus side it's a feel-good activity that two strangers can share without a trace of guilt.

Testosterone Babes

These women, usually under 35, enjoy a night out at a strip club or watching a wet T-shirt contest at a local bar as much as they would a night with girlfriends watching chick flicks. In part, the Testosterone Babe attitude is a strategy for overcoming chauvinist pigs by beating men at their own game, that is, "You can't objectify me because I objectify myself first!" Some women become Testosterone Babes because they think it's fun and subversive to act as wild and sex-crazy as men often do, or they think it's a good way to garner attention from guys. Ariel Levy, author of the book *Female Chauvinist Pigs: Women and the Rise of Raunch Culture* sees this behavior as decidedly two-dimensional, saying these women either act like "a cartoon man—who drools over strippers, says things like 'check out that ass,' and brags about having the 'biggest c–k in the building'—or like a cartoon woman, who has big cartoon breasts, wears little cartoon outfits, and can only express her sexuality by spinning around a pole"[4] Others see this Psyche as a logical next step for feminism—women finally owning and exploiting their own sexuality. Whatever your view, in a world growing increasingly raunchy, Testosterone Babes are unlikely to disappear anytime soon.

Creative Counters

There is still a strong sexual double standard when it comes to racking up conquests. Sexually prolific men don't mind their labels—stud (well, who would?) or player—but many of their female counterparts will do anything to keep from being a tramp. (Well, they'll do anything save abstinence; the last thing anyone wants to appear to be is a prude.) Some Creative Counters take refuge in the widespread use of the term "hooking up" (so vague that it can apply to just about anything from French kissing to actual intercourse). This easily bandied-about catchall allows her to compete in the bragging game while keeping her number of real sex partners (read: intercourse) within the bounds of respectability. It isn't unheard of for a Creative Counter to sleep with an ex-boyfriend rather than an exciting new prospect just to avoid adding another dreaded notch to her belt. (There is still some debate about how many notches are acceptable for a woman, but some have put it at any number that's at least two fewer than one's future spouse.) In their own way, Creative Counters are as sexually liberated as their 60s compatriots—they just choose to hide that fact. They may not like the system, but they've found a way to beat it.

Modified Monogamists

Modified Monogamists are in committed relationships (marriage or its equivalent), but they have romantic relationships outside it with their partner's consent. Call it neo-swinging or polyamory, the important fact is that regardless of the sexual acts committed by either partner, the original relationship still holds. The best guess—and that's all it is, because research is so sparse—is that somewhere between 2 and 10 percent of married couples in the United States have done something that could be called swinging. (Even if it's the smaller figure, that amounts to over a million couples. There are approximately 500 swinging clubs operating around the United States, or at least that many registered on nasca.com, a Web site devoted to linking up like-minded Modified

Monogamists with each other.) The Web is one of the major factors for some couples in making the choice to pursue alternative sexual outlets. Now partners for whatever sort of activity this Psyche has in mind can be found quickly and easily from the comfortable safety of home. According to psychologists and marriage experts, this behavior can be healthy for a stable relationship. One study found that Modified Monogamist couples stay together just as long as nonswinging ones, and with a higher level of marital satisfaction.[5] Considering that almost half of all marriages end in divorce, perhaps this Psyche has something to teach the rest of us.

Benefriends

These younger consumers are redefining the boundaries of sexual relationships. Benefriends socialize in male/female "packs," platonic social groupings that in themselves have no sexual overtones. However, within these packs various individuals generally choose one or two members to experiment with sexually. According to a 2003 survey by national research group Child Trends, the number of high school seniors who say they never go on one-on-one dates rose from 14 percent in 1993 to 25 percent that year. Among sophomores, their younger counterparts, 37 percent never go on one-on-one dates.[6] The key thing about Benefriends' sexual episodes when they do occur is that it's understood by both parties that there are no strings attached. These casual hookups appear to be becoming the norm rather than the exception: one study found that 61.7 percent of students on one college campus reported having at least one "friend with benefits" relationship, while a 2005 *People Magazine*/NBC News survey revealed that 46 percent of teens had oral sex or sexual intercourse in an otherwise casual relationship.[7] Opinions are sharply divided as to whether this new behavior is healthy or morally dubious, but for Benefriends, the notion of committing to a monogamous relationship seems outmoded or something they'll get to when they find the right person.

Kiss and Bloggers

What's the harm in a little kiss and tell, you ask? Well, what if the teller has an audience of thousands? As noted in the chapter on Innerpreneurs, there are now about 40 million active blogs in the United States, most of which are personal journals.[8] The question always is *how* personal? While a goodly number of bloggers include their romantic lives in the activities they chronicle, Kiss and Bloggers take this behavior to the extreme. They regale their readers with extremely detailed accounts of the what, when, why, and how of their sex lives. Sometimes they'll employ code names to protect the "who" but not always or not always successfully. In the case of former Capitol Hill intern Jessica Cutler, when her blog *Washingtonienne* featured thinly veiled accounts of her escapades with a fellow staffer (among others), it cost her a job. (It also won her a six-figure book deal and a contract with Sarah Jessica Parker's production company for HBO, but that's beside the point.) So be careful what you say or do on that next date. You may end up reading about it later, along with anyone with an Internet connection. Even if Kiss and Bloggers decide later to delete the entry about you, it will live on in Google's memory, wayback machines, and screen captures—at a rough estimate—forever.

Educated Sexplorers

When we want a higher test score or to master a challenging yoga position, we turn to education to make us better, stronger, or smarter. So it should come as no surprise to learn that some consumers seek out the same sort of help in achieving mind-blowing orgasms or new tricks to ensnare (or keep) the perfect lover. Perhaps it's a sign of our competitive times: simple competence is no longer enough; now we all have to be experts. Or at least Educated Sexplorers feel they do. A search for sex and "self-help" on Google will garner well over 7 million results; the same search on Amazon.com will bring you such titles as *The Lowdown on Going Down* or *Scientifically Guaranteed Male Multiple Orgasms* plus hundreds of others. The information is out there, and Educated Sexplorers can't get enough. The Sinclair Institute's "Better Sex" videos have sold over 4 million copies since 1991, and nationwide, sexual health experts are instructing on everything from the Kama Sutra to g-spot location techniques to the importance of emotional intimacy in a sexual relationship. Whether all this information leads to better sex or just to overly analytical lovemaking, we're not in a position to say.

Butterflies

We had to wait for a female surgeon general before we got a government official ballsy enough to speak about the importance of onanism (or spanking the monkey or diddling the skittle or any euphemism you like). Of course, Jocelyn Elders's frankness eventually contributed to her losing her job, but the Butterflies of America clearly got the message. Masturbation, historically considered the provenance of men, has in the last few years been revealed as the universal activity it was always meant to be. Studies suggest that anywhere from between 41 and 63 percent of women now jill off (as opposed to jack off, which only applies to boys) regularly.[9] Younger women are particularly comfortable with the idea of self-gratification and can be found casually perusing the aisles of their local drugstores (which now often stock "personal vibrating massagers"—talk about a euphemism—and all manner of lube). For Butterflies who want a little luxury for their solitary endeavors, there are even women-focused boutiques like Babeland (in New York and Los Angeles). High-end products like expensive vibrators and tactile toys are the norm there, and women are encouraged to browse and touch before they buy.

3.3 PORTFOLIO OF FOOD PSYCHES

Since we opened our doors in 1991, we've probably done more work in helping develop new food and drink products than anything else. In pursuit of the next, the new, and the no-no's of this arena, we've eaten with consumers (in all sorts of restaurants), filmed ethnographic interviews in the homes of consumers, talked to leading nutrition experts and dietitians, and toured forward-thinking food-related venues across the country. In this way we've stayed on top of the emerging trends shaping the landscape. (The "trans fat scare" was visible on the leading edge long before it made the cover of national magazines. The trend we now have our eye on is biodynamic farming.) But also in the course of these projects, we realized that this most basic and primal of human needs brings out many aspects of consumers' personalities, revealing more about them than just the way their taste buds lean. We decided to try to bucket consumers according to their similarities in how they thought about the need to nourish themselves. And in doing so, some fun and fascinating consumer Psyches surfaced (alongside the more obvious ones. The biggest movement in the food world, the organic revolution, is now so large it crosses many, many Psyches and C-Types, and therefore doesn't make an appearance in the list below).

Foodies
These eaters are at the top of the food chain—or at least at the top of the food-lovers chain, so to speak. Nobody takes food as seriously as they do, or can equal their comprehensive knowledge of world cuisines, spices, or preparation techniques. Foodies eat out more than average consumers do, which helps them stay on top of the very latest in trendy ingredients and cutting-edge cooking styles. Currently they're devotees of molecular gastronomy, a sophisticated cooking style in which chefs use dehydrators or powerful food processors to alter the texture of various foods. Eating in restaurants also allows them to enjoy food the way they feel it should be enjoyed, as part of a total experience encompassing presentation, aroma, and ambiance. And they're not shy about telling the rest of us what they've found. Sometimes it seems that every Foodie is embracing their inner Frank Bruni these days (Bruni is head restaurant reviewer for the *New York Times*) detailing his or her culinary obsessions or adventures on a food blog or writing the mini-reviews appended to restaurant listing on sites like citysearch.com or menupages.com. What all this means is that the rest of us need never again try a new bistro blind or make a trip to the supermarket without insight into the best variety of lettuce. Next time you meet a Foodie, say thanks!

Locavores
In 2005, four San Francisco eaters challenged themselves to consume only foodstuffs that came from within a 100-mile radius of where they live. They also started a Web site, which they called Locavores. The name pretty much says it all: herbivores eat plants; carnivores eat meat; locavores eat only food that's local. The purpose of the Locavore move-

ment is to encourage people to eat from the bioregion in which they live. (Much of the food most of us eat has traveled up to 1,500 miles to reach our kitchens, losing flavor and nutrients or requiring stabilizers and additives to make the trip.) Farmers markets are a great example of this thinking, and there are now more farmers markets in more cities and towns than ever before. But the Locavore mandate is as much something to be aimed for as it is something to achieve: Even if you can't only eat food that has come from within a 100-mile radius of your home, Locavores hope that you attempt to do so. They believe the vigilance it takes to at least ascertain where the foods you put in your mouth come from will be enough, over time, to effect a culturewide shift in the way all food is produced and purchased.

Fire Men

These asbestos-tongued guys seek out the spiciest foods they can find. For them it's about testing their limits as much as any culinary pleasure they derive from the experience. According to the trend-tracking Center for Culinary Development in San Francisco, ". . . there's little doubt, the American consumer is demanding more intense, less familiar flavors."[10] Even though American men *and* women are enjoying spicier foods than in years past, an appreciation of the very hottest hot sauces and dishes still seems to be a boy's club. The membership of the Chile-Heads ("a group of friendly, helpful individuals who share one unique trait: they just can't get enough of that Hot and Spicy food!") is 85 percent male. And the Patron Saint of this capsicum-obsessed subculture is Dave Hirschkop, author of *Crazy from the Heat: Dave's Insanity Cookbook* and creator of "Insanity Hot Sauce" (touted as the hottest hot sauce in the universe, and proudly featuring "the same ingredients as pepper spray").

Calorie Restrictors

The most extreme of the calorie-counting brigade, the desire of Calorie Restrictors is not to lose pounds or maintain current weight, but to extend their lives past 120 years. They're not crazy; there is some scientific evidence that being slightly underweight might contribute to longevity.

Tests have revealed that cholesterol and blood sugar levels can be vastly lowered after an extended time of caloric restriction, and a study by the Calorie Restriction Society revealed that 41- to 65-year-olds who ingested between only 1,200 and 2,000 calories a day for six years had hearts that functioned, on average, like persons 15 years younger.[11] Members of this Psyche often appear to be ill, they're so painfully skinny, but if they're right, they'll most certainly have the last laugh—about, oh, 80 years from now.

PC-tarians

For this Psyche "the personal is political" isn't an aphorism, it's a diet plan. For PC-tarians, the chicken must be free range, the beef grass-fed, and the vegetables local (and picked by laborers earning fair wages!). PC-tarians are as concerned about the health and well-being of fruit growers and migrant workers as they are about risks of ingesting pesticides from the fruit itself. A trip to the grocery store with a PC-tarian (or more likely, a trip to the health food store and/or local farmers market) can mean a crash course in the world's social ills. Or you could just pick up a copy of Jay Weinstein's *The Ethical Gourmet: How to Enjoy Great Food That Is Humanely Raised, Sustainable, Nonendangered, and That Replenishes the Earth*. Presumably "that Tastes Good" couldn't fit on the cover, too.

Spiritual Eaters

What would Jesus eat? Probably not the high-fat, high-salt, high-carb diet popular among some of his followers today. Hence the thinking behind recent bestsellers, *The Maker's Diet* by Jordan S. Rubin and *Body by God: The Owner's Manual for Maximized Living* by Dr. Ben Lerner. Lest you think these authors are only interested in saving souls, note that Rubin also markets a line of products and supplements which he claims netted him $60 million in 2005.[12] Since moral support can be important to those trying to make the lifestyle changes involved in weight loss, it's not surprising that local churches are getting into the diet business too. One of the largest programs, First Place, which started in 1981, is now working in 12,000 churches worldwide, offering participants a member's kit ($80) and a Bible study food guide ($20) which look to the content of the Bible for dining rules that early Christians were likely to have followed.[13] Some Spiritual Eaters eschew all the products, however, and depend instead on the time-tested power of prayer to help fight delicious temptations. After all, if faith can fight the devil, why not devil's food cake?

Paleodieters

The human body hasn't changed much in the past 10,000 years, but according to Colorado State University researcher Loren Cordain (author of a series of Paleo Diet books, and an expert on the diets of early humans) 70 percent of our daily calories come from foods our ancestors ate rarely, if at all. With obesity on the rise and diseases associated with aging, such as diabetes and hypertension showing up in preteens, it doesn't take a genius to figure out that something about the modern diet has to change. It turns out that a degree in anthropology may be more useful in this regard than one in nutrition. Paleodieters believe that the solution is to focus on foods that would have been regularly foraged by our ancient ancestors, things like fresh fruits, vegetables, and meat from lean, wild animals. Modern (well, relatively speaking) foods like dairy, nuts, and grains, for instance, not to mention trans fats and artificial sweeteners, turn out to be harder for the human body to digest. Paleodieters claim that by giving their bodies what they were designed to handle, they'll subsequently improve their health. The moral? Move forward, but look back.

Functional Eaters

Food can be sensuous—a delicious flavor, creamy mouth-feel, or tantalizing aroma. Those are probably the first things you notice. But tasting good is, in reality, the least important factor when it comes to health and nutrition. Functional Eaters try to transcend hedonics, focusing instead on food as fuel, as beauty aid, or as medicine. Members of this Psyche know exactly what berries have the most antioxidants, whose yogurt best aids digestion, and which vegetables are likely to give skin a healthy glow. (This Psyche is particularly prevalent among Baby Boomers determined to stay looking and feeling young.) Functional Eaters drink Pom for the heart health benefit, feast on leafy greens to help stave off cancer, and eagerly snap up bestsellers like *SuperFoods Rx: Fourteen Foods That Will Change Your Life* which claims to have identified nutritional power-houses that are the nutritional equivalent of the fountain of youth, and which will save you from cancer, heart disease, diabetes, and more. Functional Eaters may like the taste of these foods, true, but that's incidental. It's their nutritional benefits that really guarantee them a place on this Psyche's plate.

Moms-to-Be

It may seem like this is a food Psyche that only lasts nine months. But there's more to it than you might think. To begin with, of course, becoming pregnant does impose a new and different set of food-related habits on a woman. Every year the list of foods deemed "possibly dangerous during pregnancy" seems to increase: today's Moms-to-Be need to avoid tuna, shark, swordfish, king mackerel or tilefish (harmful levels of mercury), packaged cold cuts (risk of listeriosis), sushi (let's not even start), Caesar salad dressing (might contain unpasteurized raw egg), and all nuts (inconclusive evidence that suggests a mother's intake of nuts could have an effect on her baby's propensity for food allergies).

Most of these prohibited items make a reappearance after delivery, but the surprising thing is that many of the food habits which Moms-to-Be adopt remain even after giving birth. Pregnant women often begin switching, for the first time, from nonorganic to organic food and drink (especially dairy), and when it comes time to shop for baby, they continue to purchase them. According to a Media Central, Inc., study, sales of organic baby foods are expected to have more than doubled between 2000 and 2006, to over $206 million a year, and new moms make up over a third of consumers buying organic products for the first time.[14]

Urban Farmers

Few debate the benefits of eating foods locally grown and locally farmed. But there are some consumers out there who have taken this notion to the extreme and started growing their own fruits and vegetables — even right in the middle of large metropolitan areas. Advances in gardening technology and design, and new initiatives in progressive city planning, have made urban farming (on rooftops, balconies, and fire escapes) a viable alternative for city dwellers. Omlet, a company out of the United Kingdom, can provide Urban Farmers with an organically reared hen plus portable henhouse (it looks like a large dog carrier) for those who like the idea of fresh eggs every morning. AeroGarden's oxygenated growing chamber (about the size of a breadbox) will let the Urban Farmer grow anything from salad greens to chili peppers right on the kitchen counter. According to the United Nations, 15 percent of the world's food is already grown in urban areas, and that figure is only expected to rise.

Food Questers

These gastronomic adventurers will travel far and wide to sample the best, the most exotic, or the newest—whether that means a day trip to a remote 5-star restaurant 40 miles outside Paris, an 8-day hike through the Bavarian Alps to sample 20 varieties of small-batch beer, or an hour-long subway ride to a little immigrant neighborhood in an outer borough of New York to try a new kind of oxtail soup or pad thai. Food Questers think nothing of planning their entire vacations around food (and drink). According to *Restaurant News* this sort of culinary tourism is already substantially enriching the restaurants (and economies) of Vietnam, Thailand, and other Asian nations.[15] Americans regularly spend more on food than they do on lodging even when traveling domestically ($131 billion in 2004!) according to the Travel Industry Association of America.[16] This Psyche is epitomized by celebrity chef Anthony Bourdain (author of *A Cook's Tour: Global Adventures in Extreme Cuisines*), who showed that Food Questers can often be as influential as they are intrepid. This Psyche delights in sharing its hard-won culinary expertise with the rest of the world and can help in bringing foreign foods and ingredients to mainstream notice.

Posh Presenters

For these women—and they're mostly women—it's as much about how food looks as how it tastes. Inspired by head Posh Presenter Martha Stewart, they'll lavish time and energy on slicing, stacking, swirling, and

fanning out, and lavish their hard-earned dough on all the accoutrements—from exotic garnishes to plates, platters, ladles, and more. The
only qualification to a Posh Presenter's obsessive attention to detail?
These women aim to impress, and pull out all the stops only when it involves guests or a very special occasion.

Bulge Battlers

As the Baby Boom continues to spread (around the middle, that is),
there's a growing number of men fighting the battle of the bulge while
trying to maintain a manly air of indifference to the whole subject. It's
true that more women (51 percent) worry about their weight than men
(32 percent), but that's still nearly a third of men).[17] This is still a country where a "healthy appetite" is regarded as a mark of virility, and where
"watching your weight" is a phrase that carries feminine associations.
Nate Griffin, a former Army sergeant, puts it this way: "To talk about a
diet means you're really weak in a certain area."[18] Because of this cultural bias, Bulge Battlers often diet on the down low, trying to keep their
restricted calorie intake a secret from friends and coworkers. However
they handle it, though, the fact remains that there are more members of
this Psyche with every passing year, and they require new and different
marketing approaches from those for female slimmers.

Unadulterators

Led by food writers like Nina Planck, and dovetailing neatly with the influential slow food movement (which calls for a return to unprocessed,
"real" foods, and currently has 83,000 members worldwide), Unadulterators maintain that currently "taboo" foods, like whole milk, complete
eggs, and (oh, no!) lard, are healthier than skim milk, egg whites, and
reduced-fat margarine. How's that? We'll let an expert explain: "Whole
milk is what is called a complete food, because each ingredient plays its
part. Without the fat, you can't digest the protein or absorb the calcium.
The body needs saturated fat in particular (monounsaturated and
polyunsaturated fat can't do the job) to take in the calcium that makes
bones strong. Milk fat also contains glycosphingolipids, which are fats
that encourage cell metabolism and growth and fight gastrointestinal in-

fections."[19] Unadulterators embrace a diet based on fresh, whole foods — no homogeneous, industrially produced convenience foods for them — and feel that even supposedly bad high-fat, high-cholesterol foods can be the cornerstones of a truly healthy diet.

Gastro Voyeurs

Why cook when you can watch someone else do it? It's a lot easier, and a lot less fattening. Gastro Voyeurs come in all ages, shapes, and sizes, but they're all linked to their TV sets, which are invariably tuned to the Food Network or HGTV. Gastro Voyeurs are certainly interested in learning, be it about different cuisines or professional cooking tips and techniques, but they rarely (if ever) put this knowledge to use. They're neither the most adventurous home cooks nor the main market for high-end ingredients, but they're a powerful demographic when it comes to cookbook sales. They like to look at the pictures. It's understandable that the cookbook section in a bookstore is often derisively called "food porn"! Thanks to this Psyche, Emiril Lagasse is a household name and Rachael Ray (who has a show backed by none other than Oprah Winfrey) regularly receives multimillion-dollar cookbook contracts. Lest you doubt the power of the TV when it comes to cookbooks, 12 of the top 25 cookbooks for 2004 were by just five authors, all of whom have shows on the Food Network.[20] Another trend that also rates a Gastro Voyeur mention is the food photo blog. Thanks to blogs like Triplecreme (www.triplecreme.blogspot.com) or La Tartinbe Gourmande (www.beastkitchen.com/blog), Gastro Voyeurs can salivate at images of perfectly prepared foods even when they're away from the TV.

Young Men in the Kitchen

Women's work? Hardly. Well, okay, across America most meals still reach the table courtesy of mom, but the number of Gen X and Millennial men who are spending their time in the kitchen rather than in the garage is growing. Boosted by a number of high-visibility and "regular guy"-type celebrity chefs like Bobby Flay (*Boy Meets Grill*) and Jamie Oliver (*The Naked Chef*), members of this Psyche have helped make cooking an acceptable way for a man to express his creativity as well as nurture his family (or just pamper himself). They're also responsible, in part, for the current popularity of grilling.

Diet Dilettantes

For these women the question is, "Why should I stick with one diet, when there are so many popular ones to try?" Diet Dilettantes are often completely committed followers and proselytizers for whatever diet they happen to be on that day. Each new diet has its moment, during which Diet Dilettantes can expound on its every facet in detail, and explain why everyone should follow it—and then the next month rolls around. Thus, the Zone Diet gave way to the Atkins diet which gave way to the South Beach diet, and so on. For Diet Dilettantes it's more about novelty than establishing a healthy mode of eating. But their behavior sure helps cookbooks and meal plans fly off the shelves, and helps the $40 billion a year diet industry continue to grow season after season.

FoodPhobes

Bucking the tide of culinary expansion sweeping across the country, these stalwart nonfoodies want nothing but the basics. FoodPhobes' conception of bread doesn't extend beyond white (and preferably presliced), and their idea of cheese is bright orange processed American or maybe, if they're feeling adventurous, cheddar. They're completely uninterested in trying inventive new recipes or any kind of ethnic cuisine, and you should bear in mind that they still regard garlic as a foreign spice. While FoodPhobes are perfectly happy to be left alone (to enjoy their macaroni and cheese), their influence can make life difficult for friends and family planning group meals.

Allergic Abstainers

Allergy rates are rising. Current estimates by the National Institutes of Health have 6 to 7 million Americans, including 2 million school-age children, suffering from some food allergies, or about 1 percent of the total population.[21] This translates into big business. According to Packaged Facts, the total allergen-oriented market is expected to top $4 billion by 2008.[22] Certain food types (dairy, nuts, sulfates, and gluten are some of the biggest) are being regularly cut out of diets around the country. The gluten-free category alone is growing at nearly 15 percent annually, according to San Francisco–based market research group Spins Inc. Even when allergic reactions may be fairly mild, food sensitivities rather than full-on allergies, this Psyche prefers to completely avoid offending foods rather than live with even less-than-severe symptoms.

Flexitarians

Flexitarians is a useful term which has been popularized in the press for the growing ranks of "not-quite" or "sometime" vegetarians. (In fact, it topped the American Dialect Society's 2003 list of new words or phrases which most filled a need.) Margie Roswell, a Baltimore Flexitarian sums up her attitude like this: "I will go 100% vegan for a period of time, but that doesn't mean when I go to my sister's house for Thanksgiving that I won't have part of the turkey."[23] Flexitarians range from consumers who generally follow a vegetarian diet but very occasionally eat fish, to health-conscious eaters who simply try to eat two to three meatless meals a week. While only 3 percent of the U.S. population is strictly vegetarian, Charles Stahler, codirector of the Baltimore-based Vegetarian Resource Group estimates that as much as 40 percent could be considered flexitarian. And for further proof that this crossover lifestyle is flexing (forgive the pun) its muscle: the formerly vegan *Natural Health* magazine recently started printing some recipes that include meat.

Short-Order Parents

For some time it has been clear that many parents are doing a lot more than getting a decent meal on the table each night—they're getting multiple meals on the table. Declining to fight the age-old battle over what their kids will or won't eat, frustrated parents are giving in and preparing different dishes for each of their kids. The underlying belief seems to be that it's more important that kids eat something than that kids learn to eat what's placed in front of them. Unfortunately, much of what today's kids prefer to eat is not what could strictly be termed healthy, making this parental behavior a likely contributor (one of many) to the current obesity epidemic among youngsters.

NOTES

1. *Arizona Republic*, 7/13/06

2. *Herald News*, 12/21/04

3. *Newsweek*, 6/03, "No Sex, Please, We're Married"

4. *New Statesman*, 10/24/05

5. Electronic Journal of Human Sexuality (vol. 8), 12/05

6. *The Oregonian*, 10/27/05

7. *Boston Herald*, 2/14/05

8. *The New York Times*, 12/19/04

9. *The Janus Report on Sexual Behavior* (John Wiley & Sons, Inc., 1993)

10. *Press Enterprise*, 3/9/05

11. East Bay Express (California), 1/18/06

12. *The New York Times*, 4/28/05

13. *The New York Times*, 4/28/05

14. Organic Trade Association, 8/06

15. *Restaurant News*, 6/27/04

16. *BusinessWeek*, 4/3/06

17. *USA Today*, 4/26/06

18. *Kansas City Star*, 1/31/06

19. Nina Planck, *The New York Times*, 2/12/06

20. *Publisher's Weekly*, 3/21/05

21. *Food Processing*, 4/1/06

22. *Just Food*, 5/06

23. *Kansas City Star*, 11/25/04

C-TYPES
APPLIED

4.1 THE C-TYPE CONSTRUCT IN A WEB-BASED WORLD

Consciously or not, marketers have informally used the notion of consumer typing to make decisions about marketing, advertising, and innovation for a long time. In the late 70s, Revlon introduced its perfume Enjoli with an ad which indelibly defined the Enjoli woman: "I can bring home the bacon/fry it up in a pan/but never ever let you forget you're a man . . . ." The combination of sexpot and career girl that the jingle described, a woman who embraced feminism but secretly feared it might undermine her femininity, was in essence a C-Type, the forerunner of our own Ms. Independent. Outside the bounds of advertising, typing (or in this case, stereotyping, with all the inaccuracy and two-dimensionality that word connotes) has forever been a feature of the schoolyard. Kids define themselves and each other through the use of ritualized types: the geek, the jock, the stoner, the skater, the princess, the goth, and so on. The music industry does much the same thing with artists — it defines music in narrow categories to make it easier to sell to consumers. (Disco never really died, it just got relabeled.) Pop music has always spawned types, from the zoot-suited hep cats of the 40s to today's saggy-jeaned hip-hoppers. Now, neither hep cats nor hip-hoppers are a true C-Type. They're merely cartoons, but they do give you a feeling for how easy it has always been to create a culture-based shorthand for identifying consumers.

The big difference in the world today, and one which has made it possible to not only define true C-Types but to track them, is the Internet. Members of a C-Type cohort can find each other on the Web, and there they can create a cyber world that suits them perfectly. MySpace.com is the best example. With 94 million users as of this writing (almost one-third of the entire U.S. population), the site is the big kid on the cyber block. There consumers can create networks of friends or buddies with shared outlooks, interests, or attitudes, in the process creating perfect marketing niches. This behavior has not gone unnoticed. Mainstream marketers like Toyota and Verizon Wireless have created pages on MySpace to promote their newest products and services. Even the U.S. Marines have joined the club, using the site as one element in their 2006 recruiting drive.[1]

> A decade into the Age of the Graphic Browser Interface, Americans [are] congregating in enormous numbers on websites and other high-tech portals that function much like the institutions they've nudged aside. The culture's being boutiqued or, as the expression goes, "unbundled." Broadcast has given way to a proliferation of narrowcasts.
>
> *Los Angeles Times*, 5/18/05

One of the great advantages the Web has as a marketing tool over older models is its ability to serve a wider population with a broader range of choices. Unlike the limited shelf space of, let's say, even one of the new breed of super-sized bookstores, a Web bookseller can offer every single title in print. Surprisingly, the sales of obscure titles (though each one singularly may only sell one copy per annum) can add up to quite a lot of dollars. This observation, called "The Long Tail" theory of sales, was popularized by Chris Anderson, the editor of *Wired* magazine, in an article in 2004 and in a subsequent book. According to him, niche and specialty items will continue to gain ground at the expense of the mass bestsellers as Web commerce continues to overtake older retail models. It also broadens the opportunity for small yet demographically key C-Types to slowly but surely alter the buying patterns of their online buddies, one buddy at a time. As the years go by, influence on the Web is becoming indistinguishable from influence in the real world.

4.2 HOW TO USE C-TYPES TO SPARK INSIGHT

One of the most valuable ways C-Types can prove useful is as stimulus when you're brainstorming. Try using the C-Types in this book as a backdrop, a thought-starter, as you seek to find creative solutions and genuinely innovative new ideas. There are countless ways. Think about which type is *least* likely to buy your brand. Now try to sell it to them. Or take two types, merge them, and create a new hybrid. What happens when a Karma Queen hooks up with a Geek God? What products would fill their cupboards? What kind of car would they buy? What would their long-range financial plans center on?

Working on developing a new quick casual restaurant concept? Ask your team to articulate specific needs and attitudes that the type would bring to your category.

Imagine your target consumer is a Karma Queen. What would the menu look like? *Wholesome, nutritionally rich source foods that are natural or organic, and a range of herbal teas, fair-trade coffee, vegetarian options, and healthy fresh fruit-based desserts. The atmosphere? Cool, calming, and energetic all in one, with soft paint effects on the walls, comfortable wood furniture, and Moby playing in the background. Maybe there would be a quiet room or reading room included as part of the space.*

Now imagine your target is a Culture Crosser instead. *The place would pulse with interesting music. The décor would be loaded with cool objects that embody the culture crossing code. The menu would be a spin on multiple kinds of ethnic food, across a cultural smattering that would include samplers from all over the world, while the attached bar would be well stocked with both sake and Pabst Blue Ribbon, served by cool mixologists dressed in the latest fashions.*

Layered against your business needs, the C-Types as fodder will bring very different ideas and possibilities to mind. Sifting through and sorting these ideas with respect to your current situation and determining which ones have the most potential for you and your business can turn a simple brainstorming exercise like this into a far-reaching business opportunity.

Here are some examples of more involved ways you can use C-Types to explore your category or brand:

Method Market Research

Lee Strasberg revolutionized the theater world when he created "Method Acting." His theory was that performers need to become the characters they play, immersing themselves in their background and everyday life, so they could respond to stimulus with the emotional and psychological reactions of the character rather than of themselves. Actors like Brando, Hoffman, and Pacino, devotees of the Method, ate, drank, and slept in character while working on a role, even going so far as not to allow people to use their real names, and in doing so reached the pinnacle of their profession.

Consider emulating them and become a Karma Queen, Innerprenuer, Denim Dad, or Geek God for a day, or a week. Think of it as Method Market Research—a way you can truly get inside your target consumer. By forcing yourself to live as your target or type lives, shop where they shop, go through their day as they do, truly live their life, you will become keenly aware of both their functional and emotional needs and key influencers. You will be shocked at what you learn and the insights you will garner. Instead of asking a consumer in focus groups to tell you what she or he cares about, live his or her life for a day and you'll learn firsthand.

Bellwethering

Another way to use C-Types as a tool for generating insight is to think about which ones reflect a leading-edge thinker among a larger target group, an influencer who helps set the trends that mainstream consumers latch on to. Through doing this, you may just leapfrog over the obvious and get to a "thought place" for your brand or target which is significant and breakthrough.

Let's say your brand is aimed at kids, but sold to moms as gatekeeper. Think about the most extreme type of mom, the Parentocrat, and determine how she would react to your current product and the claims that are being made about it. About six years ago, we did exactly this. We sat with a significant player in the snack food industry, trying to help him discover where the category, was going (using the Parentocrat as a backdrop—this is a type that has been on our radar for about a decade), we quickly realized there were two leading-edge notions likely to take hold in the coming years. These were the negatives associated with trans fats and the notion of good fats versus bad fats. As of this writing, the first of these two concepts has already reached a tipping point, while the second still has a way to go to infiltrate the mainstream. Average consumers may not have fully gotten their heads around it, but as we watch the explosion of the nut category, it is just a matter of time until the notion of "good versus bad fats" will be on the tip of every consumer's tongue. But both thoughts were invaluable to our client, who needed to think about product formulation and marketing strategies years in advance.

With this in mind, it is interesting to think about how something moves from leading edge into the mainstream. When does trans fat go from an extreme concern of overly vigilant parents to one that every food marketer takes note of? How does one determine when the time is right to bring these kinds of notions to the fore? If your brand revolves around food or nutrition, then continually tracking Parentocrats and paying attention to the coverage of their concerns in the mainstream media is a good way to start.

Places to begin include niche periodicals like *The Nutrition Action Newsletter*. How do the stories in the magazine match up against a mainstream TV talk show like *Oprah* or *The Today Show*? Recent topics like, "Parents out of control: Cameras catch all the drama!" "Parents obsessed—how far will they go to make their kids number one?" on *Oprah*, or "Prevent summer learning loss in your kids" on *Today*, indicate that both shows take careful note of what Parentocrats are up to and use them as a key conduit to what the average American parent will be concerned about tomorrow.

Look to radicals who are to the far right or left of mainstream thought. Michael Jacobson, founder of the Center for Science in the Public Interest, who once proudly proclaimed, "CSPI is proud about finding something wrong with practically everything," is just such a figure. When he began ranting years ago about childhood obesity in this country, he was a voice in the wilderness. Now *TV Magazine* shows and chat fests address the issue from every possible angle, and it's Topic A for schools, parent-teacher organizations, health classes, and more. It reached a seminal moment in 2006, to become part of the food zeitgeist. The time to have begun preparing new products and strategies targeting childhood obesity was years earlier. Sensing the moment an idea or cause is about to jump from the fringe to the center is a tricky business, but a necessary one if you are to stay competitive. Tracking the C-Types that matter most to your brand, and staying close to the attitudes that are close to their hearts, will ensure that you're never caught by surprise.

4.3 BRINGING YOUR TARGET TO LIFE THROUGH TYPING

As we have noted, this book contains the nine consumer types that we think are important. This does not mean that only these nine have validity or that the tools of consumer typing cannot be profitably applied to your specific category. Doing so will help you identify how better to market your brand to your current consumer. A fully fleshed out target can be the decisive factor in both generating truly breakthrough insights and delivering your message in ways that are useful and relevant.

In all of our years of reviewing background data from Fortune 100 clients, we have seen very few who have managed to create a true portrait of their key consumer. Most have quite detailed studies that aptly summarize brand essence or equity; some have behavior and attitude studies that reflect key purchase drivers; some even have segmentation studies that slice up category users by key demographics. But rarely have we seen businesses that have rolled all these factors into a multidimensional picture of a consumer type. On the rare occasions that we have seen this notion brought to bear, it has proved to be invaluable. One major beverage company shared a study in which it identified the three different types of consumers who form its key constituency. And, importantly, the descriptions of these types were not solely focused around the consumer's interaction with its brand, or even the beverage category in general. They included the consumer's attitude toward food, health, and nutrition, toward exercise and fitness, toward sex and sensuality. They talked about the magazines the type read, movies they related to, celebrities they admired, etc. They even had a "mood board" of imagery to help bring color and texture to the dry prose. Given the benefit of this level of sophistication around the consumer target, our job of generating insights was made immeasurably easier. Everything we brainstormed could be filtered through these key consumers. Would they approve? Would they care? What words would they use to describe this idea?

The lesson is simple: When you understand your consumer as a multidimensional type, your ideas and insights are that much richer. By using typing to better define your brand's target, you'll have a handy barometer with which to measure ideas against. By understanding your target fully, you'll intuitively surface innovations that will be compelling and highly marketable. By continually updating and refreshing your view of your target, how your brand plays out in their life, you will always stay ahead of the curve. In a postmarketing world, in which it seems like all needs and desires have been met, talking to mainstream consumers about their behaviors and attitudes usually proves less than fruitful. A better bet is to talk to leading-edge category radicals as you generate hypotheses and formalize your ideas and then take those ideas for testing in the mainstream.

So how, exactly, does one begin to apply the principles of typing to your target? For us, it all comes back to the Consumer Immersion process. As noted in the introduction, our company, Consumer Eyes, pioneered the Consumer Immersion as a way to bring a variety of vantage points to our consideration of a project goal. Consumer Immersion enables us to see leading-edge phenomena before they reach the mainstream, because we speak not only to consumers themselves but also to people who write about them, sell to them, befriend them, and analyze them. A typical Consumer Eyes brand or innovation Consumer Immersion includes expert interviews as well as consumer ethnographies plus experiential visits and a trend tour of category-related hot spots where consumers gather. Our immersions have taken us all over the world, from Sao Paulo to Bangkok, from New York City to Madison, Wisconsin, but our modus operandi is always the same: to try to inform our project goal through a series of thought-provoking experiences and real-world consumer interactions.

You can use this same approach for your brand. The step-by-step process might look something like this:

1. *Desk research:* What do you know about the demographics of your core target? The who, what, where, and when of your brand usage? How has this evolved over the years?

2. *Web searching:* Has your brand target appeared in chat rooms? Who is talking about it and why? What are they saying? Who seems positive? Negative? Why? If your target is not interested in chatting on the Internet, ask yourself why. Are they tech phobic? Or merely old-fashioned?

3. *Online consumer feedback:* What can you learn if you put together an interesting usage, behavior, and attitude study or segmentation study that goes beyond the obvious? Conduct some base level research to learn more about who is using your brand and your competitor's brand. Our sister company BuzzBack Market Research has been a pioneer in blending qualitative and quantitative research in a way that helps point up both functional and emotional behaviors and attitudes among respondents. Look to new, forward-thinking Internet-based research companies to set up studies that go beyond the obvious.

4. *Conduct ethnographies with key brand loyalists:* Make sure they are ultra loyal, almost extreme in their fanaticism about the brand and

category. Visit with them, and talk with them in their homes, but be sure to explore their world, not just your category. Take videos, take photos, and get to know them. Explore their bookshelves with them, their CD racks, their garage.

5. *Conduct expert interviews:* Talk with people whose opinions may have direct impact on your category or consumer, or whose expert-ise can raise awareness about the functional and psychological or subtle underpinnings of your brand.

6. *Conduct internal brand interviews:* Talk to the people who have been involved in the brand from its earliest days—from your side and your agency partner side. Learn from the past. Who has historically been the target? How has it evolved over the years? How is it different than in the past? Often, the earliest keepers of the brand keys have moved on or left the company, and often these folks are loaded with infor-mation that can create a shortcut to insight and information. Find them and tap into them.

7. *Conduct experiential visits and trend tours:* Shop the fringes, shop the mainstream; shop, look, and listen by informally talking with con-sumers and shopkeepers/sales clerks.

8. *Have a party (or barbecue or family gathering, etc.):* Bring your brand to your next party. Informally observe the behavior of your friends, family, and colleagues; then talk with those who you think are most interested in your brand. If you know the person well, create a link from his or her personality to your brand. If you don't, then try to get to know this person in order to identify a link. "Grandmother Research" (informally interviewing and/or observing friends and family) is often more valuable than formal research. Yes, it lacks the research rigor around screening, category usage, and so forth. But you know these people, you know their attitudes and lives, and tap-ping into that and how your brand plays out can prove to be uniquely valuable. Formal research presents consumers as a blank slate and puts their behavior into a checklist. Grandmother research is full of depth and knowledge around the person and the brand as part

of their lives. It puts brands into a deeper context that is virtually impossible to discern when you conduct traditional qualitative research.

9. *Press the flesh*: Bring a living, breathing target consumer to your next meeting. Have this person interact with the most senior level executives in your company.

10. *Video vitals*: Create a video compendium of your consumer—with clips and bits that help bring it to life from a variety of consumer interviews.

11. *Type-o-graphy*: Create a simple one-page type key that will enable everyone to quickly understand how your consumer interacts with your brand, with his or her family, with popular culture, with society, and so on. By doing all of this, you will be viewing your target holistically, as a friend of the brand who matters. And once you're clear on who your consumer is, you will be able to make more intuitive decisions about advertising, marketing efforts, line extensions, and innovations.

4.4 C-Types: Windows on the Future

So, you've reached the end of the book. Now what?

First and foremost, we hope we've inspired you to think a little differently about consumers—where they're coming from and where they're headed in the future. But more than that, we hope that we've given you some new tools for looking at the consumer landscape, for generating breakthrough new business insights. We hope this book has sparked your inner sociologist and anthropologist and will continue to resonate as you begin to create your own consumer constructs and hypothesize about the consumer types that will most affect your business and brand.

Obviously, the nine consumer types detailed in this book do not represent the entire world—not even close. But, as you think about marketing and innovating, we think these nine are among those that are most important for you to take into consideration no matter what marketplace category you work in. These types are today's thought leaders, and we think you will gain a lot simply by exploring their depths. By examining the far reaches of consumer behavior, you might just stumble onto the leading edge of tomorrow's mainstream.

Think about your friends, family, and acquaintances, and see where they fit in the gallery of C-Types. Do you know a Karma Queen or Culture Crosser? Do you work with a Ms. Independent? Just for kicks, try to figure out which type you come closest to. Think about your brand to determine which, if any, of these types are most relevant to it and its future health. Check out the places, spaces, and Web sites that are referenced throughout. Play these types against your view of the world and consumer trends. How do they come together? Where do they diverge?

C-Types are not a silver bullet or magic black box. They are but one tool among many that can inform your judgment, inspire your creativity, and help you reach your marketing goals. The purpose of this book has been to enlighten and inform, but most importantly to introduce you to a new sort of consumer construct, one that you can bring to bear upon any and all new experiences you have in the future. Keep your eyes open. Seek out those who see the world differently. New C-Types are emerging all the time. Only by constantly reaching out to the fringes of the consumer world will you uncover who and what's coming next.

NOTE

1. Associated Press Online, 7/24/06

Ron Rentel is the founder of Consumer Eyes, a leading brand and innovation consultancy, which creates customized methodologies that can encompass both long-term strategy and pipeline work and/or highly specific near-in product execution and tactics. He is also cofounder of BuzzBack Market Research, an online market research company. Visit Ron Rentel at consumereyes.com.